Getting Started with Oracle WebLogic Server 12c: Developer's Guide

Understand Java EE 6, JDK 7, and Oracle WebLogic
Server 12c concepts by creating a fully-featured
application with this step-by-step handbook

Fabio Mazanatti Nunes

William Markito Oliveira

[PACKT] enterprise 88
PUBLISHING
professional expertise distilled

BIRMINGHAM - MUMBAI

Getting Started with Oracle WebLogic Server 12c: Developer's Guide

First published: September 2013

Production Reference: 1190913

Published by Packt Publishing Ltd.
Livery Place
35 Livery Street
Birmingham B3 2PB, UK.

ISBN 978-1-84968-696-9

www.packtpub.com

Cover Image by J.Blaminsky (milak6@wp.pl)

Credits

About the Authors

Fabio Mazanatti Nunes: With more than two decades of experience in system design and development, Fabio worked in a wide range of projects and architectures (mainframe, client-server, distributed architecture, and SOA) for large corporations in Brazil, and for the last dozen years, he specialized in the architecture and implementation of Java EE and SOA solutions, mainly using BEA and Oracle products. You can find more material related to these topics on his blog, `http://mazanatti.info`.

I'd like to thank my wife, Valesca, for her constant support and for keeping calm and distracting the little ones while I was focused on writing this book, my kids, Gabriela and Caio, for being such wonderful people and a joy in my life, and my parents, for always being there for us.

A great thank you to my friend and co-author, William, for not letting my acid comments corrode his will to get this book done and for being such a curious and committed individual, raising the bar for everyone who happen to work with him.

I'd also like to thank the technical reviewers of the book, especially my friends Vinicius Santos and Daniel Amadei for accepting this tricky task and for being such nice lads to work with.

Finally, I'd like to mention the honey badger as our role model for this project, because he just takes what he wants, and sometimes in life, that's what we should do—in a positive way, of course!

William Markito Oliveira has more than 15 years of experience in software development, including solution architecture and consulting. For the last few years, he had focused on Service Oriented Architecture (SOA) solutions, Enterprise Application Integration (EAI), and system optimization.

Currently, he is looking into cloud systems with specific focus on in-memory data grid and Java EE. He is also a member of the Java EE Tutorial documentation team, helping with write-ups and code examples about new Java EE technologies and can be reached at Twitter (@william_markito) or through his blog, http://blog.markito.info.

He has authored another book, *The Java EE 6 Tutorial: Advanced Topics, Fourth Edition, Addison-Wesley Professional, 978-0-13708-186-8*.

I'd like to thank my wife Rebeca, as she was always supportive and encouraged me several times during the writing, helping me by distracting our little man when he tried to type his own words for the book.

Antônio, my son, who also behaved and understood things beyond his age, by letting me write the book while watching Toy Story several times in a row. Love you both more than anything.

Also, a special mention to my family, especially my mother, father, and stepfather. Regina, Antônio, and Vanderlei, thank you for giving me the best and for always being supportive during my night hacks.

Thanks to the reviewers, who prevented us from publishing some silly errors and gave us great ideas on how to write things in a clear way, especially my friend and the best man, Daniel Amadei.

And of course, I'd like to thank the Honey Badger and Fabio, for always being so inspirational and hustler on the way we look at computers and programming in general.

About the Reviewers

Daniel Amadei is a Senior Principal Consultant working for Oracle Consulting Services in Brazil and has more than 10 years of experience in the IT market, being a specialized consultant and solutions architect for SOA and Enterprise Applications. He has strong analytical and problem-solving abilities with solid experience in the development and architecture of applications.

He is a specialist in SOA and EAI Oracle middleware products, web services and related technologies, and the Java Platform, especially Java EE. He has been working with Java since 1999, and SOA/EAI since 2007, and has, at the time of this book's writing, eight certifications related to his specialties, including Oracle Certified SOA Architect, Oracle SOA Foundation Practitioner, and Sun Certified Enterprise Architect for J2EE.

You can write to him at daniel.amadei@gmail.com, and read about his works at http://www.amadei.com.br.

> I'd like to thank the authors for giving me the chance to learn a lot by reviewing the book.

Wickes Potgieter has worked as a product specialist for over 12 years. His main focus was on the BEA WebLogic suite of products, and after the Oracle acquisition of BEA Systems, he focused on the Oracle Fusion Middleware suite of products. His experience ranges from Solution Architecture, Infrastructure Design, administration, development, pre-sales, and training to performance tuning of the Oracle Fusion Middleware products, JVM, and custom applications. He specializes in Oracle WebLogic Server, JRockit, Service Bus, SOA, AIA, BPM, BAM, Enterprise Manager 11*g*/12c, WebCenter, Identity & Access Management, and Application Performance Management.

They have formed a specialized consulting company in 2003 with offices in the United Kingdom and South Africa, covering customers in the EMEA region. They are in partnership with Oracle Gold and have a team of specialized Oracle Fusion Middleware consultants servicing customers both onsite and offsite.

The website of TSI-Systems is `www.tsisystems.co.uk`, and Wickes can be contacted on `wickes@tsisystems.co.uk`.

I would like to thank my wife Mary Jane for her patience and for assisting me through all the late nights. Thank you to all my friends and family for constant encouragement.

Vinícius Rodrigo dos Santos has been working on software development since 1999 on high school projects and has developed his career focusing on middleware and EAI ever since.

He has worked for companies as a Software Engineer in South America and North America, creating and maintaining critical systems that served clients around the world.

After dedicating the last 5 years almost exclusively to SOA, he is now focused on multiplatform mobile development and cloud computing solutions.

The solutions he has worked with have served companies mainly focused on Vehicle Engineering, Home Broker, Telecommunications, and the Government.

He now owns a startup named IstyaTech (`http://www.istya.net`) in Brazil that serves customers on mobile and cloud computing solutions.

I would like to thank my parents, my mother Elisabete Brito dos Santos and my father Raimundo Nonato dos Santos, for giving me support in my young years so I could one day participate in a project as satisfying as this one. Of course my special thanks goes to my loving wife Cristiane Danna who has given me strength to carry on; I love you.

www.PacktPub.com

Support files, eBooks, discount offers and more

You might want to visit www.PacktPub.com for support files and downloads related to your book.

Did you know that Packt offers eBook versions of every book published, with PDF and ePub files available? You can upgrade to the eBook version at www.PacktPub.com and as a print book customer, you are entitled to a discount on the eBook copy. Get in touch with us at service@packtpub.com for more details.

At www.PacktPub.com, you can also read a collection of free technical articles, sign up for a range of free newsletters and receive exclusive discounts and offers on Packt books and eBooks.

http://PacktLib.PacktPub.com

Do you need instant solutions to your IT questions? PacktLib is Packt's online digital book library. Here, you can access, read and search across Packt's entire library of books.

Why Subscribe?

- Fully searchable across every book published by Packt
- Copy and paste, print and bookmark content
- On demand and accessible via web browser

Free Access for Packt account holders

If you have an account with Packt at www.PacktPub.com, you can use this to access PacktLib today and view nine entirely free books. Simply use your login credentials for immediate access.

Instant Updates on New Packt Books

Get notified! Find out when new books are published by following @PacktEnterprise on Twitter, or the *Packt Enterprise* Facebook page.

Table of Contents

Preface

Oracle WebLogic Server has been the most innovative and important application server in the market since its conception in 1995. In release 12c, which brings support for Java EE 6 platform and JDK 7, it provides developers and administrators several new and powerful functionalities along with long-awaited improvements to existing features.

With this book you will learn some of the basic WebLogic Server concepts such as domains, managed servers and node managers, and dive into more practical topics such as how to expose and consume web services and how to use and protect JMS queues, exploring Java EE 6 APIs and features such as context dependency injection (CDI), EJB 3.1, JPA 2.1, and others. This is done through an incremental development of a business case, building up a sample application with very detailed steps and screenshots, so readers can follow and apply them to real-world solutions.

What this book covers

Chapter 1, Overview of WebLogic Server 12c and Related Technologies, presents an overview of the latest Java Development Kit (JDK) 7 and Java EE 6 technologies, along with an introduction to the most relevant features of Oracle WebLogic 12c. It also positions WebLogic Server 12c in the Oracle Cloud Application Foundation (CAF) architecture.

Chapter 2, Setting Up the Environment, explains how to install and configure Oracle WebLogic Server and an IDE (Eclipse OEPE), setting them up to be able to develop and run the sample applications we will build throughout the book. We also set up a database (MySQL) and an LDAP Server (OpenLDAP).

Chapter 3, Java EE Basics – Persistence, Query, and Presentation, defines the business case used as a background to the technical features and implementation details that will be covered throughout the remaining chapters, giving an overview of some of the basic features of Java EE and WebLogic Server—how to create and use an optional package, the creation of a web application and a persistence layer project, including how to deploy and do sanity checks on them.

Chapter 4, Creating RESTful Services with JAX-RS, shows how to create and expose an Enterprise JavaBean as a RESTful web service through the usage of JAX-RS annotations, representing the business entities as JSON or XML instances leveraging JAXB parsing.

Chapter 5, Singleton Bean, Validations, and SOAP Web Services, explains the concepts of the validation framework, showing how to use the built-in rules and how to create custom validations. The chapter demonstrates how to persist an entity to the database and the transactional aspects involved in this operation. There is also the development of a JAX-WS service and an example of a Java EE singleton bean.

Chapter 6, Using Events, Interceptors, and Logging Service, shows how to use Java EE interceptors by creating a logging annotation that can be attached to classes or methods, how to publish and observe events by using CDI, how to create and use asynchronous methods on an EJB, and details about the logging services available in WebLogic Server.

Chapter 7, Remote Access with JMS, explains the different modes of remote connection presented by WebLogic Server, creating a standalone Java application to post messages to a JMS Queue and then enhancements to avoid problems when the server is down by keeping the message local using the SAF client.

Chapter 8, Adding Security, covers the basics of the Java EE Security model with step-by-step instructions on how to configure it on a WebLogic server, creating an authentication mechanism using LDAP, and integrating it on the sample application.

Chapter 9, Servlets, Composite Components, and WebSockets, shows how to create and apply reusable web components by applying JSF templates, how to create and test a WebSocket component, and includes a few tips about the new Servlet specification.

Chapter 10, Scaling Up the Application, explains how to create and configure a WebLogic Server cluster using a software load balancer to distribute requests among the servers, how to make session replication more scalable by using Coherence*Web, and how to use the WebLogic Singleton Service.

Chapter 11, Some WebLogic Internals, covers a few features brought by WebLogic Server and Java EE 6 that helps the development process by cutting deployment time, optimizing class redefinitions without the need to restart the whole application, finding classloader issues, and monitoring server resources in a simple way.

What you need for this book

The following are the software applications we will use to develop and test the sample applications of this book:

- Oracle Java JDK Version 7u21 or newer
- Oracle WebLogic Server Version 12.1.2
- Oracle Enterprise Pack for Eclipse (OEPE) Version 12.1.2
- MySQL server and client packages, Version 5.1 or newer
- PrimeFaces Version 3.5
- OpenLDAP Version 2.4.x

We need to run at least one instance of Oracle WebLogic Server, the development environment, Eclipse with OEPE (Oracle Eclipse Pack for Eclipse), MySQL server, and OpenLDAP. You may be able to run all this on a machine with 2 GB of RAM, but consider at least 4 GB to have a smoother experience.

Who this book is for

This book is intended for entry level and intermediate Java EE developers who want to learn how to develop for and use Oracle WebLogic Server by showing how to apply its concepts and features to a real-world scenario. The book is also intended for those who want to learn about the new features of 12c and Java EE 6 releases, and how those updates make things easier and more productive, both at design and runtime.

Conventions

In this book, you will find a number of styles of text that distinguish between different kinds of information. Here are some examples of these styles, and an explanation of their meaning.

Code words in text, database table names, folder names, filenames, file extensions, pathnames, dummy URLs, user input, and Twitter handles are shown as follows: "You can find the logging configuration file at `$JAVA_HOME/jre/lib/logging.properties`."

A block of code is set as follows:

```
package com.packt.store.log;

@Inherited
@InterceptorBinding
@Retention(RetentionPolicy.RUNTIME)
@Target({ElementType.METHOD, ElementType.TYPE})
public @interface Log {
    @Nonbinding
    LogLevel value() default LogLevel.FINEST;
}
```

When we wish to draw your attention to a particular part of a code block, the relevant lines or items are set in bold:

```
package com.packt.store.log;

@Inherited
@InterceptorBinding
@Retention(RetentionPolicy.RUNTIME)
@Target({ElementType.METHOD, ElementType.TYPE})
public @interface Log {
    @Nonbinding
    LogLevel value() default LogLevel.FINEST;
}
```

Any command-line input or output is written as follows:

```
/oracle/jdk1.7.0_21/bin/java/java -jar wls_121200.jar
```

New terms and **important words** are shown in bold. Words that you see on the screen, in menus or dialog boxes for example, appear in the text like this: "By clicking on the **Print** button the selected reservation will be printed."

> Warnings or important notes appear in a box like this.

> Tips and tricks appear like this.

Reader feedback

Feedback from our readers is always welcome. Let us know what you think about this book—what you liked or may have disliked. Reader feedback is important for us to develop titles that you really get the most out of.

To send us general feedback, simply send an e-mail to feedback@packtpub.com, and mention the book title via the subject of your message.

If there is a topic that you have expertise in and you are interested in either writing or contributing to a book, see our author guide on www.packtpub.com/authors.

Customer support

Now that you are the proud owner of a Packt book, we have a number of things to help you to get the most from your purchase.

Downloading the example code

You can download the example code files for all Packt books you have purchased from your account at http://www.packtpub.com. If you purchased this book elsewhere, you can visit http://www.packtpub.com/support and register to have the files e-mailed directly to you.

Errata

Although we have taken every care to ensure the accuracy of our content, mistakes do happen. If you find a mistake in one of our books—maybe a mistake in the text or the code—we would be grateful if you would report this to us. By doing so, you can save other readers from frustration and help us improve subsequent versions of this book. If you find any errata, please report them by visiting http://www.packtpub.com/submit-errata, selecting your book, clicking on the **errata submission form** link, and entering the details of your errata. Once your errata are verified, your submission will be accepted and the errata will be uploaded on our website, or added to any list of existing errata, under the Errata section of that title. Any existing errata can be viewed by selecting your title from http://www.packtpub.com/support.

Piracy

Piracy of copyright material on the Internet is an ongoing problem across all media. At Packt, we take the protection of our copyright and licenses very seriously. If you come across any illegal copies of our works, in any form, on the Internet, please provide us with the location address or website name immediately so that we can pursue a remedy.

Please contact us at copyright@packtpub.com with a link to the suspected pirated material.

We appreciate your help in protecting our authors, and our ability to bring you valuable content.

Questions

You can contact us at questions@packtpub.com if you are having a problem with any aspect of the book, and we will do our best to address it.

1
Overview of WebLogic Server 12c and Related Technologies

In this chapter, we're going to see some basic information about the subject of this book, including:

- A brief history of Oracle WebLogic Server
- The most significant additions to Java SE Version 7
- New features of Java EE 6, the specification implemented by the WebLogic Server
- The improvements added to Version 12.1.2, the latest release of the product

Before we get into the new features of Oracle WebLogic Server 12c, let's do a quick recap on how it all started.

Introducing Oracle WebLogic Server 12c

In a very brief history of WebLogic, we must remember that it came to Oracle through the acquisition of **BEA** (**B**ill, **E**dward, **A**lfred). Although the name WebLogic is widely associated with BEA, they didn't create the product.

In fact, WebLogic itself was a company formed in 1995 (same year as BEA) that created a middle-tier server to enhance communication between applets and servers providing implementations for SNMP, JDBC drivers, and ping. This server was named Tengah but also had a codename, **T3Server** (the three-tier server) and used a custom proprietary network protocol called **T3**. This server later evolved to be a Java application server as we know today and right after BEA acquired WebLogic (the company) in 1998, Tengah was officially renamed to WebLogic (Version 4.5). Later, BEA acquired a high performance JVM (BEA JRockit, now Oracle JRockit) that was certified against WebLogic and received various performance awards.

The last BEA release of WebLogic Server was Version 10.0, a full Java EE 5 application server.

WebLogic Server @ Oracle

After BEA's acquisition in 2008, Oracle announced WebLogic as the strategic application server to replace Oracle Application Server (OC4J), and it also became the foundation for Oracle Fusion Middleware and Oracle Fusion Applications, the main families of Oracle products.

The first release under Oracle's brand was WebLogic Server 10gR3 (10.3.0), soon followed by Version 11g. Here's a figure showing all 11g and 12c releases till now:

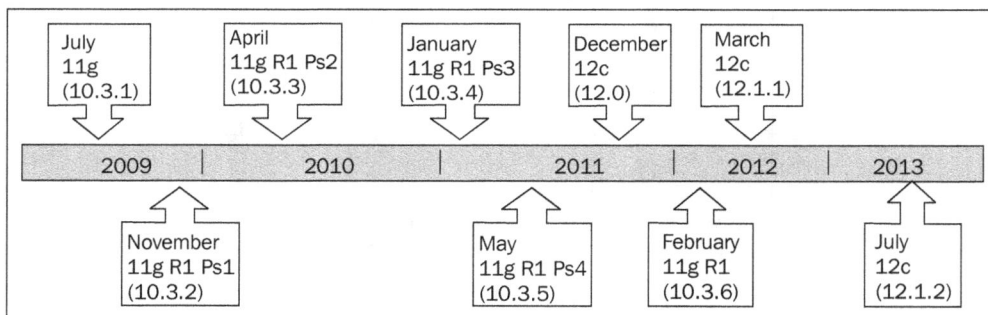

The focus of this book is WebLogic Sever 12c, which is approximately the eighth release by Oracle and has lots of new and improved features, as shown in the next section.

Most relevant features

Here is a list of the most important features of Oracle WebLogic Server 12c Version 12.1.2, the most current version and the focus of this book:

- **Full Java EE 6 support**: WebLogic 12c is the first release to implement Java EE 6 specification, delivering all its features. The next section of this chapter is going to explain new and relevant additions to Java EE 6.

- **Certified with JDK 6 and JDK 7**: Through the use of JDK 7, developers can leverage all language optimizations available in the new version of the JDK, including features already converged from JRockit—the proprietary JDK that came from BEA.

- **JDBC Store for JTA logs**: WebLogic supports JDBC Store to persist transaction logs (TLOGs) in a database, and leverages replication and high availability on the underlying database. It also simplifies disaster recovery since the synchronization happens at the database level.

- **Built-in Classloader Analysis Tool (CAT)**: WebLogic CAT is a web-based application that can filter the different classloaders available (JVM, application server, applications) showing the classes loaded by each one of them. This functionality enables the analysis of common classloader issues such as conflicts. The tool even offers suggestions on how to fix problems.

- **Coherence 12.1.2**: This release includes support for Coherence Servers Management through WebLogic Management Framework, including security and application deployment through GAR (Grid Archive) files. It offers asynchronous backup, multiple Coherence REST applications, integration with Oracle Universal Installer, and support for ECID (Execution Context ID) for correlation with Oracle Fusion Middleware. Other than these, it still offers WebLogic integration for HTTP session management (Coherence*Web) and Oracle TopLink Grid as a JPA mechanism.

- **Glassfish to WebLogic deployment descriptor support**: WebLogic offers support for Glassfish deployment descriptors so you can seamlessly deploy web applications written for Glassfish Server on WebLogic Server.

- **Enhanced WebLogic Maven support**: In this release, one of the most important changes is that it's not required to generate the WebLogic Maven plugin anymore; there is now a bundled version under `/wlserver/server/lib/`. Also, several new tasks were added to the plugin, including support for server installation from zip files, domain creation, start/stop servers, and execution of inline WLST scripts.

- **WebSockets support**: The newest release 12.1.2, brings support for the WebSocket protocol, which provides two-way and full-duplex communication over a single TCP connection between clients and the server. With this, we can open a direct connection between a browser and the server, receiving and sending information in an asynchronous way, opening possibilities to create Rich Internet Applications (RIA).

- **OSGi bundles**: The OSGi architecture is now available as a WebLogic feature, providing us a way to create a set of configurations to define our own modules and use its API to, for instance, start and stop modules and acquire data sources. The implementation that comes with WebLogic Server is Apache Felix 4.0.3.

- **Server templates and dynamic servers/clusters**: To make Oracle's Cloud Application Foundation more flexible, Version 12.1.2 of WebLogic Server introduced these concepts that basically give us an easy way to scale up a WebLogic domain. Up to this version, we had to manually create and configure managed servers to distribute workload; now, we create a server template once, setting up a few basic points of information such as name prefix, and create a dynamic cluster based on this template. When the workload reaches a peak, we just instruct the environment to fire up additional servers based on these configurations, and it's done. It's quick and easy.

- **Dynamic clustered JMS Servers**: Another improvement that involves ease of configuration when dealing with dynamic clusters is that now a JMS Server — the component used to deploy JMS resources such as queues and topics to a server — can be targeted to a WebLogic cluster. Previous versions only accepted a managed server as a target for such components, and now management and migration tasks are a lot easier to perform.

Overview of JDK 7

Version 7 of JDK was a huge release for Java, providing great functionality for a wide group of developers and platforms, and Oracle WebLogic Server has been certified on this version since WebLogic 11*g*. Even though this isn't a brand new feature, it is an important one, so let's check some of the main features of this release:

- For those who work at the JVM level, InvokeDynamic (JSR 292) is the big name, providing extensions for dynamically-typed languages (such as Ruby, Perl, and Groovy) to perform at almost the same level as a pure Java program.

- The new class loader architecture introduces safe multithreaded class loading, among other related improvements.

- Concurrency and collections updates (JSR 166) create new classes that support the fork/join structure, new synchronization barriers, and a utility class `ThreadLocalRandom` that generates random numbers in applications invoking it from multiple threads.

- New APIs for filesystem access, part of NIO.2 (JSR 203), with support file metadata, symbolic links, multicast datagrams, and socket-channel binding. Also, there is a new file system provider for zip/jar files and enhancements to the Watch Service API that allows you to register for file change notifications.

- **SDP (Socket Direct Protocol) support**: An implementation of a high performance network protocol that streams data over InfiniBand connections on Linux and Solaris. To enable SDP you just need to set a JVM system property and a configuration file.

> InfiniBand is a communications link used in high-performance computing (HPC) systems and datacenters that delivers low latency, scalable throughput between processor nodes and I/O systems, with transmission speeds up to 300 GBps.

- On the security side, there are many important enhancements, including support for Elliptic Curve Cryptography (ECC), TLS 1.1/1.2, and NLTM (Microsoft's security protocol).

- The JDBC was upgraded to Version 4.1, enabling the developer to use `try-catch` structures when dealing with the objects of `Connection`, `Statement`, and `ResultSet` — no need to write `finally` blocks to release these components anymore.

- Enhancements to the current **MBeans** (**Management Beans**) available at `com.sun.management` to access information about CPU usage on the system and the JVM.

- There was a minor update on the XML stack, including **JAXP 1.4** (JSR 206), **JAXB 2.2a** (JSR 222), and **JAX-WS 2.2** (JSR 224).

> That's a pretty extensive list but it leaves out tons of **RFEs** (**Request for Enhancement**) that were addressed in JDK 7; the complete list can be found at `http://www.oracle.com/technetwork/java/javase/jdk7-relnotes-418459.html#jdk7changes`.

The Project Coin

The objective of Project Coin is to define a set of simple changes to the Java language that would make the developer's life easier. Some of these changes make their way to JDK 7, and some are expected to be released with Version 8.

Let's explore some of these enhancements with quick examples.

The diamond operator

Following the DRY (Don't Repeat Yourself) principle, the diamond operator (<>) allows developers to have protection at compile time by inferring types from **generic collections** without repeating the declared type. Before JDK 7, if we had to declare a map that contains a list of Strings, it would look something like this:

```
Map<String, List<String>> words = new HashMap<String,
   List<String>>();
```

In JDK 7 it can be replaced with the following statement:

```
Map<String, List<String>> words = new HashMap<>();
```

The try-with-resources statement

The **try-with-resources** feature is also known as **Automatic Resource Management** because it's focused on resources such as connections, files, input/output streams, but in the end a so-called `resource` can be defined as an object that needs to be closed after being used. Basically, any object that implements the `java.lang.AutoClosable` interface can benefit from the `try-with-resources` statement.

The feature allows you to simplify resource management by closing one or more resources that were declared within a `try` block right after their use, without having to write code to release the resources (usually inside `finally` blocks), avoiding insertion of potential leaks.

A quick example on how this feature can be applied to execute a query is as follows:

```
try (Statement st = con.createStatement()) {
   ResultSet rs = st.executeQuery(q);

  // Process the results
} catch (SQLException e) {
    logger.error(e);
}
```

In the preceding example, a JDBC Statement is created within the `try` context and then used by a SQL query. After execution, the `Statement` will be automatically closed by JVM. In previous versions, we had to manually dispose of the Statement resource when it was no longer necessary, confirming that it isn't null and then releasing it.

> The `try-with-resources` statement can still use `finally` blocks just like the traditional `try` statement; the difference is that any `catch` or `finally` block is now executed after the resources declared have been closed.

Strings in switch statements

Strings in `switch` statements is a long-awaited feature that you should have already asked yourself: Why don't we have strings in a Java `switch` statement? Some might say it is a performance issue or something like that, but there's not much sense discussing an optimization that sometimes even the Java compiler doesn't care about. Besides, even cell phones are multi-core nowadays, so processing power really isn't a factor here.

So, developers can have a good time when crafting their code now; if we need to test against a list of possible Strings, we can use one `switch` statement and save many `if` and `else` blocks:

```
for (Order order : orderList) {
  switch (order.getStatus()) {
  case "NEW":
    processNewOrder(order);
    break;
  case "PENDING":
    processPendingOrder(order);
    break;
  case "CLOSED":
    processClosedOrder(order);
    break;
  default:
    processErrorOrder(order);
    break;
  }
}
```

Of course it's a simple example, but remember that you would need to replace the `case` blocks with several cumbersome `if` and `else` statements.

Manipulating binary integral literals

The use of binary number manipulation is common in some programming domains (compression encoding, network protocols, or any other type of bitmapped application), though, Java supported the use of only other numeric representations such as decimal, hexadecimal, and octal.

The idea of adding some methods to let the programmer write the numbers directly in binary format is much more practical, and avoids injection of bugs, because the programmer doesn't need to keep in mind that a special variable with numbers in hexadecimal is in fact a number to be translated to binary.

Exception handling with multicatch statements

Usually it's a common requirement to write code that needs to catch multiple exceptions and deal with error handling using a common approach (the same piece of code replicated a few times). Until JDK 7, the simplest option was to write a common method to reuse the same error treatment (or re-throw the exception) for some common exceptions or even use the `finally` block (which is pretty nasty — getting your code executed even with no exceptions? Please don't!). With multicatch, it is possible to catch multiple exceptions and avoid this duplicated code in `catch` clauses.

A common exception handling block from Java 6 would look like this:

```
try {
  // try-code throwing IOException or SQLException
} catch (IOException ex) {
    logger.severe(ex.getMessage());
    throw ex;
} catch (SQLException ex) {
    logger.severe(ex.getMessage());
    throw ex;
}
```

After JDK 7 the same code can be written like this:

```
try {
  // try-code throwing IOException or SQLException
} catch (IOException | SQLException ex) {
    logger.severe(ex.getMessage());
    throw ex;
}
```

Delving into Java EE 6

This topic deserves special attention because of the huge impact Java EE 6 made into the way we develop enterprise Java applications by adding new, powerful technologies and features to its specification. Several topics are mentioned here, and most of them will be demonstrated throughout the next chapters:

- **Java API for RESTful Web Services (JAX-RS, JSR 311)**: This enables lightweight web services' development following the **Representational State Transfer** (**REST**) architectural paradigm. The concept of manipulating resources through different networks using a standard protocol such as HTTP, is a growing paradigm and an alternative to the traditional SOAP-based services.

- **Context and Dependency Injection for Java EE Platform (CDI, JSR 299)**: This provides a built-in **dependency injection** mechanism for Java EE that offers a set of services that bind several components (for example, EJB and JSF Managed Beans) to lifecycle contexts. Another facility provided by CDI is a loosely coupled event mechanism that works with annotation and simple **POJOs** (**Plain Old Java Object**). In a nutshell, the main objective of CDI is to create a unified programming model for EJB and JSF while keeping other important services (transactions, for instance) available to all Java EE tiers.

- **Bean validation (JSR 303)**: Developers tend to validate objects in many layers. Sometimes they generate duplicated code and may even forget to replicate a validation logic to one of the layers, which can lead to catastrophic consequences. To solve such problems, the bean validation framework provides a standard set of validation rules that can be shared by all layers; so the same rule can be applied to the user interface (through JSF and managed beans) and more internal tiers (attached to JPA, for instance), avoiding duplicated code.

- **Enterprise JavaBeans 3.1**: In this update of the EJB specification, the main focus was to make it simple and easy to use. The most noticeable change is that EJBs now can be packaged in WAR files, removing the need to produce specific packages for EJBs and combine them in an EAR file. But other important features were added, such as the following:

    ○ **Singleton beans**: These are the EJBs that can primarily be shared and support concurrent access, with the guarantee that the container will have only a single instance per JVM

    ○ **Embeddable API for Java SE**: With some limitations, it runs client code and EJB instances in the same JVM on SE environments using an embeddable container

- ° **EJB Lite**: Since Java EE 6 has the concept of profiles, specific vendors can choose to implement the full container or the Lite version with a subset of EJB API

- **Servlet 3.0**: Servlets are one of the main components of Java EE since its initial release, but few changes were made to its specification since then, except for adding filters and web application events. Servlet 3.0 adds important changes into the API such as the following:

  - ° **Support for annotations**: It's now possible to declare a servlet by just adding an annotation (@WebServlet) to a Java class. There are also annotation for filters, listeners, and parameters.

  - ° **Asynchronous processing**: Servlets now allow asynchronous method calls. This feature helps applications to scale up, since it releases the caller while the processing is done by the server, allowing other requests to be accepted by the released thread.

- **Java Persistence API 2.0**: JPA 2.0 has some major enhancements over the previous version. These new features include new annotations for mappings, enhancements to **Java Persistence Query Language** (JPQL), typed queries, shared cache, integration with bean validation, and probably the most powerful feature, Criteria API for dynamic strongly-typed query creation.

- **Java Server Faces 2.0**: JSF 2.0 brings some important features long awaited by the community such as official integration with **Facelets** (an XML-based view declaration language), more options for error handling, better integration with Ajax, and many more. In this release, there is a new concept of **resource** and how you can integrate the different kinds (stylesheets, images, and JavaScript files). Componentization and composites form the main theme, with an easy API that supports the creation of UI components for reuse.

> Under the topic of Java EE 6, we could list and discuss several updates and enhancements in other areas, but that would be out of the scope of this book. We'll be showing examples on most of what we have seen here during the construction of case studies and the main application that will be built along with the book.

Other technologies in the book

To be able to develop the application throughout this book, other products and technologies will be used. A few of them are discussed in the following sections.

Oracle Enterprise Pack for Eclipse

Oracle Enterprise Pack for Eclipse (**OEPE**) is a set of plugins for the Eclipse IDE that enables Java EE application development and leverages the toolset of Oracle specific technologies for Oracle Fusion Middleware.

The following is a list of key features that OEPE supports:

- Oracle WebLogic Server (including WLST, SCA, and shared libraries)
- Oracle Cloud
- Oracle Database
- Object Relational Mapping (ORM)
- Spring 3.2 integration
- Oracle Coherence

Oracle Coherence

Coherence provides a replicated and distributed data management and caching services, on top of a peer-to-peer clustering protocol, shared across multiple servers but with very high throughput, low response times, and predictable scalability.

In this book we're going to show examples of **Coherence*Web**, which is an HTTP session management module dedicated to managing the session state in clustered environments. This module integrates with WebLogic Server and provides a pluggable mechanism to scale up Java EE applications, having the benefit of not requiring any application instrumentation or changes to be activated.

PrimeFaces

PrimeFaces is a popular, free, and open source JSF component suite that provides several extensions and has a rich set of components, including an HTML editor and animated charts. It's very lightweight (only one jar, less than 2 MB) with no required dependencies other than JSF itself, making it a breeze to use and create Java EE web user interfaces.

MySQL

Since the very early years of the Web, MySQL empowers millions of websites and systems worldwide, being considered the world's most used open source database. It is a relational database system and supports many high profile products such as Wikipedia, Google, Twitter, Facebook, and YouTube.

MySQL offers a huge and rich set of features, but one of the most important features is the cross-platform support. So you can run the same product on Microsoft Windows, GNU/Linux, FreeBSD, or even Apple's OS X.

The Cloud Application Foundation (CAF)

WebLogic Server is part of **Oracle Cloud Application Foundation** (**CAF**), which is defined as a superset of products provided by Oracle that enable the infrastructure for building cloud environments for private or public clouds, hosting end-user applications.

Here's a graphical representation of the CAF stack, followed by a description of each component:

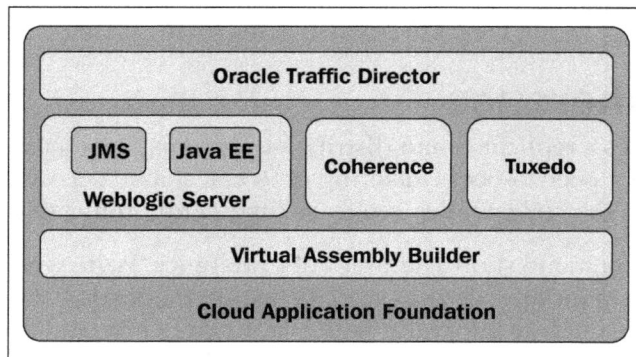

Oracle Traffic Director

Oracle Traffic Director is a high-speed, layer-7 (the application layer of the **OSI Model**) load balancer that can be set as the main entry point for HTTP and HTTPS traffic for large volumes, low latency, and mission-critical systems. It is optimized for Oracle Exalogic Elastic Cloud and leverages InfiniBand fabric for more throughput.

It can be configured to do traffic routing and to offload SSL/TLS, acting as the termination point for HTTPS requests, reducing the overhead of security processing on the application server. Also, it can improve performance for clients through content caching and reducing impact on the backend servers.

Oracle Tuxedo

Oracle Tuxedo runs mission-critical C/C++/COBOL applications in x86 servers or cloud environments, with ultra-high performance and linear scalability. It provides service-oriented infrastructure to manage distributed transaction processing, tracking participants, and monitoring XA two-phase commit, thus, ensuring that transactions are all committed or rolled back properly.

Oracle Virtual Assembly Builder

Oracle Virtual Assembly Builder provides an easy way for system administrators to configure new environments of multitier applications in cloud and virtualized environments. It allows drawing blueprint diagrams of the application topology and wire logical connections between the different appliances that compose the architecture.

Oracle Exalogic and WebLogic 12c

Oracle Exalogic is an engineered system, which means that it provides the best-of-breed components (storage, compute nodes, network, operating system, and software products) that are tested, tuned, and optimized to deliver extremely high performance. It can be considered as the evolution of Oracle Grid architecture as it moves into a concept of a **Private Cloud in a Box** platform, ideal for consolidation of mission-critical and cloud systems.

WebLogic 12c is fully supported on Oracle Exalogic and has many enhancements that can be enabled through WebLogic's **Administration Console**. These enhancements leverage the Exalogic architecture and tune WebLogic Server to perform using the benefits of SDP API, for example.

> SDP or **Socket Direct Protocol** is a low-level network technology that provides higher throughput. It is supported by JDK 7 and can be used for inter-process communication in WebLogic.

Other major features that can be enabled for Exalogic are as follows:

- **Scattered reads and gathered writes**: This feature allows us to increase the efficiency during I/O in environments with high network throughput

- **Lazy deserialization**: This feature allows us to increase efficiency for session replication

- **Self-tuning thread pool optimization**: This feature allows us to increase efficiency of the self-tuning thread pool by aligning it with the Exalogic processor architecture threading capabilities

This book will not discuss WebLogic 12c features that are specific to Exalogic systems, but it is important to know what can be accomplished through the use of Oracle-engineered systems.

Web resources

For further reading about the topics discussed in this chapter, here is a list of links with documentation or tutorials freely available on the Internet.

Java and Java EE 6

- Your First Cup: An Introduction to the Java EE Platform
    - http://docs.oracle.com/javaee/6/firstcup/doc/
- The Java EE 6 Tutorial
    - http://docs.oracle.com/javaee/6/tutorial/doc/
- Java API docs
    - http://docs.oracle.com/javaee/6/api/
- Java EE 6 Specification
    - http://www.jcp.org/en/jsr/detail?id=316
- Java SE 7 Specification
    - http://download.oracle.com/otndocs/jcp/java_se-7-final-eval-spec/index.html
- Support for Dynamically Typed Languages Specification
    - http://www.jcp.org/en/jsr/detail?id=292
- Class file Specification
    - http://www.jcp.org/en/jsr/detail?id=202
- Concurrency Utilities Specification
    - http://www.jcp.org/en/jsr/detail?id=166
- More New I/O APIs Specification
    - http://www.jcp.org/en/jsr/detail?id=203
- JAXB 2.0 Specification
    - http://www.jcp.org/en/jsr/detail?id=222
- JAX-WS 2.0 Specification
    - http://www.jcp.org/en/jsr/detail?id=224
- JAX-RS Specification
    - http://www.jcp.org/en/jsr/detail?id=311

- JSR 206: JavaTM API for XML Processing (JAXP) 1.3
    - `http://www.jcp.org/en/jsr/detail?id=206`
- Context and Dependency Injection Specification
    - `http://www.jcp.org/en/jsr/detail?id=299`
- Bean Validation Specification
    - `http://www.jcp.org/en/jsr/detail?id=303`
- The WebSocket Protocol
    - `http://tools.ietf.org/html/rfc6455`
- Code Samples
    - `http://www.oracle.com/technetwork/java/javaee/documentation/code-139018.html`

WebLogic 12c

- Documentation
    - `http://docs.oracle.com/middleware/1212/wls/index.html`
- Developing applications
    - `http://docs.oracle.com/middleware/1212/wls/wls-developdeploy.htm`
- What's new
    - `http://docs.oracle.com/middleware/1212/wls/NOTES/index.html#NOTES254`
- YouTube channel
    - `http://www.youtube.com/user/OracleWebLogic`
- WebLogic Server community
    - `http://www.oracle.com/technetwork/middleware/weblogic/community/index.html`
- Creating dynamic clusters
    - `http://docs.oracle.com/middleware/1212/wls/CLUST/dynamic_clusters.htm`
- Exalogic overview
    - `http://www.oracle.com/us/products/middleware/exalogic/oracle-exalogic-brochure-1934171.pdf`
- Using the Maven plugin
    - `http://docs.oracle.com/middleware/1212/wls/WLPRG/maven.htm#WLPRG586`

Coherence

- Developer's guide
  - ° http://docs.oracle.com/middleware/1212/coherence/coherence-developdeploy.htm
- Knowledge base
  - ° http://coherence.oracle.com/display/COH/Oracle+Coherence+Knowledge+Base+Home
- Coherence Incubator
  - ° http://coherence.oracle.com/display/INC10/Home
- Webcasts
  - ° http://www.oracle.com/technetwork/middleware/coherence/coherence-webcasts-098958.html

Other tools

- Oracle Enterprise Pack for Eclipse
  - ° http://www.oracle.com/technetwork/developer-tools/eclipse/overview/index.html
- MySQL
  - ° http://dev.mysql.com
- PrimeFaces
  - ° http://primefaces.org

Summary

This chapter presented an overview of the latest Java SDK 7, Java EE 6 technologies, and Oracle WebLogic 12c features. Most of them will be covered in this book. It also positions WebLogic Server 12c in the Cloud Application Foundation architecture, showing how co-related products such as Oracle Coherence can be integrated into a cohesive solution.

In the next chapter, we're going to set up the development environment with all the necessary components to create the application that will be used to demonstrate several features of WebLogic Server in the book.

2
Setting Up the Environment

In this chapter we're going to set up all the software required to implement and execute the code that we will be writing along the book. More specifically, we're going to:

- Install JDK Version 1.7, which will be used by the application server and the development environment
- Install Oracle WebLogic Server and Eclipse OEPE binaries
- Install a MySQL RDBMS server and configure a database
- Create and configure a WebLogic domain
- Configure the Eclipse IDE to recognize the WebLogic Server
- Install and configure an OpenLDAP server

About the directory structure

While writing this book, a couple of Unix-like operating systems were used, more specifically Mac OS X and Ubuntu. So, when referencing a directory path, the format adopted is /some/folder. If you are a Windows user, the equivalent path would be C:\some\folder.

The base folder used in the book is /opt/packt/. Inside it, we're going to add a few more folders to accommodate the necessary components. Here's the basic structure you have to create before moving on to the next section:

```
/opt/packt/
    |- domains
    |- etc
    |- install
    |- workspace
```

Of course, you don't need to follow the preceding definitions. If so, just remember to change the references accordingly, when mentioned.

> **Microsoft Windows users**: Whenever asked to choose a directory name, remember to select or create one without spaces to avoid potential problems later on.

Installing JDK 1.7

Since Oracle WebLogic Server 12c offers support to both Java SE 6 and 7, we're going to use the newest version, so we can code using a few developer-friendly features, such as the diamond operator and multicatch statements, as outlined in the *The Project Coin* section in *Chapter 1, Overview of WebLogic Server 12c and Related Technologies*.

1. Access the download page at `http://www.oracle.com/technetwork/java/javase/downloads/index.html`

2. Click on the **DOWNLOAD** button at the top of the page, or the one in the **JDK** column inside the **Java Platform, Standard Edition** table. At the time of writing, the newest JDK version was 7u21.

> Remember that we need a JDK, not a JRE.

3. On the next page, click on the **Accept License Agreement** option button and select the appropriate package for your system inside the **Java SE Development Kit 7u21** table:

> **Downloading the example code**
>
> You can download the example code files for all Packt books you have purchased from your account at `http://www.packtpub.com`. If you purchased this book elsewhere, you can visit `http://www.packtpub.com/support` and register to have the files e-mailed directly to you.

Java SE Development Kit 7u7

You must accept the Oracle Binary Code License Agreement for Java SE to download this software.

Thank you for accepting the Oracle Binary Code License Agreement for Java SE; you may now download this software.

Product / File Description	File Size	Download
Linux x86	120.62 MB	jdk-7u7-linux-i586.rpm
Linux x86	92.86 MB	jdk-7u7-linux-i586.tar.gz
Linux x64	118.8 MB	jdk-7u7-linux-x64.rpm
Linux x64	91.59 MB	jdk-7u7-linux-x64.tar.gz
Mac OS X	143.46 MB	jdk-7u7-macosx-x64.dmg
Solaris x86	135.4 MB	jdk-7u7-solaris-i586.tar.Z
Solaris x86	91.86 MB	jdk-7u7-solaris-i586.tar.gz
Solaris x64	22.51 MB	jdk-7u7-solaris-x64.tar.Z
Solaris x64	14.95 MB	jdk-7u7-solaris-x64.tar.gz
Solaris SPARC	135.69 MB	jdk-7u7-solaris-sparc.tar.Z
Solaris SPARC	95.15 MB	jdk-7u7-solaris-sparc.tar.gz
Solaris SPARC 64-bit	22.75 MB	jdk-7u7-solaris-sparcv9.tar.Z
Solaris SPARC 64-bit	17.47 MB	jdk-7u7-solaris-sparcv9.tar.gz
Windows x86	88.34 MB	jdk-7u7-windows-i586.exe
Windows x64	90.03 MB	jdk-7u7-windows-x64.exe

> The main difference between a 32-bit and a 64-bit version is memory addressing — the former can address up to 4 GB of memory, and the latter, 16 exabytes. As we're not going to run stress tests or highly demanding processes, the 32-bit version gives us plenty of room to play with.

5. After the download completes, unpack the file into the desired folder — /opt/packt/install is the directory adopted by the book — or if you chose an executable file, double-click on it and follow the installation process.

6. We now have a functional JDK installed as a sub-folder of the install directory. If you want, add a JAVA_HOME environment variable to your system pointing to your JDK root — that would be /opt/packt/install/jdk1.7.0_21 if you're following the book's pattern. You don't strictly need to do this in order to follow the book.

> It is recommended to create a JAVA_HOME environment variable for most cases so you can update your Java versions without further impacts. For the rest of the book, we're going to refer to Java's installation folder as $JAVA_HOME.

Installing Oracle WebLogic Server

Oracle WebLogic Server's installation is pretty straightforward; we just need to pay attention to the Java SDK selection in order to use the one we just installed.

1. Navigate to the download page at `http://www.oracle.com/technetwork/middleware/weblogic/downloads/index.html`.

2. Click on the **Accept License Agreement** option button.

3. Right below the option box, there's a drop-down list with five entries. Select the entry **Generic WebLogic Server and Coherence installer (880MB)** and click on the **Download File** button.

> Another option is to download the zip distribution; with barely one fifth the size of the generic installer, it includes all core artifacts, leaving out samples, the Derby database, and web server plugins, among other features. Also, there's no way to apply patches to this installation.
>
> If bandwidth is a concern, go ahead and get this file instead of the generic one. Check the README.txt file inside the package for instructions on how to install and configure a domain—the steps described in this chapter don't apply.

4. You will be redirected to a login page where you must enter your Oracle credentials (if you don't have one yet, sign up for an account now; you just need to fill up a short form).

5. When the download is completed, execute the installer using the Java binary installed in the previous section:

   `/oracle/jdk1.7.0_21/bin/java/java -jar wls_121200.jar`

6. The first step of the installation asks you to set up an **inventory**, which is the engine used by Oracle (along with **OPatch**) to apply upgrades and patches to its software. Enter `/opt/packt/inventory` as **Inventory Directory**, select a system group, and click on **OK**.

> You may proceed and run the inventory script created in the folder you entered, or just go ahead and continue the installation process—we're not going to apply any patches to the installation, so this step is optional.

7. Click on **Next** on the **Welcome** screen.

8. Enter the installation directory for the software, `/opt/packt/install`, and click on **Next**.

> The path you just entered is called **Oracle Home**, where the WebLogic Server binaries will be installed. If you are familiar with the previous versions of WebLogic, this is what was called **Middleware Home**, and earlier still, it used to be the **BEA Home**. In a nutshell, this folder is the root point where other Oracle products, such as SOA Suite, can be installed later, using the software that is already present as its starting point.
>
> If you're using Windows, remember to choose a folder name with no spaces in it. This is critical to run things smoothly.

9. On the **Installation Type** screen, you can choose between the default **WebLogic Server Installation** and **Complete Installation**; the difference between them is that the latter installs everything from the former plus the samples for both WebLogic and Coherence. Now click on **Next**.

10. The **Prerequisite Checks** screen does a basic validation of the environment, showing warning messages for those that don't pass; for instance, if you're using Ubuntu, which is not a certified platform, a warning is shown, and can be safely ignored. If no other warnings or errors are present, go ahead and click on **Next**.

11. You may want to register with Oracle Support in order to receive security updates. If you don't want to, just uncheck the **I wish to receive security updates via My Oracle Support** option and click on **Next**.

12. A summary is presented. Go ahead and click on **Install** to start the installation process.

> If this sequence is going to be repeated frequently, you can create a response file by clicking on the **Save Response File** button at the bottom of the summary tree, and execute a silent install later. Get a link to the official documentation in the *Web resources* section at the end of the chapter.

13. After it finishes, uncheck the **Automatically Launch the Configuration Wizard** checkbox and click on **Finish** to close the installer.

> It is recommended to export an environment variable pointing to your WebLogic's installation folder. Inside Oracle's documentation and usually in real environments, this is referred to as **MW_HOME** (the middleware home). For example: `export MW_HOME=/opt/packt/install`. This is how we will refer to this folder from now on.

Installing Oracle Enterprise Pack for Eclipse (OEPE)

The installation package we got doesn't come bundled with a development environment (Oracle JDeveloper, NetBeans, or Eclipse/OEPE). To create the book's applications, we decided to use Eclipse along with Oracle's application server plugin, OEPE, which is a great tool for Java EE development, integrating the IDE with WebLogic Server and other Java EE application servers. Perform the following steps to install it:

1. Navigate to `http://www.oracle.com/technetwork/developer-tools/ eclipse/downloads/index.html`.
2. Click on the option button for **Accept License Agreement**, choose the Eclipse version that runs on your system, and click on it to start the download.
3. After the download completes, unzip the installer in the directory `$MW_HOME/ oepe` and it's done.

> OEPE's newest version, 12.1.2.1, is based on Eclipse 4.3 Kepler, the most up-to-date version of Eclipse.

Installing MySQL

In order to explore Java Persistence, we need to install and configure a database server, and MySQL is a logical choice, being widely adopted and lightweight.

The software is available to several operating systems: Microsoft Windows, Debian, SUSE Linux Enterprise Server, Red Hat, Solaris, Mac OS X, and so on.

Installing on Linux using a package manager

If you are using a Linux distribution such as Ubuntu or Red Hat, most likely you already have the software available, you just need to install it with a command like this (you may want to update your repositories and packages to be sure that your system is up-to-date):

```
sudo apt-get install mysql-server mysql-client
```

> The stable version at the time of writing is 5.5.27, but most likely the repositories have older versions, for instance, 5.1 on Ubuntu 11. This version is pretty much enough to run the code we're going to explore throughout the book, so you can go ahead and install it.

The system is going to suggest a lot of other packages, but we don't need them. Just press *Y* to start the procedure. When applying the changes, the installation procedure will ask you to enter a password for user **root** (MySQL's administration user):

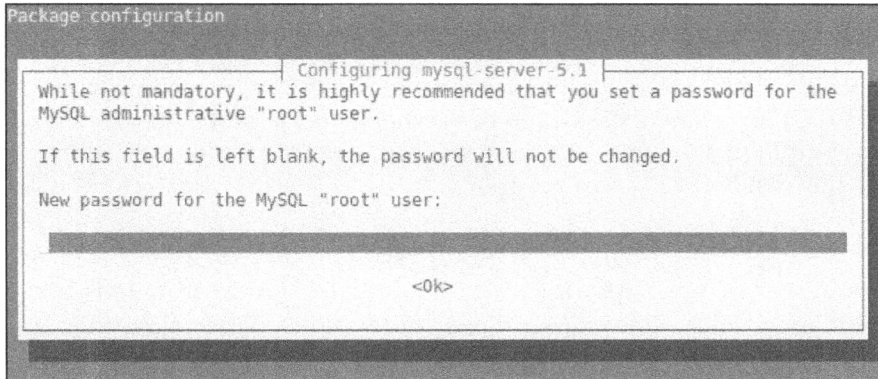

Downloading and installing manually

If your system doesn't provide a package manager, perform the following steps to manually download and install the product:

1. Access MySQL's download page at `http://dev.mysql.com/downloads/mysql/`.

2. At the **Generally Available (GA) Releases** tab, select your platform. The list of available downloads will be updated automatically.

3. Find the package that best fits your needs and click on **Download**.

4. A login page is presented. If you don't have or don't want to create an account, click on the **No thanks, just start my download.** link.

> You have to download both **MySQL Server** and **Client Utilities** packages, if the selected platform doesn't have a unified package.

5. The detailed installation procedure for every platform can be found at `http://dev.mysql.com/doc/refman/5.5/en/installing.html`; just follow the instructions.

Disabling case sensitivity for tables on Unix/Linux

If you are using a UNIX or Linux distribution, most likely the filesystem you're using differentiates between lower case and upper case in filenames.

As MySQL databases and tables persist as folders and files, respectively, we must instruct MySQL to ignore these differences when handling table names by editing the engine's configuration file—/etc/mysql/my.cnf is default—and adding the following line inside the mysqld group:

```
lower_case_table_names=1
```

Restart the server with the appropriate command for your environment, and we're good to go:

```
sudo service mysql restart
```

Some Windows specifics

If you are using Microsoft Windows, here are the points to note when running its installer:

1. We will not use any special feature of the product, so selecting **Standard Configuration** is good enough:

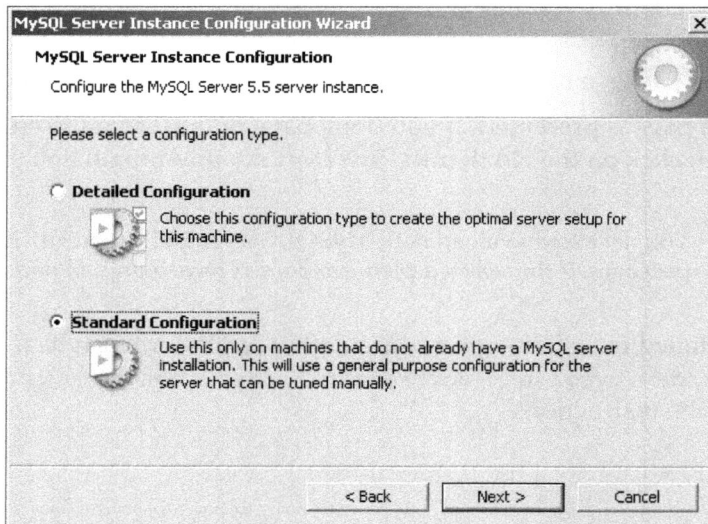

2. You can set it to start at system startup by leaving both **Install as Windows Service** and **Launch the MySQL Server automatically** flags enabled:

3. Finally, set a password for root access (MySQL's administrator user) and write it down to use in the next section:

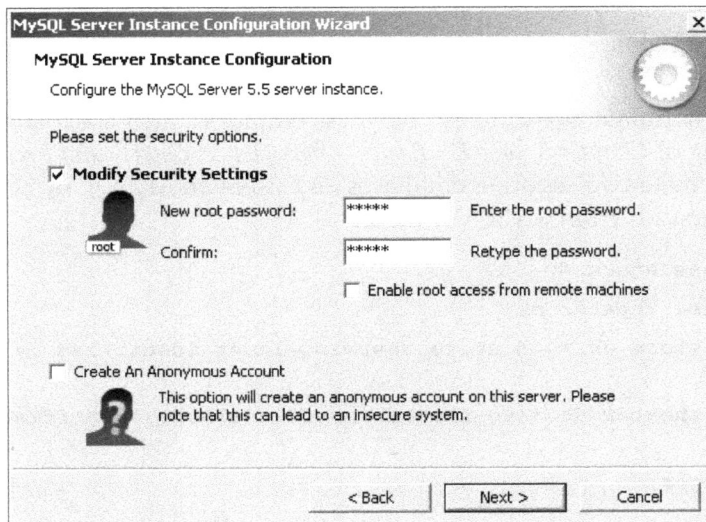

4. Click on **Next**, then **Execute**, and the installation process will begin. Close the wizard by clicking on **Finish**.

Configuring MySQL databases

If you chose to set it up as a service, or if this is the nature of your platform, then MySQL is already running upon completion of the installation procedure. To check this, open a terminal and enter the following command to start MySQL Monitor:

```
mysql -u root -p
```

If a message resembling **ERROR 2002 (HY000): Can't connect to local MySQL server through socket '/var/run/mysqld/mysqld.sock' (2)** shows up, you must start the server by issuing the proper command for your platform:

```
sudo service mysql start
```

Then, run the first command again. Enter the password you typed when installing MySQL, and you should be connected to the server.

> By default, MySQL listener is bound to the **loopback interface**, so only local access is allowed. If you want to access the database from another machine, edit the configuration file (/etc/mysql/my.cnf or equivalent) and change the line:
> ```
> bind-address     = 127.0.0.1
> ```
> To point to the desired network address:
> ```
> bind-address     = 192.168.0.5
> ```
> Save the file and restart MySQL.

We're going to simulate two different business entities (which is explained in detail at the beginning of *Chapter 3, Java EE Basics – Persistence, Query, and Presentation*), so we need to create two separate databases and users on MySQL by running the following commands from MySQL Monitor:

```
create database store_db;
create database theater_db;
grant all on store_db.* to store_user@localhost identified by
   'store';
grant all on theater_db.* to theater_user@localhost identified by
   'theater';
flush privileges;
quit;
```

> In case you are planning to connect from a machine or host other than `localhost`, change the command to:
>
> ```
> grant all on store_db.* to store_user@'%' identified by
>     'store';
> grant all on theater_db.* to theater_user@'%' identified
>     by 'theater';
> ```

We've just created the users, the databases, and granted the corresponding access.

Now, to create and populate the data structures, we're going to use the same command, but pass a script as the parameter for each database. From the command prompt run:

```
mysql -D store_db -u store_user -p < store_db.sql
mysql -D theater_db -u theater_user -p < theater_db.sql
```

> Files `store_db.sql` and `theater_db.sql` are located in the code bundle, available for download at the Packt Publishing website www.packtpub.com.

You should not see any error messages while the script is running. When the scripts end, the databases are configured and loaded with data.

Preparing PrimeFaces

PrimeFaces is a suite of components built on top of JSF 2.x, giving you lots of first-class widgets to use on a **Rich Internet Application** (**RIA**) solution, such as charts and mind maps. Its only requirement is to choose between **Oracle Mojarra** and **Apache MyFaces**, both JSF 2.0 implementations, and to reference the chosen one. The current implementation version at the time of writing is 3.5.

> Oracle WebLogic Server 12c comes with a JSF 2.0 implementation (Oracle Mojarra) enabled at its classpath, so we don't need to download anything but PrimeFaces.

Downloading the binaries

To use PrimeFaces, we must download it from http://www.primefaces.org/downloads.html. You can choose between **Binary**, **Source**, and **Bundle** packages.

> To follow the book, getting the binaries is enough, but if you plan to use PrimeFaces for real work, the **Bundle** option would be a good idea, since it includes the binaries, source code, API Javadocs, and taglib documentation.

The official documentation is a PDF available at `http://www.primefaces.org/documentation.html` with details on every component of the framework. And the most valuable source of information is the **ShowCase** page, with samples and working code for every component, available at `http://www.primefaces.org/showcase/ui/`.

PrimeFaces can be configured with JQuery's **ThemeRoller** (`http://jqueryui.com/themeroller/`), and there are lots of predefined themes available at `http://primefaces.org/themes.html`. You can also access the showcase mentioned previously and see how the themes feel like by selecting different names from the top left drop-down box.

Theme packages can be downloaded from `http://repository.primefaces.org/org/primefaces/themes/`. Grab the themes that appeal to you by clicking on the folder with the same name, then clicking again on the highest version number and selecting the file with extension `.jar`.

> Download at least one theme; we're going to use it in the next section to compose a shared library—**ui-lightness** is the authors' choice.

Creating a shared library

Shared libraries are a handy way to make different types of resources available between applications deployed on the same domain, avoiding the need to add them inside each application package or to change the classpath (and the unavoidable restart to make the new libraries available).

There is another way to share libraries called **optional packages**, where you can deploy a single plain JAR file as a library, and reference it from your application. The main difference between the two concepts is that a shared library can be a Java EE module (have a few EJBs, for instance), and an optional package is a standard Java library that can be shared by many applications without having to put the library inside the deployment package or adding it to the server's classpath.

> As we're going to use PrimeFaces and at least one theme package, the more sensible way to go is to construct a shared library.

For a full list of available modules, the differences between shared libraries and optional packages, and detailed specs on how to build and reference them, refer to `http://docs.oracle.com/middleware/1212/wls/WLPRG/libraries.htm`.

> We're going to use `/opt/packt/etc` as the base folder to keep files that do not directly relate to installation procedures or the development workspace.

The following steps show how to create the shared library:

1. Create a folder to hold the contents of the library and a few subdirectories:

```
cd /opt/packt/etc
mkdir ./primeSL
cd primeSL
mkdir ./META-INF
mkdir ./WEB-INF
mkdir ./WEB-INF/lib
```

2. Copy the JAR files downloaded in the previous section—`primefaces-3.5.jar`, `ui-lightness-1.0.10.jar` and any other themes you chose—to the `lib` folder.

3. Create a file named `MANIFEST.MF` inside `META-INF` with the following content:

```
Manifest-Version: 1.0
Extension-Name: primefaces
Specification-Version: 3.5
Implementation-Version: 3.5
```

4. Compress the contents of `/opt/packt/etc/primeSL` into a file named `primefacesSL.war`:

```
cd /opt/packt/etc/primeSL
zip -r primeSL.war */*
```

> Make sure that folders `META-INF` and `WEB-INF` are at the highest level of the WAR file.

5. The shared library is ready to be deployed.

Now that we have the assembled package, here's some insight about the MANIFEST.MF file we just created:

- The extension-name attribute is the name that we're going to use to reference the shared library at our projects

- The specification-version attribute is used to indicate which version this library exposes

- Finally, entry implementation-version is related to package versioning, so the developer can pin to a specific build version, if necessary

> Usually, this last entry is not declared, you only need to stick to a spec version. If a new release of PrimeFaces, let's say version 3.5.1, is made available, and we only declared specification-version, there's no need to update MANIFEST.MF.

Setting up a WebLogic domain

As you may know, after finishing the installation of Oracle WebLogic Server, you have the necessary binaries to start a container, but there is no configured server to deploy your code yet (unless you installed the samples, but we're not going to use them). To accomplish this, you have to create a **domain** consisting of one or more server instances. Your code runs on these instances.

We're going to use a basic domain template, consisting of just one instance, since we don't have any scalability or high availability requirements for the time being.

> Concepts related to how to configure an Oracle WebLogic Server environment — domains, clusters, machines, and so on — are covered in *Chapter 10, Scaling Up the Application*. For now, we only have to know that we need an instance to run the projects on, and it is part of a domain, which is the component that OEPE links to.

To create it, follow the ensuing steps:

1. Start the Configuration Wizard script, config.cmd (Windows) or config.sh (others), located at $MW_HOME/wlserver/common/bin/.

2. Leave the **Create a new domain** option, enter /opt/packt/domains/tickets as **Domain Location** and click on **Next**:

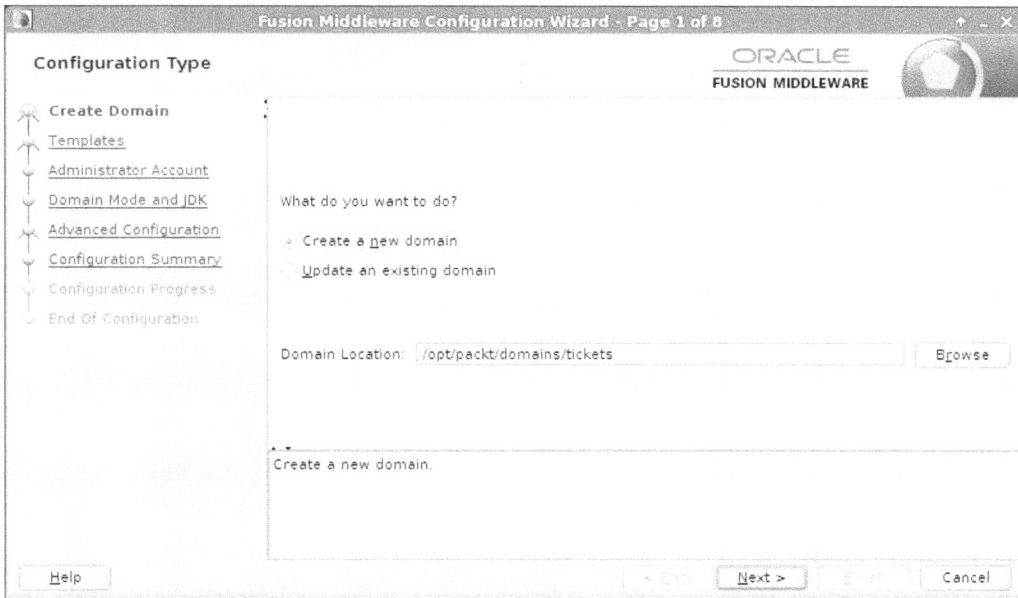

3. We are going to use only the **Basic WebLogic Server Domain** template:

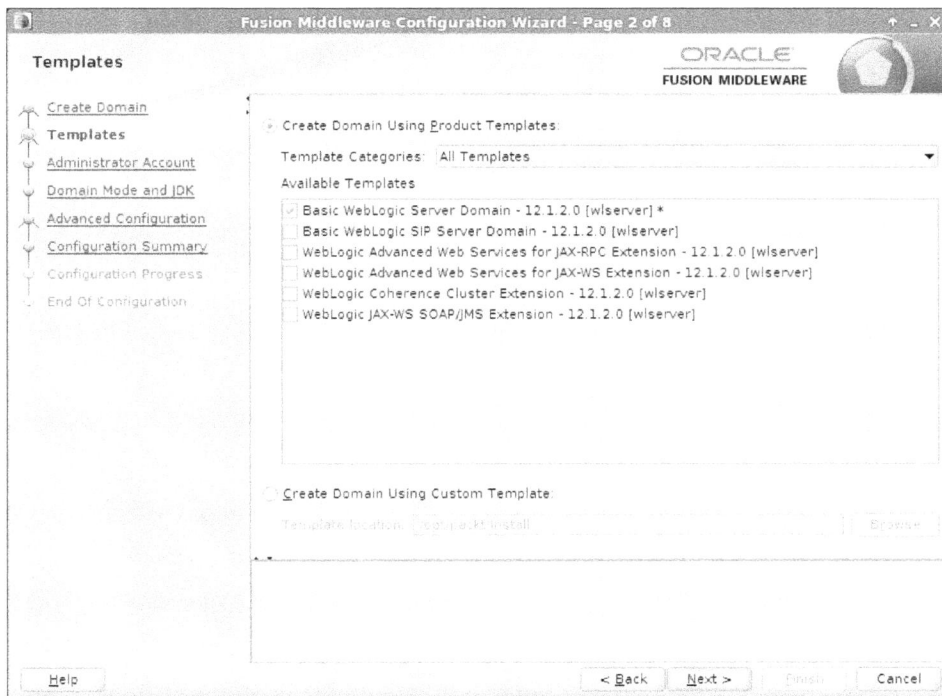

4. Configure the administrator's name (login) and password and navigate to the next page.

5. Leave the **Development** option selected under **Domain Mode**, make sure that the 1.7 JDK we installed at the start of this chapter is selected and click on **Next** twice.

6. On the **Configuration Summary** screen, click the **Create** button to start the process.

> By default, the server instance is bound to TCP port 7001. If you have other software using this port, check **Administration Server** on the **Advanced Configuration** screen, click on **Next** and change the **Listen port** field to another value.

7. When the process is done, click on the **Next** button to show information about the brand new domain, and click on **Finish** to close the wizard.

> It is recommended to export an environment variable DOMAIN_HOME that points to the domain you are currently working on, tickets in this case. For example: export DOMAIN_HOME=/opt/packt/ domains/tickets.

Configuring Eclipse and OEPE

The next step is to configure the Eclipse IDE so it knows about Oracle WebLogic Server's installation, the domain we created, and PrimeFaces' shared library.

Linking WebLogic's runtime environment

First, we're going to tell Eclipse where to find WebLogic's runtime environment:

1. Launch the Eclipse IDE by running the following command:

   ```
   $MW_HOME/oepe/eclipse
   ```

   Or open the shortcut created by the installation process.

2. Enter /opt/packt/workspace on the **Workspace Launcher** screen.

3. Open the Preferences screen using the menu – Window → **Preference**.

4. In the filter field, type server, click on the **Runtime Environment** entry and then the **Add...** button.

5. In the new window, type `12c` in the filter field, select the entry **Oracle WebLogic Server 12c (12.1.2)** and click on **Next**.

6. Fill the field **WebLogic home** with the path where you installed the server — `$MW_HOME/wlserver` — and the other fields should be filled automatically:

7. Click on **Finish** to close this window and return to the **Preferences** screen.

Adding a reference to the PrimeFaces' shared library

Now we're going to set up the PrimeFaces shared library, so we can reference it from our projects:

1. On the **Preferences** screen, type `shared` to filter the entries, and click on **Shared Libraries**.

2. The list of configured shared libraries is going to show up. Click on **Add...** to insert a new one.

3. On the pop-up window, type in the full path of your `primeSL.war` file, or find it using the **Browse...** button.

> The location of the file is `/opt/packt/etc/primeSL/primeSL.war` if you're following the book's pattern.

4. The information we entered in the `MANIFEST.MF` file will be shown along with the JAR files that compose the shared library:

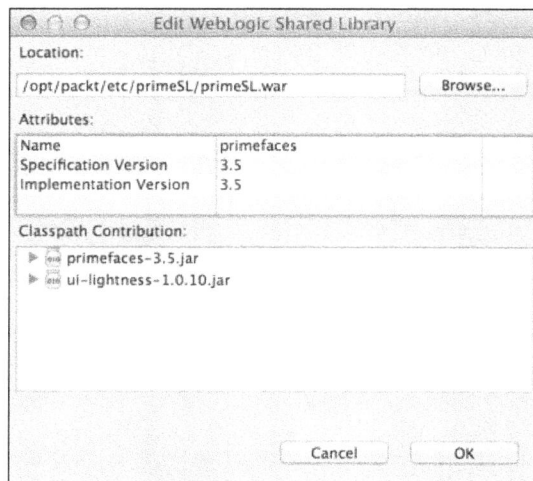

5. Click on **OK** to confirm the procedure, and then click on **OK** again on the **Preferences** window to close it.

Linking WebLogic Server's instance

In order to start and stop the server from within Eclipse, along other actions such as package, deploy, and debug applications using the environment, we must inform the IDE about WebLogic's configured domain and server. To accomplish this, perform the following steps:

1. Navigate to **Window | Show View | Other...** and type `server` in the **Filter** field; now double-click on the **Servers** entry.

2. The **Servers** tab is going to show up. Click on the **No servers are available. Click this link to create a new server...** link inside it to open the **Define a New Server** window.

3. As we only have one runtime environment configured, Eclipse suggests it at the first screen. Just click on **Next**.

4. Now, enter your domain path—the whole value of /$DOMAIN_HOME—and click on **Finish**. Here's the final configuration:

> We left the **Local** server type on this screen, meaning that OEPE has direct access to the server. If you need to connect to a development server, for instance, **Remote** is the way to go. Remember that OEPE still needs to access WebLogic Server's modules and libraries to compile your projects, so a local copy of it must be present, even though you will deploy them to a remote server.

5. The new server is going to appear at the **Servers** tab. Right-click on it and select the **Properties** entry from the context menu.

6. On the **Properties** window, click on **Weblogic** then **Publishing**, and select **Publish as an exploded archive** from the **Publishing mode** group:

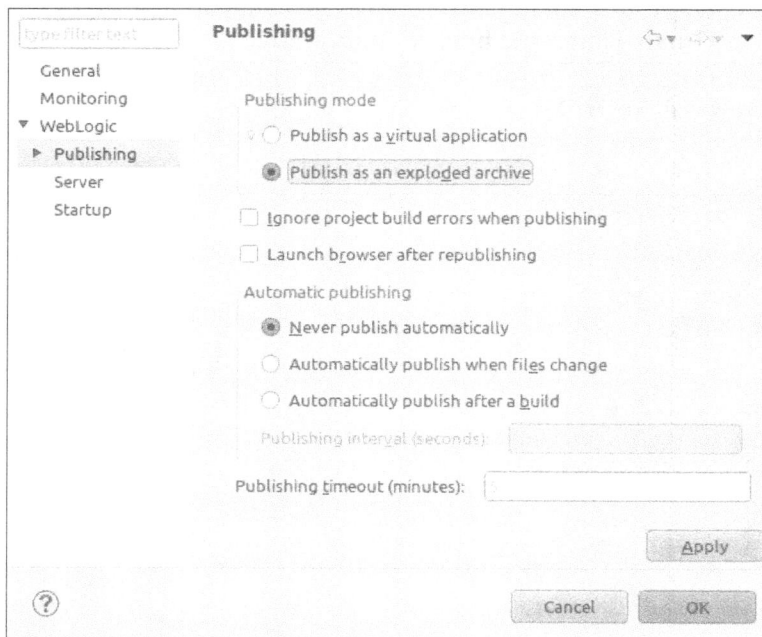

7. Click on **OK** to close the window, and it's done.

Referencing MySQL databases

The last step is to configure the data sources that the application is going to use at WebLogic, and create links to these databases at Eclipse. This kind of connection is a **data source (DS)** inside WebLogic Server.

> In earlier versions of WebLogic Server, you were supposed to configure both a **connection pool** and a data source. Now, both concepts are contained within a data source, which is a logical move—sharing a pool of connections but not the link to it (the data source) may lead to problems, since no application could predict if others were using the underlying pool, and worst yet, how.

Creating WebLogic data sources

As we just finished enabling the domain at Eclipse, we can start the server from there:

1. In the **Servers** tab, right-click on the domain name and then **Start** from the context menu, or if you prefer to start it manually, OEPE will synchronize to show that the server is up and running.

2. The focus will switch to the **Console** tab. After 15 to 30 seconds, a message stating that the server is running is going to show up (**<BEA-000360><The server started in RUNNING mode.>**) and the focus will get back to the **Servers** tab.

3. Right-click again on the server name, select **Go To**, and then **Admin Console** to open a browser window pointing to the administration console.

    > The default address of the administration console is
    > `http://localhost:7001/console`.

4. Enter your administrator's credentials (the username and password you set when creating the domain) and click on **Login**. The initial page shows you a list of basically every resource you can configure. Find the link **Data Sources** inside the **Services** group and click on it.

5. On the new page, click on **New**, then click on **Generic Data Source** and then on **Next**.

6. Fill the fields as follows and click on **Next**:
    - **Name**: Store DS
    - **JNDI Name**: jdbc/tickets/store
    - **Database Type**: MySQL

7. Leave the default value for the driver, **MySQL's Driver (Type 4) Versions: using com.mysql.jdbc.Driver**, and click on **Next**.

    > Oracle WebLogic Server already comes with a MySQL driver, so we don't need any additional downloads in order to create a Data Source that points to this database engine.

8. Select the **Logging Last Resource** option and go to the next page.

> As we're using a driver that doesn't support **global** (distributed) transactions — transactions that coordinate several resources as a single unit — we will emulate its behavior by enabling the **Emulate Two-Phase Commit** option.
>
> The **Logging Last Resource** option is an alternative to this emulation that brings performance and reliability improvements. For detailed advantages and considerations about it, check the **Web resources** section at the end of the chapter.

9. Enter the following values and click on **Next**:
    - **Database Name**: store_db
    - **Host Name**: localhost
    - **Port**: 3306 (this is the default value)
    - **Database User Name**: store_user
    - **Password and Confirmation**: store

10. There's no need to change any values here. Click on the **Test Configuration** button at the top of the page and a message **Connection test succeeded** must show up right above the test button. Click on **Next**.

> If the test returned an error, you must check the message and figure out what went wrong — an invalid credential, MySQL server is down or a typo are the most likely causes.

11. Finally, select the server on which the resource is to be made available — **AdminServer** is the only one on our domain — and click on **Finish** to commit the changes.

12. Now, create another data source following the same steps, but changing these fields:
    - **Name**: Theater DS
    - **JNDI Name**: jdbc/tickets/theater
    - **Database Name**: theater_db
    - **Database User Name**: theater_user
    - **Password and Confirmation**: theater

You must have a list of data sources like the following one by now:

Data Sources (Filtered - More Columns Exist)

New ⌄	Delete			Showing 1 to 2 of 2 Previous | Next
☐	**Name** ⌃	**Type**	**JNDI Name**	**Targets**
☐	Theater DS	Generic	jdbc/tickets/theater	AdminServer
☐	Store DS	Generic	jdbc/tickets/store	AdminServer
New ⌄	Delete			Showing 1 to 2 of 2 Previous | Next

Adding database connections to Eclipse

Now we're going to inform Eclipse/OEPE about the databases, so we can use its wizards later. Go back to Eclipse and execute the following steps:

1. Find or open the **Data Source Explorer** view (In the menu, navigate to **Window | Show View | Other | Data Source Explorer**).

2. Right-click on **Database Connections** and select **New...** in the context menu.

3. Select **MySQL**, type `MySQL - Store` as **Name** then click on **Next**.

4. Click on the **New Driver Definition** button beside the **Drivers** dropdown.

5. Select **MySQL JDBC Driver version "5.1"** and go to the **Jar List** tab.

6. Select the entry **mysql-connector-java-5.1.0-bin.jar** and click on **Remove JAR/Zip**, then click on **Add JAR/Zip**.

7. On the pop-up window, navigate to `$MW_HOME` and continue to the subdirectory `./oracle_common/modules/mysql-connector-java-commercial-5.1.22/`.

8. Select the file `mysql-connector-java-commercial-5.1.22-bin.jar` and click on **OK**.

9. The **New Connection Profile** window is going to pop up, change the following fields:

   ° **Database**: `store_db`

   ° **URL**: `jdbc:mysql://localhost:3306/store_db`

   ° **User name**: `store_user`

   ° **Password**: `store`

° Check **Save password**

Specify a Driver and Connection Details

Select a driver from the drop-down and provide login details for the connection.

Drivers: MySQL JDBC Driver

Properties

General | Optional

Database: store_db

URL: jdbc:mysql://localhost:3306/store_db

User name: store_user

Password: •••••

☑ Save password

☑ Connect when the wizard completes   Test Connection

☐ Connect every time the workbench is started

⊘   < Back | Next > | Cancel | Finish

10. Click on **Test Connection**, and you should see a **Ping succeeded!** message.

> If this is not the case, go back, check if you entered the correct values and run the test again. You may need to start up the MySQL Server.

11. Click on **Finish**.

Now we need to execute the same steps mentioned earlier, but this time pointing to the Theater database. Here are the fields you need to change:

- **Connection name**: MySQL - Theater
- **Database**: theater_db
- **URL**: jdbc:mysql://localhost:3306/theater_db
- **User name**: theater_user
- **Password**: theater

The last step is to create and configure an OpenLDAP server, which will be accessed by WebLogic's instance when we discuss security features.

Using OpenLDAP

OpenLDAP is a cross-platform, free, and open source implementation of a **Lightweight Directory Access Protocol (LDAP)** server, released under a BSD license. It was started in 1998 and since then has had active development and constant releases, being widely adopted by many commercial-grade systems and applications.

Although WebLogic server includes its own embedded LDAP server for default security management, it's neither used nor recommended for application-specific security management. That's when third-party LDAP servers and products are recommended and offer much more flexibility and features for a real-world scenario.

> Note that you can use WebLogic embedded LDAP for the examples in this book, although we do recommend the experience of creating and configuring an Authentication Provider outside WebLogic.

In this section we're going to provide general guidelines for OpenLDAP configuration, but due to the way different operating systems package the software, some configuration files may not be present at the same paths. Such differences may not impact the ideas expressed in this section.

Installing OpenLDAP

The OpenLDAP software is available to several operating systems: Microsoft Windows, Debian, SuSE Linux Enterprise Server, Red Hat, Solaris, Mac OS X, and so on.

It can easily be installed through package managers such as RPM, APT, or MacPorts on Linux and Mac using the following commands:

For Linux with APT:

```
sudo apt-get install slapd ldap-utils
```

For RPM-based systems:

```
sudo yum install openldap-servers openldap-clients nss_ldap
```

For Mac OSX:

```
sudo port install openldap
```

Windows users can download and install the executable package available at `http://userbooster.de/en/download/openldap-for-windows.aspx`.

> The installation may ask for a password that will be used for the **rootdn** user, which is the main user for an OpenLDAP installation. Take note of this password as we're going to use it later.
>
> We are currently using version 2.4.35 but any 2.4+ release of OpenLDAP will be sufficient for the features we're going to implement.

Configuring an OpenLDAP server

Under some distributions, OpenLDAP provides `ldap.conf` and `slapd.conf` files with standard values. There are cases where these files must be copied or renamed from default files that come as part of the distribution. For example, on a Mac OS X system, the following files must be copied or renamed:

- `/private/etc/openldap/ldap.conf.default` to `ldap.conf`
- `/private/etc/openldap/slapd.conf.default` to `slapd.conf`
- `/private/var/db/openldap/openldap-data/DB_CONFIG.example` to `DB_CONFIG`

On Ubuntu Linux, these steps can be skipped as the configuration files are already at the `/etc/ldap` directory.

> It's worth mentioning that there are even YouTube videos explaining how to do the basic setup of an LDAP server on Ubuntu and other popular Linux distributions. Refer to them if you have problems on performing the basic operations and check this section again in order to make the specific configurations for our usage.

Files `ldap.conf` and `slapd.conf` are the most important ones on an OpenLDAP configuration, with `DB_CONFIG` being the file-based database that stores runtime configuration such as users and groups.

After copying or renaming the files, open the `ldap.conf` (under `/private/etc/openldap` on Mac or `/etc/ldap/ldap.conf` on Ubuntu/Linux) so we can set or uncomment the BASE value used for an LDAP tree. Note that we're going to use `example.com` as our base domain values:

```
## Make sure you have the BASE uncommented
BASE    dc=example,dc=com
#URI    ldap://ldap.example.com ldap://ldap-master.example.com:666
```

Use the command `slappasswd` to generate an encoded password or use the default password `secret` when asked for a password on the next command. Depending on your OS you may have already set this password during the installation.

Example:

```
$ slappasswd -s welcome1
{SSHA}Pcvcy4CpSL4BVLA0MWLtKM9XbV3Tw3q+
```

> Note that this hash will change every time this command is executed.

Now we're going to use this hashed value on `rootpw` variable in the configuration file. Also check or set `suffix` and `rootdn` values on `slapd.conf` as follows:

```
suffix          "dc=example,dc=com"
rootdn          "cn=Manager,dc=example,dc=com"
# Use of strong authentication is encouraged
rootpw          {SSHA}Pcvcy4CpSL4BVLA0MWLtKM9XbV3Tw3q+
```

Still in `slapd.conf` there is a section that includes schemas used by this instance of OpenLDAP. Enable additional schemas to store other commonly required information and structures under the directory service:

```
#
# See slapd.conf(5) for details on configuration options.
# This file should NOT be world readable.
#
include /private/etc/openldap/schema/core.schema
include /private/etc/openldap/schema/cosine.schema
include /private/etc/openldap/schema/nis.schema
include /private/etc/openldap/schema/inetorgperson.schema
```

> On Ubuntu these steps can be done through the following commands:
> ```
> ldapadd -Y EXTERNAL -H ldapi:/// -f /etc/ldap/schema/
>     cosine.ldif
> ldapadd -Y EXTERNAL -H ldapi:/// -f /etc/ldap/schema/
>     inetorgperson.ldif
> ldapadd -Y EXTERNAL -H ldapi:/// -f /etc/ldap/schema/
>     nis.ldif
> ```

In order to test what we have configured so far, we need to restart the OpenLDAP server by issuing a command like the following:

```
sudo /etc/init.d/slapd restart
```

Or as follows:

```
sudo /usr/libexec/slapd -d3
```

> A common error when setting these under Linux environments is when the starting script does not load your configuration files. In order to prevent those problems take a quick look at the code present under /etc/init.d/slapd.

Loading sample entries and testing

Now you can load the default entries from the export file provided with the book bundle using the following command:

```
sudo ldapadd -c -D "cn=Manager,dc=example,dc=com" -W -f
  ldap_export.ldif
```

And after that you can list all the entries using a command like this:

```
ldapsearch -z 0 -b "dc=example,dc=com" -D "cn=Manager,
  dc=example,dc=com" -W "(objectclass=*)"
```

If you followed all the steps and imported the file we're providing with the book, the output should look like this:

```
Enter LDAP Password:
# extended LDIF
#
# LDAPv3
# base <dc=example,dc=com> with scope subtree
# filter: (objectclass=*)
# requesting: ALL
#

# example.com
dn: dc=example,dc=com
objectClass: organizationalUnit
objectClass: dcObject
dc: example
ou: example
```

```
# people, example.com
dn: ou=people,dc=example,dc=com
objectClass: top
objectClass: organizationalUnit
ou: people

# groups, example.com
dn: ou=groups,dc=example,dc=com
objectClass: top
objectClass: organizationalUnit
ou: groups

# robert@example.com, people, example.com
dn: cn=robert@example.com,ou=people,dc=example,dc=com
objectClass: top
objectClass: person
objectClass: organizationalPerson
objectClass: inetOrgPerson
cn: robert@example.com
sn: Robert
mail: robert@example.com
userPassword: XXXX

# admin, groups, example.com
dn: cn=admin,ou=groups,dc=example,dc=com
objectClass: top
objectClass: groupOfNames
cn: admin
member: cn=superuser@example.com,ou=people,dc=example,dc=com
ou: admin

# john@example.com, people, example.com
dn: cn=john@example.com,ou=people,dc=example,dc=com
objectClass: top
objectClass: person
objectClass: organizationalPerson
objectClass: inetOrgPerson
cn: john@example.com
sn: john
userPassword:: XXXX
```

> As with other commands in this section, the command to test may change depending on your operating system.

And that's it, we now have every required piece of software installed and configured.

Web resources

- Oracle WebLogic Server Certification Matrix
  - ○ http://www.oracle.com/technetwork/middleware/ias/
    downloads/fusion-certification-100350.html
  - ○ http://www.oracle.com/technetwork/middleware/fusion-
    middleware/documentation/fmw-1212certmatrix-1970069.xls

- Exploded Deploy
  - ○ http://docs.oracle.com/middleware/1212/wls/INTRO/
    deploying.htm

- Creating Shared Java EE Libraries and Optional Packages
  - ○ http://docs.oracle.com/middleware/1212/wls/WLPRG/
    libraries.htm
  - ○ http://blogs.oracle.com/jamesbayer/entry/weblogic_
    server_shared_librari_1

- Logging Last Resource Transaction Option
  - ○ http://docs.oracle.com/middleware/1212/wls/JDBCA/
    transactions.htm

- Configuring Your Domain For Advanced Web Services Features
  - ○ http://docs.oracle.com/middleware/1212/wls/WSGET/jax-ws-
    setenv.htm#CACHCAJD

- Features and Standards Supported by WebLogic Web Services
  - ○ http://docs.oracle.com/middleware/1212/wls/WSOVR/
    weblogic-web-service-standards.htm

- PrimeFaces
  - ○ http://www.primefaces.org/downloads.html
  - ○ http://www.primefaces.org/documentation.html
  - ○ http://www.primefaces.org/showcase/ui/

- OpenLDAP
  - ° `http://www.openldap.org/`
  - ° `http://www.openldap.org/doc/admin24/quickstart.html`

- OpenLDAP for Windows
  - ° `http://userbooster.de/en/download/openldap-for-windows.aspx`

- OpenLDAP configuration on Ubuntu
  - ° `https://help.ubuntu.com/community/OpenLDAPServer`

Summary

At this point, we have installed and configured the Oracle WebLogic Server, an IDE (Eclipse OEPE), and the additional pieces of software needed to develop our applications.

The following is a table with all paths and environment variables that you may have defined in your environment in this chapter:

Variable	Path
JAVA_HOME	/opt/packt/install/jdk1.7.0_21
DOMAIN_HOME	/opt/packt/domains/tickets
MW_HOME	/opt/packt/install

In the next chapter, we're going to set up the projects that will evolve throughout the book, develop the business entities, and use the libraries and packages we've just created. These projects will be deployed to the server and we will run a simple test to make sure everything is properly configured.

3
Java EE Basics – Persistence, Query, and Presentation

In the previous chapter, we set up all the necessary software to develop and execute the applications that will be developed throughout the book. In this chapter, we will:

- Take a look at the business case used as a background to the technical features and implementation
- Create an entity project to provide isolation and reuse of business entities, defining a persistence layer
- Create a web project with a simple query page that would access the entities we just created
- Deploy and run both projects to make sure every component—database, application server, and libraries—is configured and working as expected

The business scenario – movie ticket system

To explore the features delivered by the WebLogic Server and its associated technologies/products, we're going to develop a system to search and reserve movie tickets with two main business entities — the customer and the theater:

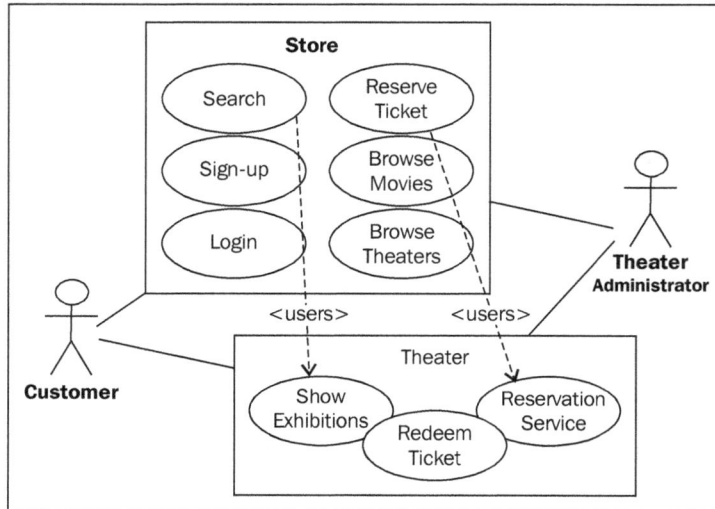

The main focus of the business is to provide a central point for movie theater customers to browse, search, and reserve tickets. In order to show up as a search result, a theater location (or chain) must close a deal with us. By doing so, they don't have to keep all the necessary structure to have an online presence, and we get our income from a monthly fee paid by each theater plus a small percentage of each ticket we sell.

Some of the data, such as the list of movies and locations are located at the central module, Store, and others, such as seat availability are held by each theater. Upon closing a partnership, we hand over a small application module that the theater's IT personnel must set up. So, when a customer queries about a specific exhibition, the theater module is accessed by the store module to get up-to-date information on available seats, and so on. When a reservation is made, the store sends the necessary information to the selected theater so that it can mark the seat as taken. Here is a high-level modular view of our solution:

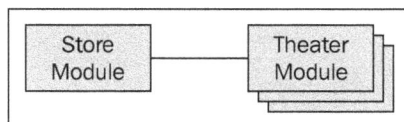

The basic use case scenario goes like this:

1. The customer accesses the web page to search for a movie, chooses between the available criteria to compose the query, and submits it to the store module.

2. Some of the information (movie and theater data) is located at the store module and is validated upon the arrival of the request. After checking for data consistency, the local data is retrieved and a query to the appropriate theater is issued.

3. The theater module receives the request, processes it by getting the necessary information from its database, and sends the response back.

4. The store module receives the data and shows it to the customer. If he/she wants to proceed and reserve the ticket, another command is sent to the store module, which in turn sends the data to the theater module.

5. The remote module sends the request to the theater's proprietary system and after the reservation is confirmed, a response is sent back to our store module, which saves the transaction along with a unique control number.

6. A confirmation message is presented to the customer with the generated control number. This is a proof that the transaction was completed successfully. Upon arrival at the theater's booth, the customer presents the control number to the clerk, who verifies the validity of the reservation using his own system. If everything's ok, the customer pays for the tickets and the entrance is granted.

Business entities of the system

When we think about a diagram with the main entities (domain model) of this system, their definitions and relationships should look like this:

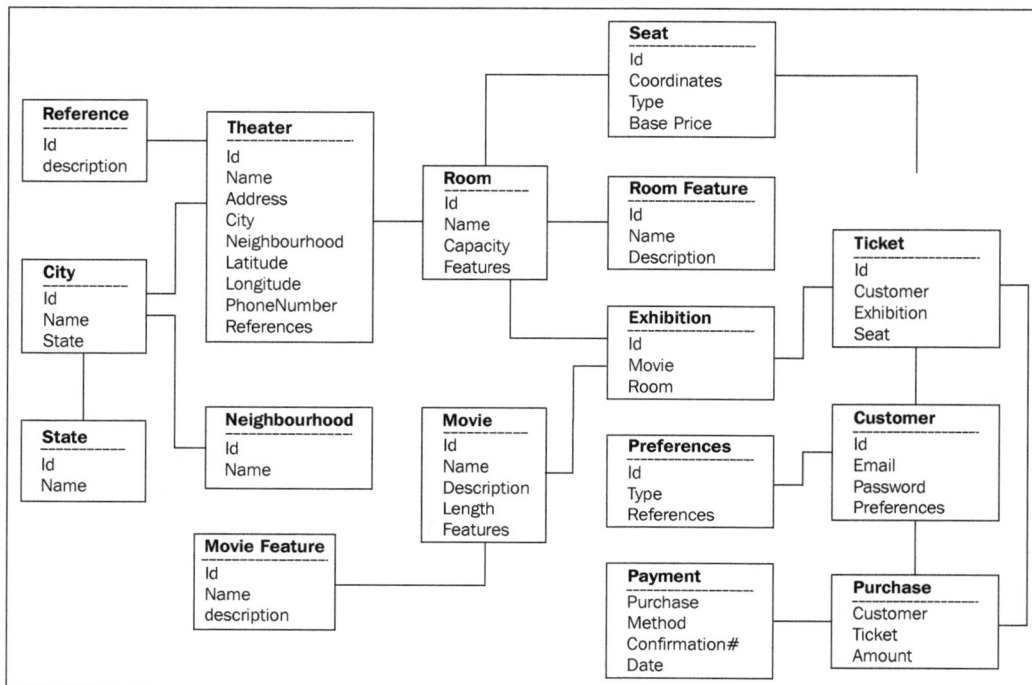

The preceding graphic is a fairly complete representation of the entities that a real-world system would need to implement the business scenario we just presented. As the goal of the book is to help the understanding and usage of the WebLogic Server 12c, we're going to simplify the business model a little bit so that we can keep the focus on what really matters.

So, here is the set of entities we are going to use throughout the book:

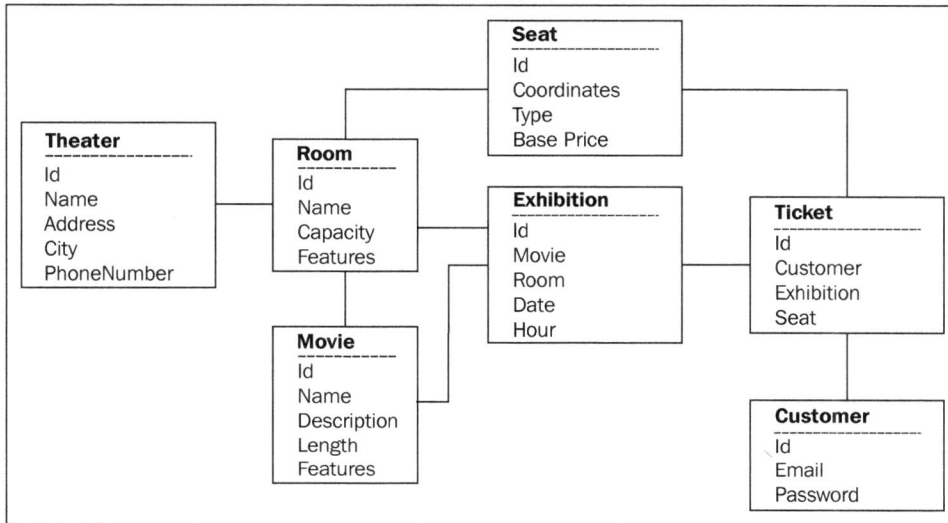

The mapping of these entities to relational tables is pretty straightforward, but as we have two modules, each module will use a subset of the tables as shown here:

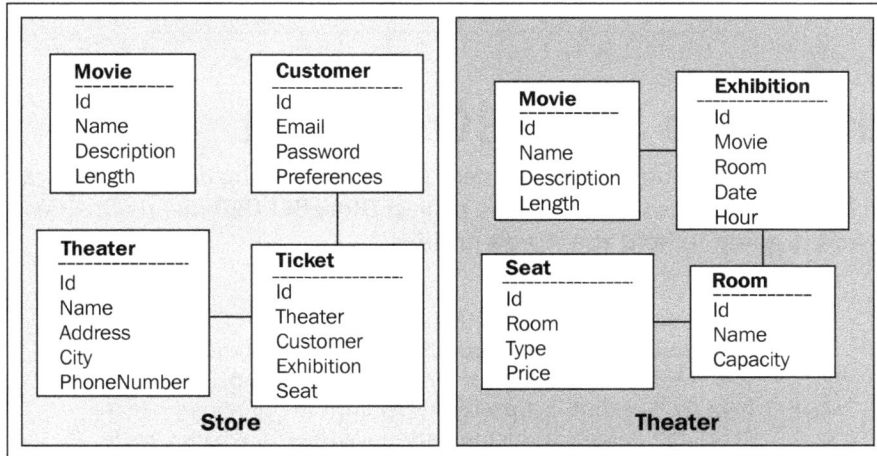

Keep in mind that even with this simplified model, we will be able to present the intended features of the application server. Having a complex model would just demand repetitive coding effort. That said, let's discuss one last detail about the project's structure using Eclipse before we start generating actual code.

Organizing projects in Eclipse

The application architecture points to two isolated modules: the central module, which we will name **Store** and a remote module that each theater must set up and run at its own installation, aptly named **Theater**. So, it is a natural decision to have two projects, each implementing one module.

These two modules will be implemented as web applications, holding screens, web services, and business logic. The business entities will reside in projects of their own. This is a common pattern when mapping domain entities that virtually any project of your company will have to access at some point in time. In the development phase, this approach helps avoiding concurrency between developers editing source code and isolates sensitive code if security is a concern. When the systems are up and running, maintenance is also simplified. Instead of repackaging every module that uses the common library, just one update is necessary.

Our entities are mostly isolated by modules, but we're going to apply this general principle in order to show you how to configure/reference them so that two entity projects will be deployed as **Java optional packages**. Here is a visual representation of the projects we are going to create:

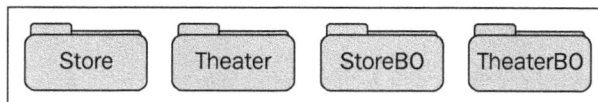

Creating the StoreBO project

To implement even the most basic business functionality, the domain entities must exist and be available. So, let's create the project **StoreBO** (BO means Business Objects) that is going to hold the store's entities.

> As we're going to use the Java Persistence API (JPA), it's good to know that the default JPA implementation shipped with Oracle WebLogic Server 12c is Oracle TopLink, which is heavily based on EclipseLink. Up until the previous release (11*g*), the default implementation was Kodo, which Oracle bought along with other BEA products.

The Oracle Enterprise Pack for Eclipse gives us a couple of handy features to create a **JPA Project**. By selecting this project type, we basically instructed Eclipse to add the **JPA facet** to the project, enabling features such as a tool to map relational tables to classes.

> Keep in mind that JPA 2.0, which is the layer that enables EJB 3.x persistence features, is not directly linked to Java EE — you can use the persistence layer on a pure Java project without having to use an application server.

Fire up your OEPE and perform the following steps:

1. Navigate to **File | New | Project…**.
2. Type JPA in the textbox, select **JPA Project** and click on **Next**.
3. On the **New JPA Project** screen:
    1. Enter StoreBO in **Project name**.
    2. **Target Runtime**: select **Oracle WebLogic Server 12c (12.1.2)**.

    > By doing this, we're telling Eclipse where it is supposed to look for dependencies/libraries when Project Facets or Shared Libraries are used.

    3. Click on the **Modify…** button next to the **Configuration** dropdown menu and make sure that the **Java** facet is set to Version **1.7**, changing it if necessary, then click on **Finish**.
4. Click on **Next**.
5. We don't need to change the default values for source folders, so just click on **Next**.
6. On the **JPA Facet** screen:
    1. Select **EclipseLink 2.4.x/2.5.x** as **Platform**.
    2. Under **JPA implementation**, select **Disable Library Configuration**.
    3. In the **Persistent class management** group, select **Annotated classes must be listed in persistence.xml**.
    4. Click on **Finish**.
7. Click **Yes** to open the **JPA Perspective**.

Let's take a closer look at the options presented by the **JPA Facet** screen:

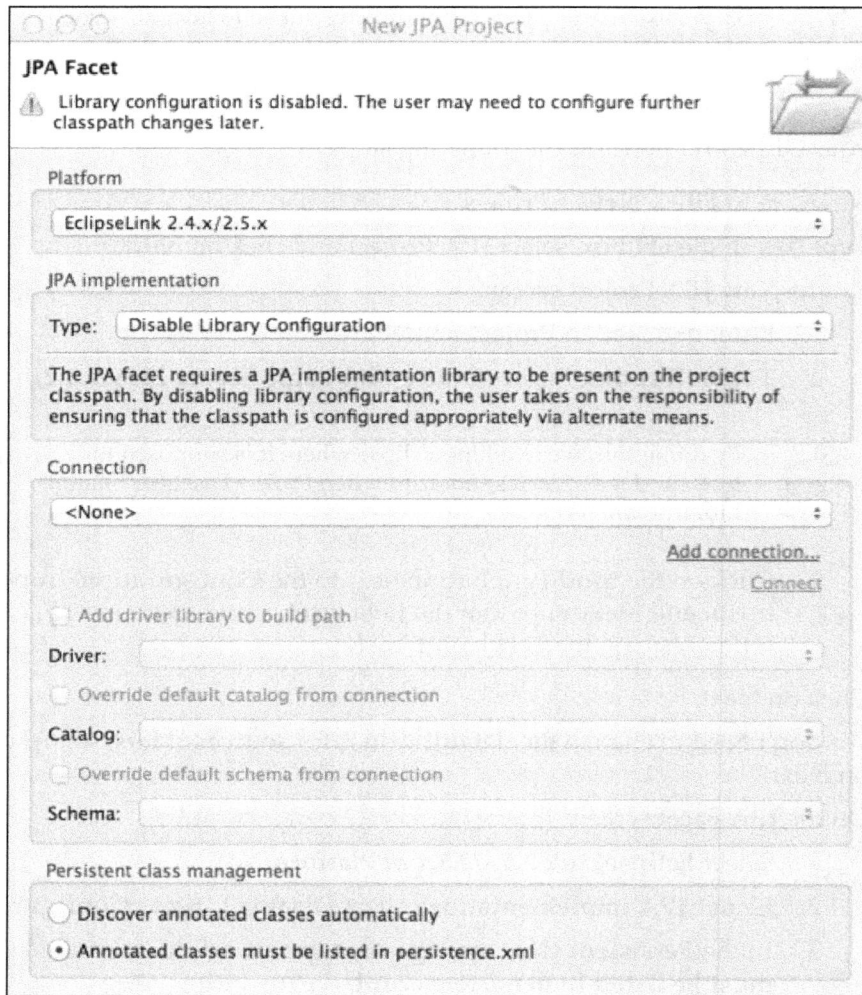

The default value for **Platform** is **Generic 2.0**, which means Eclipse/OEPE will give you the most basic configuration options when you open the `persistence.xml` file to edit. The other options are for specific versions of **EclipseLink** — an **Object-Relation Mapping** framework — giving you more graphical resources to edit the file.

Oracle WebLogic Server 12.1.2 ships with **Oracle TopLink** Version 12.1.2, which is the base for this book and is built upon EclipseLink 2.4.2. So, we selected the **EclipseLink 2.4.x** option to enable the features related to this version.

[
EclipseLink 2.4.2 added a lot of new features, such as
support for NoSQL, REST, and JSON development.
]

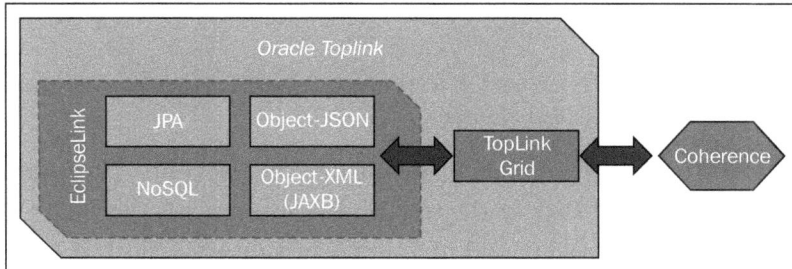

We disabled the configuration related to the **JPA Implementation** because OEPE doesn't give us a direct option to use the libraries provided by WebLogic. We could have selected **User Library** instead and installed one of the EclipseLink versions shown, but that defeats the idea of using WebLogic modules.

After walking through the other options of this screen, we're going to add the necessary module reference.

The **Connection** drop-down menu gives us the option to select one of the connections listed in the **Data Source Explorer**. If you are not running your application inside a Java EE container, you can set the transaction-type attribute as RESOURCE_LOCAL, which means that the entity managers or data sources used by the application are not capable of providing JTA services. Changing this property under the connection tab will populate the related entries in the persistence.xml. A good use case for this transaction type is **unit testing**.

According to the JPA 2.0 specification (**JSR 317**), the default value for this attribute in the Java EE environment is JTA and the default value for the Java SE environment is RESOURCE_LOCAL. Since we're going to use the WebLogic Server's **Data Source** to access data, we can leave it as JTA or empty.

Finally, the **Persistent class management** option configures the persistence.xml file to instruct the container to discover annotated beans by scanning the packages that compose the deployment/project. This is controlled by the exclude-unlisted-classes entry and the default behavior is to scan the packages. By setting the screen option to **Annotated classes must be listed in persistence.xml,** we are telling the container to stick to the classes listed in the file.

> The package scanning feature is only supported by Java EE
> application containers. So, if you plan to use Entities on standalone
> applications, you must explicitly name them in `persistence.`
> `xml` — the `exclude-unlisted-classes` tag is ignored.

The last step to configure the project is to reference WebLogic's persistence library,
so we can compile the generated classes:

1. Right-click on the project name and click on the last entry, **Properties**.
2. Click on **Java Build Path** in the tree.
3. Click on the **Libraries** tab and then the **Add Library…** button.
4. Select **WebLogic System Libraries** and click on **Next**.
5. Select the **javax.persistence** library and click on **Finish**.

> If the library is not available, click on the Add button (the plus sign)
> in the top-right portion of the screen, type `javax.persistence` in
> the **Module id** field, and click on **Finish**.

6. Click on **OK** to close the **Properties** window.

Generating classes from database tables

With the project properly configured, we can use the database tables as a starting
point to create the entities.

> Make sure the tables from the `store_db` database are loaded
> and Eclipse's connection to MySQL is properly configured. These
> procedures are explained in the *Configuring MySQL databases* section
> in *Chapter 2, Setting Up the Environment*.

To generate the classes:

1. Right-click on the project name and select **JPA Tools**, then select **Generate
   Entities from Tables…** from the submenu.
2. Select the **MySQL - Store** connection. If the connection is not yet active, the
   button just below the **Connection** drop-down menu will be enabled. If this
   is the case, click on it.
3. Select the **store_db** entry from the **Schema** drop-down menu, then select all
   the business tables — **customer**, **movie**, **theater**, and **ticket** entries — and click
   on **Next**:

Select Tables

Select tables to generate entities from.

Connection: | MySQL - Store

(Note: You must have an active connection to select sche

Schema: | store_db

Tables:
- ☑ customer
- ☑ movie
- sequence
- testewlstore
- ☑ theater
- ☑ ticket

☑ Update class list in persistence.xml

Restore Defaults

? | < Back | Next > | Cancel | Finish

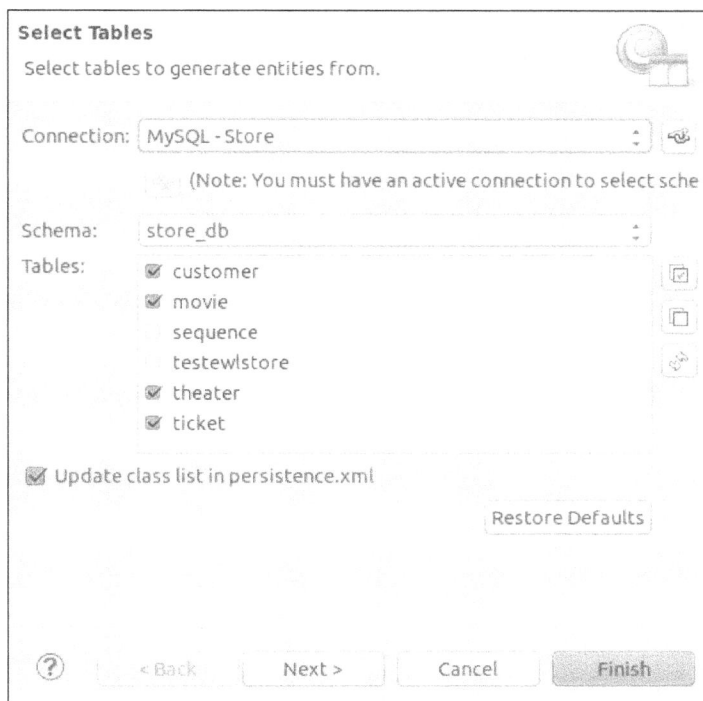

4. On the **Table Associations** screen, click on the **New Association** button and do the following:

   1. Select **Simple association** as **Association kind**.

   2. Click on the button at the right side of **Table 1** and select **ticket**.

   3. Click on the button at the right side of **Table 2** and select **theater**.

   > If you just type in the table names, the next screen will **not** work as expected — you must select the table name from the list.

   4. Click on **Next**.

   5. On the **Join Columns** screen, click on the **Add** button, change the value of the column `ticket` to `theaterRef` and the column `theater` to `id`, then click on **Next**.

   6. The **Association Cardinality** asks you the type of relationship between the tables. The default **Many to one** is the one we need, **Each theater has many ticket**. Click on **Finish**.

5. We must execute the same preceding steps to create the second and last relationship:

1. Click on **New Association**.

2. Select **Simple association** as **Association kind**.

3. Click on the button at the right side of **Table 1** and select **ticket**, click on the button at the right side of **Table 2** and select **customer**, then click on **Next**.

4. On the **Join Columns** screen, click on the **Add** button, change the value of the column `ticket` to `customerRef` and column `customer` to `id`, then click on **Finish** (the cardinality is already set up, **Each customer has many ticket**). The list of associations should look like this:

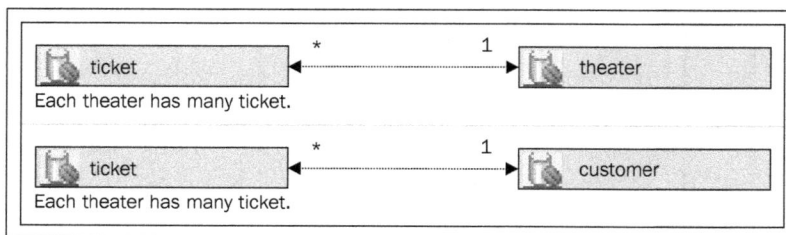

5. Click on **Next**.

6. Select **table** for **Key generator**, and enter `com.packt.domain.store` in the **Package** field.

7. Click on **Finish**.

We now have the base code to execute a query against the database. Let's check the relevant pieces of code of one of the classes, `Theater`:

```
@Entity
@Table(name="theater")
public class Theater implements Serializable {
```

This is how you create a JPA entity — you just need to annotate your POJO class with `javax.persistence.Entity` and `javax.persistence.Table`, and it's done.

> Actually, if your class and the underlying table have exactly the same name (down to capitalization, depending on the database engine/configuration), you don't need to add the `@Table` annotation.

A few more details about the generated entity class that are implicit to the code we just saw:

- The class must be public and top-level (can't be an inner class)

- The class can't be final

- The class must implement the `Serializable` interface — most likely, it will be transferred between applications, network, or business layers, so as a best practice, always implement this interface

- The class must have a no-argument constructor

Then we have the declaration of the primary key, which is also pretty straightforward:

```
@Id
@GeneratedValue(strategy=GenerationType.TABLE)
private int id;
```

The `Id` annotation states that the field is a primary key, and `@GeneratedValue` indicates the `strategy` and parameters the persistence provider must use to generate unique identifiers when inserting a record. This is the same as declaring a `generated-value` tag inside the `orm.xml` descriptor file. Use this file if you don't want to annotate your classes or if you want to change a definition without having to edit source code and repacking the binaries.

> The possible strategies for `@GeneratedValue` and their meanings are as follows:
>
> **AUTO** (default): The persistence provider chooses the best strategy considering the target database.
>
> **TABLE**: A table is used to generate unique values. You can use another annotation, `TableGenerator`, to override the default values for table name, schema, and so on.
>
> **SEQUENCE**: A database sequence is used to create the primary keys. You can fine tune its behavior by using the `SequenceGenerator` annotation.
>
> **IDENTITY**: You must use this when the provider is not supposed to generate a value, but instead read it back from the database after inserting the record. Usually, the table field is declared using a native mechanism; for example, `AUTO_INCREMENT` or `SERIAL` on MySQL, or `IDENTITY` on the Microsoft SQL Server.

Do you remember that we left out a couple of tables at the **JPA Generate Entities** wizard? One of them, the SEQUENCE table, is the default table used by EclipseLink when you select AUTO or TABLE as the strategy. This table must have a record prior to issuing an insert command, depending on the strategy selected, with specific values:

Strategy	Content of SEQ_NAME Column
AUTO	SEQ_GEN
TABLE	SEQ_GEN_TABLE

> You can let the persistence provider worry about these details by inserting the property `eclipselink.ddl-generation` with value `create-tables` in `persistence.xml`. If any of the referenced objects are missing, TopLink/EclipseLink will try to create them.
>
> This is okay to use when starting the development phase, but for other environments such as quality assurance or production, it is not a recommended practice.

The last snippet of code worth mentioning is the one that declares the relationship between the Theater and Room entities:

```
//bi-directional many-to-one association to Ticket
@OneToMany(mappedBy="theater")
private List<Ticket> tickets;
```

> On the last screen of the JPA wizard, you can select either `java.util.Set` or `java.util.List` to materialize the relationships. The main difference between them, in this context, is that the first doesn't allow duplicates. `List` is the default value.

The JPA wizard's default behavior when creating relationships is to make them bi-directional. So, if you check the `Ticket.java` file, you will find the reference back to Theater:

```
@ManyToOne
@JoinColumn(name="theaterRef")
private Theater theater;
```

> To make the relationship uni-directional, in the **JPA Generate Entities** wizard, once the association is created, select it from the list of **Table associations** and uncheck the proper checkbox. For the first relationship **Ticket to Theater**, the text next to it is **Generate a reference to a collection of ticket in theater**.

The basic entities and their mappings are ready. The usage of MySQL's **auto_increment** and **foreign** keys were left out on purpose to show how relationships and identities are manually created. In the next chapter, we're going to see how they are taken into account when generating classes.

Creating named queries

A **named query** is also called a **static query,** in the sense that its declaration is attached to the entity either by using the named query annotation or by `named-query` tags inside a JPA mapping file that maps the entity.

> As the queries are created inside entities and entities are tied to a persistence unit, the name of each query must be unique inside that persistence unit. A good practice is to prefix the query name with the entity's name.

To keep things simple, let's see how we declare a query using annotations:

```
@Entity
@NamedQuery(name=Movie.findAll, query="SELECT M FROM Movie M")
public class Movie implements Serializable {
    public final static String findAll = "Movie.FindAll";
...
```

This code snippet returns all the `Movie` instances available. This is a very basic query that we're going to use to check if all the persistence components are correctly configured. There are several possibilities to explore when creating a query — inner joins, aggregation functions, inheritance, subqueries, and so on — and we will use some of them as we evolve our sample applications.

> Remember that although there's a similarity with the **Structured Query Language (SQL)**, we're dealing with **Java Persistence Query Language (JPQL)** constructs. So, the name of the object referenced at the query — `Movie` — maps to the class `Movie` and not the underlying table.

When we ask the persistence provider to execute a named query, we need to inform the name of the desired query. You can have more than one `NamedQuery` annotation inside a class, provided you group them using the `@NamedQueries` decoration:

```
@Entity
@NamedQueries({
    @NamedQuery(name=Movie.findAll, query="SELECT M FROM Movie M")
    @NamedQuery(name=Movie.findPremiere, query="SELECT M FROM ...")
})
```

> To avoid errors, a good practice is to create a `public static final String` variable to hold the query's name, use it to declare the query and later to reference it.

There is a similar query declared inside the `Theater` class to retrieve all `Theater` instances available:

```
@NamedQueries({
    @NamedQuery(name=Theater.findAll, query="SELECT T FROM Theater
        T")
})
public class Theater implements Serializable {
    public final static String findAll = "Theater.FindAll";
...
```

Tweaking the persistence.xml file

The last piece of configuration we have to tweak is the `persistence.xml` file used by the persistence provider to identify which connections must be used to access each entity and fine-tune its behavior.

Here are the file contents after creating the entities using the wizard:

```
<persistence version="2.0">
    <persistence-unit name="StoreBO">
        <provider>org.eclipse.persistence.jpa.PersistenceProvider
            </provider>
        <class>com.packt.domain.store.Customer</class>
        <class>com.packt.domain.store.Movie</class>
        <class>com.packt.domain.store.Theater</class>
        <class>com.packt.domain.store.Ticket</class>
    </persistence-unit>
</persistence>
```

The persistence unit's name is the same as the project `StoreBO`; no need to change it. But, do you remember that we didn't select a connection when creating the project? As the JPA Project wizard does not allow us to choose a WebLogic data source, we now have to configure it:

1. Open the `persistence.xml` file inside the **JPA Content** project's tree node.

2. Click on the **Connection** tab.

3. Select **JTA** as **Transaction type**.

4. Enter `jdbc/tickets/store` in the **JTA data source** field.

As the entities were explicitly declared by the JPA wizard, we can disable package scanning. To do so, perform the following steps:

1. Go to the first tab, **General**.

2. Expand the **Managed Classes** group.

3. Click on the **Exclude unlisted classes** checkbox.

Save the file, and it's done.

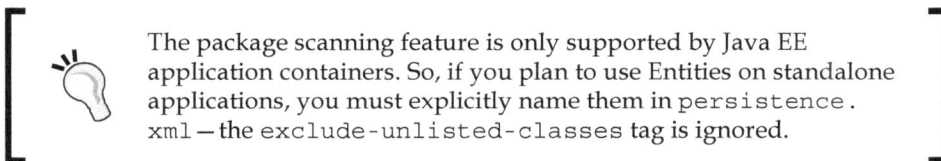

> The package scanning feature is only supported by Java EE application containers. So, if you plan to use Entities on standalone applications, you must explicitly name them in `persistence.xml` — the `exclude-unlisted-classes` tag is ignored.

Packing the project

Now we just have to pack the project and deploy it to the WebLogic Server as an **optional package**.

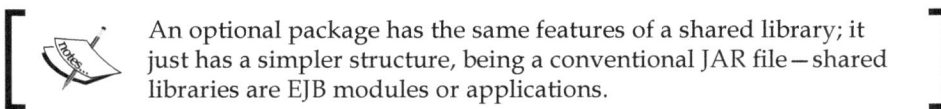

> An optional package has the same features of a shared library; it just has a simpler structure, being a conventional JAR file — shared libraries are EJB modules or applications.

To make the library adherent to the standard, create the `MANIFEST.MF` file inside the `src/META-INF` folder and add these lines:

```
Manifest-Version: 1.0
Extension-Name: storeBO
Specification-Version: 1.0
Implementation-Version: 1.0.0
```

This is the same configuration we made when creating PrimeFaces' shared library in the previous chapter, and it's the only requirement to make a plain JAR file an optional package.

You may use the **JAR Export** wizard provided by Eclipse to generate the package or create it using an Ant script as the example in the next info box, or a compression application, such as WinZip or 7Zip. Either way, make sure the packaged MANIFEST.MF file has exactly the same content (and sequence of lines) as we just showed. Without the specific tags we added in that specific order, the deployment will complete successfully but WebLogic will not be able to resolve the dependency when deploying a project that references the optional package.

Here's a simple Ant script that can be used to create the package:

```xml
<?xml version="1.0" encoding="UTF-8"?>
<project>
    <property name="jarName" value="StoreBO.jar"/>
    <target name="clean">
      <delete dir="build"/>
    </target>
    <target name="compile">
      <mkdir dir="build/classes"/>
      <javac srcdir="src" destdir="build/classes"/>
    </target>
    <target name="jar">
      <mkdir dir="build/jar"/>
      <jar manifest="src/META-INF/MANIFEST.MF"
         destfile="build/jar/${jarName}"
         basedir="build/classes" />
    </target>
</project>
```

The final package must have the structure depicted in the following figure:

Notice that we didn't add the `persistence.xml` file to the JAR package — the file must be present in the EJB project using the entities, not here.

> According to JPA 2.0 specifications, the JAR package or directory holding the `persistence.xml` file is called the **root** of the persistence unit, and it cannot be a JAR file external to the application — or, more specifically, a referenced library. That's why we have to add the `persistence.xml` file to the project that uses the entities.

Based on the rule above, here are some of the places you can place the `persistence.xml` file:

- The classes directory inside the `WEB-INF/classes` folder, when used by a Web Project (WAR)
- A JAR file placed in `WEB-INF/lib` of a Web Project
- A JAR file inside `APP-INF/lib` of an Enterprise Project (EAR)

> The `APP-INF` folder inside an EAR is a WebLogic-specific feature that helps in sharing libraries among the modules of an enterprise package. You can have a `lib` folder with several JARs and a `classes` folder with individual classes.

If you're going to pack a `persistence.xml` file into a JAR, make sure it is inside the `META-INF` folder, and that this folder is at the root of the package. Anywhere else, the container will not find it.

The last step to complete the enablement of an optional package is to register it in the WebLogic Server. To do so, access the WebLogic Administration Console and perform the following steps:

1. Click on **Deployments** in **Domain Structure**.
2. Click on the **Install** button at the top of the **Deployments** list.
3. Click on the link **upload your file(s)** inside the **Note** phrase.
4. Click on the first **Choose File** button next to **Deployment Archive**.
5. Navigate to the folder where you saved the `StoreBO.jar` file, select it, click on **Open** and **Next** on the main page.
6. The **Path** field shows the complete path to our JAR file. Click on **Next**.
7. This page shows the options to change the deployment strategy. But as the default settings are just fine, we don't need to change any of them, so go ahead and click on **Next**.

> The deployment assistant is the same for any kind of package—WAR, JAR, and so on—so we can ignore the message at the top of the page (**Issues were encountered while parsing this deployment to determine module type. Assuming this is a library deployment.**). WebLogic's guess is right.

8. Click the **No, I will review the configuration later** option and then click on **Finish**. The wizard automatically targets the deployment to the single instance available, **AdminServer**.

> Remember that a resource always has to be targeted to one or more WebLogic instances in order to be visible and active. Automatic targeting is not a feature present for every resource creation sequence, though - Data Sources, for instance, must be explicitly targeted, or else they will not be available for use.

After the deployment is completed, the **Deployments** screen is reloaded and you should see the new module and its **State** as **Active** as shown in the following screenshot:

	Name ⌃	State	Health	Type	Deployment Order
	storeBO(1.0,1.0.0)	Active		Library	100

> If you see only the library name without the version info — the numbers stating specification and implementation versions — go back and check the MANIFEST.MF file of your package; the lines are certainly mixed up.

If you followed the installation procedures in *Chapter 2*, *Setting Up the Environment*, you may be thinking that if an optional package is basically the same as a shared library, why didn't we create it the same way we did earlier using Eclipse/OEPE?

Well, the two main reasons:

- The way we reference a shared library from a project isn't the same way we reference an optional package. We're going to see how it is done in the next section.
- To show you how to deploy an optional package using WebLogic's Administration Console, since there is no automatic deployment of an optional package from Eclipse/OEPE.

Now that we have our entities available, let's create the main project and the basic code to test the environment.

The Store web project

We're now going to create the structure of our central application and add a basic query to make sure everything up to this point is running smoothly:

1. Click on the **File** menu, then navigate to **New** | **Dynamic Web Project**.

2. On the **Dynamic Web Project** screen:

    1. Enter Store in the **Project Name** field.
    2. The **Target runtime** should be **Oracle WebLogic Server 12c (12.1.2)** already. If not, select this entry.
    3. Select **JavaServer Faces v2.1 Project** from the **Configuration** drop-down menu.
    4. Click on **Next**.

3. Click on **Next** again—no need to change folder settings.
4. Change **Context root** to store.
5. Click on **Next**.
6. In **JSF Capabilities**, select **Disable Library Configuration** from the **JSF Implementation Library** field, then remove the existing entry from **URL Mapping Patterns** and create a new one with the value *.jsf.

> WebLogic Server 12c comes with JSF 2.1 enabled by default as part of its classpath (Mojarra 2.1.5 being the implementation). So, we don't need to reference any libraries here—it's just there, ready to be used.

7. Click on **Finish**.

Adding references to PrimeFaces' shared library

As we already created the shared library within OEPE, we just need to add the necessary references to the project. First, we make the library visible to the OEPE's design-time compiler:

1. Right-click on the **Store** project, select **Properties**, then **Java Build Path** entry at the tree, and click on the **Libraries** tab.
2. Click on the **Add Library...** button, select the **WebLogic Shared Library** entry and click on **Next**.
3. Click the **Browse...** button, select **primefaces** from the list and click on **OK**.
4. The fields **Name** and **Specification Version** will be populated. Leave all the fields as they are and click on **Finish** to add the library.
5. Click on **OK** to close the **Properties** window.

Then, we must tell WebLogic Server that our project depends on this library so that the proper linkage will be done when deploying and running the application. In order to do so:

1. Open the `weblogic.xml` file of the project `Store` — you can find it in the `WebContent/WEB-INF` folder.

2. Add the following lines inside the `weblogic-web-app` tag:

```
<wls:library-ref>
    <wls:library-name>primefaces</wls:library-name>
    <wls:specification-version>3.5</wls:specification-
        version>
    <wls:exact-match>true</wls:exact-match>
</wls:library-ref>
```

3. Save the file.

Adding references to StoreBO

To reference an optional package, the procedure is a little bit different. To do so:

1. Open the `MANIFEST.MF` file inside the folder `WebContent/META-INF` and paste the following lines making sure that you don't leave empty lines between the ones already there and the new ones:

```
Extension-List: storeBO
storeBO-Extension-Name: storeBO
storeBO-Specification-Version: 1.0
storeBO-Implementation-Version: 1.0.0
```

> If you leave blank lines between entries on this file, the deployer will not process the lines after the first blank one and `java.lang.IllegalStateException` is likely to be raised, associated with a somewhat misleading message, such as `Could not find backup for factory javax.faces.context.FacesContextFactory`. If you see it when deploying, check your `MANIFEST.MF` file.

2. Save the file.

With this setting, we are instructing WebLogic Server to link the optional package to our application upon deployment.

But Eclipse's compiler does not process this configuration, so we need to add another reference to be able to use the entities inside our code. The easiest way to accomplish this is to create a dependency between the Store and StoreBO projects:

1. Right-click on the **Store** project, navigate to **Properties | Java Build Path**, and click on the **Projects** tab.

2. Click on the **Add...** button.

3. Check the **StoreBO** project and click on **OK**.

4. Click on **OK** again to close the **Properties** screen.

And that's it. Now we can use the entities both during development and runtime.

Referencing the persistence configuration file

As mentioned before, we need to have an explicit reference to the `persistence.xml` file inside our project to be able to use the declared persistence unit. Here's what must be done:

1. Create for a `META-INF` folder inside the folder `/Java Resources/src` and make sure you can see the new folder in **Project Explorer**.

2. Expand the `src/META-INF` folder of the project **StoreBO**.

3. Copy the `persistence.xml` file from **StoreBO** and paste it inside the `META-INF` folder of the project **Store**.

This way, we make sure the persistence configuration will be found and processed as it should.

> You may want to create a link from one project to the other so that you have just one physical copy of the file. To do so, when doing a drag-and-drop action, hold the *Ctrl* and *Shift* keys down. Be aware that the actual reference is bound to your operating system, so the source project may not be 100% portable.

To enable data access and use these functionalities on a web page, we need to create a class to run the necessary queries against the persistence layer we just enabled. The next section shows how to accomplish this.

Creating a named bean

The concept of **Context and Dependency Injection (CDI)** is not new to the Java EE platform—the JSR that defines it, # 299, was bound to Java EE 5 and was called **Web Beans**. Here's a quote from the specification that clearly explains how we're going to use it:

> "*The use of these services significantly simplifies the task of creating Java EE applications by integrating the Java EE web tier with Java EE enterprise services. In particular, EJB components may be used as JSF managed beans, thus integrating the programming models of EJB and JSF (King, 2009).*"

Previously, when programming with JSF, you had to create **managed beans** that were specific to this technology. With the introduction of CDI, we can integrate JSF and EJB, unlocking all the features exposed by the EJB container, such as transaction demarcation and concurrency.

> You can still create managed beans by using the `javax.faces.bean.ManagedBean` annotation, but keep in mind that this is a JavaServer Faces mechanism. If you're creating a new project or application, the best bet is to use CDI over managed beans.

To expose a bean to be used by our JSF pages, we need to:

1. Annotate a class with `javax.inject.Named`.

2. Inform the container that the application/package where the bean resides is a **bean archive**—this can be a library, EJB, or an application package, or even a classpath directory, as long as a `beans.xml` file is present inside its `META-INF` folder or inside the folder `WEB-INF` of a WAR file. By doing this, we instruct the container to discover beans inside that package.

To accomplish the first item, perform the following steps:

1. Click on the **File** menu, then navigate to **New | Class**.

2. Type `com.packt.store.search` as **Java package**.

3. Enter `SearchManager` as the **Class name** and click on **Finish**.

4. In the class editor, enter the following lines:

```
import java.io.Serializable;
import javax.enterprise.context.SessionScoped;
import javax.inject.Named;
```

```
@Named("search")
@SessionScoped
public class SearchManager implements Serializable {
}
```

5. Save the file.

By decorating the class with the `Named` annotation, we made it recognizable by the container as a CDI-enabled bean. The decoration argument, `"search"`, tells the container by which name the bean will be referenced from JSF pages.

> When you do not provide a value for `@Named`, the name of the bean becomes a lower camel case version of the class name. The bean we just created would be named `searchManager`.

As we will hold static lists to populate the page — theaters and movies — we changed the scope of the bean to session by using the `SessionScoped` annotation so that we don't need to go to the database every time a new request is made.

> The default scope of a bean is **Dependent**, meaning that its instantiation is bounded to the scope of the object which carries a reference to it. For instance, when a JSF page refers a dependent bean, it can be instantiated several times when rendering the page, one for each JSF expression found.
>
> There are other longer scopes, such as Request, Session, Application, and so on. To check the complete list and behavior of these scopes, refer to `http://docs.oracle.com/javaee/6/api/index.html?javax/enterprise/context/SessionScoped.html`.

The second and final step to enable CDI is to inform the container that the application/package where the bean resides is a **bean archive**. For our web project, we just need to create an empty `beans.xml` file inside the `WebContent/WEB-INF/` folder.

> Empty means completely empty — zero bytes. If you create the file using Eclipse's **New XML File** wizard, which is a logical choice considering the file type, you end up with the basic `<?xml>` tag. If you don't remove it, upon deployment an `IllegalStateException` error will be thrown.

There are definitions we can enter in the `beans.xml` file, but none of them are relevant to our scenario; so we will let it empty by now — more on this in *Chapter 6, Using Events, Interceptors, and Logging Services* , when we discuss **interceptors**.

Here is the full code needed to execute a basic functionality test:

```java
@Named("search")
@SessionScoped
public class SearchManager implements Serializable {
    @PersistenceContext(unitName="StoreBO")
    EntityManager em;

    private List<Theater> theaters;
    private List<Movie> movies;

    private int movie;
    private int theater;

    @SuppressWarnings("unchecked")
    public List<Theater> getTheaters() {
        if (theaters == null)
            theaters = em.createNamedQuery(Theater.findAll).
                    getResultList();

        return theaters;
    }

    @SuppressWarnings("unchecked")
    public List<Movie> getMovies() {
        if (movies == null)
            movies = em.createNamedQuery(Movie.findAll).
                    getResultList();

        return movies;
    }

    public int getTheater() {
        return theater;
    }

    public void setTheater(int theater) {
        this.theater = theater;
    }

    public int getMovie() {
        return movie;
    }

    public void setMovie(int movie) {
        this.movie = movie;
    }
}
```

The `PersistenceContext` annotation injects the persistence unit that goes by the provided name into an **Entity Manager**, and with this instance we can query, create, and delete object instances, among other actions.

> If you have only one persistence unit referenced by your project, you don't need to set the `unitName` attribute.

The `getTheaters` and `getMovies` methods return a list of objects that will populate the query screen using the named queries we created earlier, if the corresponding variables, `theaters` and `movies`, aren't loaded yet. The other variables, `theater` and `movie`, along with their getter and setter methods, must be created to hold the values selected from each drop-down menu.

Configuring the Web descriptor

There are a lot of options available to configure the behavior of an application that goes inside the `web.xml` file. As we're trying to do a basic sanity test right now, we need to tweak it just a little bit:

1. Open the `web.xml` file located in the folder `WebContent/WEB-INF`.

2. Remove the list of `welcome-file` tags leaving just one entry, and change its value to `index.jsf`.

3. Save the file.

We just instructed the container to process the `index.jsf` file when the user enters the project's root URL, `http://localhost:7001/store/`.

Here's the content of `web.xml` at this point:

```xml
<?xml version="1.0" encoding="UTF-8"?>
<web-app xmlns:xsi="http://www.w3.org/2001/XMLSchema-instance"
    xmlns="http://java.sun.com/xml/ns/javaee"
    xmlns:web="http://java.sun.com/xml/ns/javaee/web-app_2_5.xsd"
    xsi:schemaLocation="http://java.sun.com/xml/ns/javaee/
        web-app_3_0.xsd" version="3.0">
    <display-name>Store</display-name>
    <servlet>
        <servlet-name>Faces Servlet</servlet-name>
        <servlet-class>javax.faces.webapp.FacesServlet
            </servlet-class>
        <load-on-startup>1</load-on-startup>
    </servlet>
    <servlet-mapping>
```

```
    <servlet-name>Faces Servlet</servlet-name>
    <url-pattern>*.jsf</url-pattern>
  </servlet-mapping>
  <welcome-file-list>
    <welcome-file>index.jsf</welcome-file>
  </welcome-file-list>
</web-app>
```

> You may also instruct PrimeFaces to use one of the themes you may have added to the shared library built in *Chapter 2, Setting Up the Environment*. To do so, add this block of code just after the `welcome-list` tag, referring to the theme that you packed into the shared library:
>
> ```
> <context-param>
>     <param-name>primefaces.THEME</param-name>
>     <param-value>ui-lightness</param-value>
> </context-param>
> ```
>
> If you don't do so, PrimeFaces will use the **Aristo** theme, which comes packed within its base library, `primefaces-3.5.jar`.

Defining the test page

Finally, edit (or create) the `index.xhtml` file under the `WebContent` folder and enter the following code:

```
<!DOCTYPE html PUBLIC "-//W3C//DTD XHTML 1.0 Transitional//EN"
    "http://www.w3.org/TR/xhtml1/DTD/xhtml1-transitional.dtd">

<html lang="en" xmlns="http://www.w3.org/1999/xhtml"
                xmlns:f="http://java.sun.com/jsf/core"
                xmlns:h="http://java.sun.com/jsf/html"
                xmlns:ui="http://java.sun.com/jsf/facelets"
                xmlns:p="http://primefaces.org/ui">

<h:head />

<h:body>
    <p:fieldset legend="Basic Query">
        <p:panelGrid columns="2">
            <h:outputLabel for="theater" value="Theater:" />
```

```
            <p:selectOneMenu id="theater"
               style="width: 350px;"
               value="#{search.theater}">
               <f:selectItem itemLabel="Select one"
                  itemValue="0" />
               <f:selectItems value="#{search.theaters}"
                  var="n"
                  itemLabel="#{n.name}"
                  itemValue="#{n.id}" />
            </p:selectOneMenu>

            <h:outputLabel for="movie" value="Movie:" />
            <p:selectOneMenu id="movie"
               style="width: 350px;"
               value="#{search.movie}">
               <f:selectItem itemLabel="Select one"
                  itemValue="0" />
               <f:selectItems value="#{search.movies}"
                  var="n"
                  itemLabel="#{n.name}"
                  itemValue="#{n.id}" />
            </p:selectOneMenu>
         </p:panelGrid>
      </p:fieldset>
   </h:body>
</html>
```

> If you don't want to type the entire page's code, go ahead and get the accompanying source code from the Packt Publishing's website, www.packtpub.com.

The relevant pieces of code here are:

- The declarations at the top of the file, where we tell which tag libraries we're going to use on this page. This is the basic set defined by JavaServerFaces and PrimeFaces:

```
<html lang="en" xmlns="http://www.w3.org/1999/xhtml"
   xmlns:f="http://java.sun.com/jsf/core"
   xmlns:h="http://java.sun.com/jsf/html"
   xmlns:ui="http://java.sun.com/jsf/facelets"
   xmlns:p="http://primefaces.org/ui">
```

- The JSF's `<h:head>` tag must be declared so that PrimeFaces can inject its dependencies into the page.

> If you declare HTML's basic `<head>` tag or forget to include the `<h:head>` tag, you will see a lot of text that wasn't supposed to be there.

- The `<p:fieldset>` entry is a PrimeFaces tag used to group fields, with support for skinning and events. We use it here to give a more polished look to our query page.

- PrimeFaces's `<p:panelGrid>` tag allows us to easily create a table—we just need to define the number of columns (2, in your sample), and it will distribute the tags declared inside it, one inside each cell, creating a new line after processing each pair of tags. This component has support for header, footers, colspan, and rowspan (ways to group cells horizontally or vertically).

- The two blocks that define the dropdown boxes for Theater and Movie— the `<p:selectOneMenu>` tag. Each drop-down menu has a reference to our bean and uses a getter to retrieve the data—the `search.theaters` entry will be translated to `searchManager.getTheaters()`, which is the method we implemented. The properties `name` and `id` of each entry are also defined inside the `Theater` class.

- Finally, each `selectOneMenu` component is attached by its `id` parameter to a variable of the bean that will have the key of the selected entry upon form submission (this will be done in a later chapter).

You may have noticed that the page extension is `.xhtml`, although we are calling it using the prefix `.jsf`. This is due to the JSF engine, which translates the request to an internal suffix, `.xhtml` being the default value.

You may change this behavior by adding the following lines of code into your `web.xml` file, declaring the extension that suits your needs better:

```
<context-param>
    <param-name>javax.faces.DEFAULT_SUFFIX</param-
name>
    <param-value>.jsf</param-value>
</context-param>
<context-param>
    <param-name>javax.faces.FACELETS_VIEW_MAPPINGS
    </param-name>
    <param-value>*.jsf</param-value>
</context-param>
```

Deploying and testing the application

To run the application, we must tell Eclipse that the configured WebLogic Server is the target container to deploy and run it. To do so, perform the following steps:

1. Open the **Servers** view and navigate to **Window | Show View | Servers**.

2. Right-click on the server name and click on the **Add and Remove...** entry from the context menu.

3. Select the **Store** project from the **Available** list and click on **Add >**.

4. Click on the **Finish** button.

The window will close and the deployment will start automatically. You should see the status **Publishing** at the end of the line in the **Servers** view. If everything goes well, the status will change to **Synchronized**.

You can now navigate to `http://localhost:7001/store/` using a browser, or right-click on the **Store** project, select **Run As** from the context menu, and then click on **Run on Server**. A browser page will open inside Eclipse showing the query page:

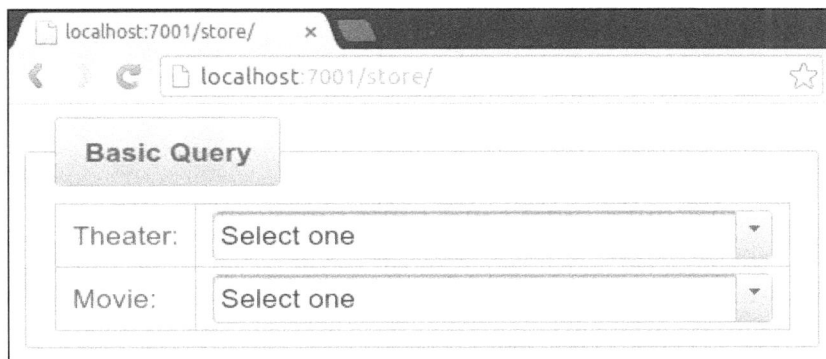

Take a look at the dropdown boxes; they should have a few entries each. This means that every component—shared library, optional package, persistence data, and configuration—is working as expected.

Web resources

Here are some references to help you get into the details of the features and resources covered in this chapter.

- Oracle TopLink Documentation
    - `http://www.oracle.com/technetwork/middleware/toplink/overview/index.html`

- Using Oracle TopLink with WebLogic Server
    - `http://docs.oracle.com/middleware/1212/toplink/TLADG/tlandwls.htm`

- Oracle TopLink Grid with Oracle Coherence
    - `http://docs.oracle.com/middleware/1212/coherence/COHIG/tlg_integrate.htm`

- Oracle TopLink JPA Certification
    - `http://www.oracle.com/technetwork/middleware/ias/jpa-082702.html`

- EclipseLink JPA User's Guide
  - `http://wiki.eclipse.org/EclipseLink/UserGuide/JPA`
- JSR 317: Java Persistence API, Version 2.0
  - `http://download.oracle.com/otndocs/jcp/persistence-2.0-fr-oth-JSpec/`
- Java EE 6 Tutorial – Persistence API
  - `http://docs.oracle.com/javaee/6/tutorial/doc/bnbpz.html`
- Enterprise JavaBeans (EJBs)
  - `http://docs.oracle.com/middleware/1212/wls/INTRO/ejbs.htm`
- Java EE 6 Tutorial – Singleton Example
  - `http://docs.oracle.com/javaee/6/tutorial/doc/gipvi.html`

Summary

We have completed a brief view of some of the basic features of Java EE and the WebLogic Server—how to create and use an optional package, the definition and coding of a persistence layer, how to wrap everything up into a web project, and deploying and testing the project.

In the next chapter, we will check how to communicate with other modules using remote services exposed with the **REST** architecture.

4
Creating RESTful Services with JAX-RS

At this point we already have the business case defined, a web application reading information from a database and every needed component running in WebLogic Server. Some other inner concepts are well developed and exemplified, such as modularization (web module, entities module) and dependency injection with CDI.

The objective of this chapter is to enhance the application created in the previous chapter, **Store**, by adding more information to the search page based on a remote call to a new application, **Theater**, which exposes a **RESTful web service** that provides movie exhibition dates.

> By definition, a web service is designed to support machine-to-machine communication in a platform-independent way. The decision to design such services using REST or SOAP standards are beyond the scope of this book, although readers will get an example of each type of service and can compare the benefits and drawbacks of each approach.

So, in this chapter we're going to:

- Create two new projects, TheaterBO and Theater, to hold the entities of this business domain and expose the interfaces consumed by the central module, respectively
- Develop a RESTful Web Service with **JAX-RS** while adjusting the entities to be able to produce XML or JSON output along the way using **JAXB**
- Extend the **Store** project to consume and display data from the new web service using **JAX-RS Client** API

Creating Theater entities

In *Chapter 3, Java EE Basics – Persistence, Query, and Presentation*, we have already created a JPA project that has entities from the Store module. Now we need to create a similar project for the Theater module, mapping entities of the corresponding database schema. We're going to do it using a few other concepts of **Java Persistence API (JPA)**. Let's get started.

> Before proceeding, make sure you have already loaded the tables into the databases and configured OEPE's (Eclipse) connection to MySQL. These procedures are explained in *Chapter 2, Setting Up the Environment*.

1. In Eclipse, create a new JPA project and perform the following steps:

   1. Enter `TheaterBO` as the **Project name**.

   2. Remember to set the **Target runtime** to point to your **WebLogic 12c Runtime** configuration.

   3. At the **JPA Facet** configuration page, select the same JPA library and implementation you already used in *Chapter 3, Java EE Basics – Persistence, Query, and Presentation* — that would be **EclipseLink 2.4.x/2.5.x** for **Platform**.

   4. Select **Disable Library Configuration** in **JPA Implementation Type**.

   5. Set the connection to **MySQL - Theater**.

   6. Finish the wizard.

2. Add a reference to WebLogic's persistence library, so we can compile the generated classes:

   1. Right-click on the project name and click on the last entry, **Properties**.

   2. Click on **Java Build Path** in the tree.

   3. Click on the **Libraries** tab and then click on the **Add Library...** button.

   4. Select the entry **WebLogic System Libraries** and click on **Next**.

   5. Select the **javax.persistence** library and click on **Finish**.

6. If the library is not available, click on the add icon (the plus sign) in the top-right portion of the screen, type `javax.persistence` in the **Module Id** field, and click on **Finish** to close this window and get back to the **Properties** window:

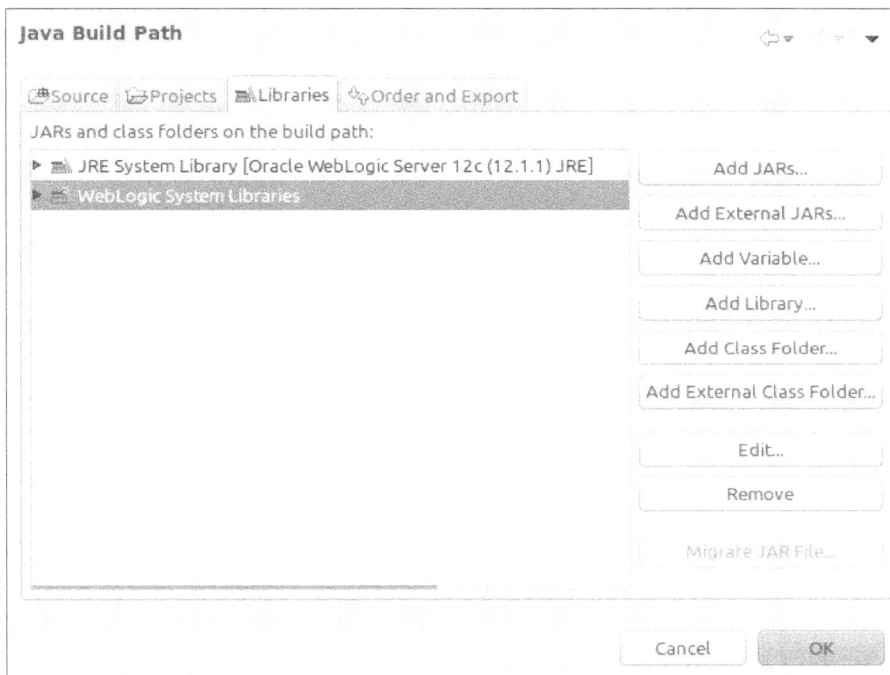

Java Build Path

Source | Projects | Libraries | Order and Export

JARs and class folders on the build path:

▶ JRE System Library [Oracle WebLogic Server 12c (12.1.1) JRE]

▶ WebLogic System Libraries

| Add JARs... |
| Add External JARs... |
| Add Variable... |
| Add Library... |
| Add Class Folder... |
| Add External Class Folder... |
| Edit... |
| Remove |
| Migrate JAR File... |

Cancel   OK

---

7. Click on **OK** to close the window.

3. Right-click on the project name and select **JPA Tools**, then select **Generate Entities from Tables...** from the submenu.

4. Now select the **MySQL - Theater** connection. Make sure you have *not* selected the **MySQL - Store** connection. If the connection is not yet active, the button just below the connection drop-down menu will be enabled. If that's the case, click on it to activate the connection.

5. Select the **theater_db** entry from the **Schema** drop-down menu, then select tables **exhibition, movie, room, seat, and theater** and click on **Next**:

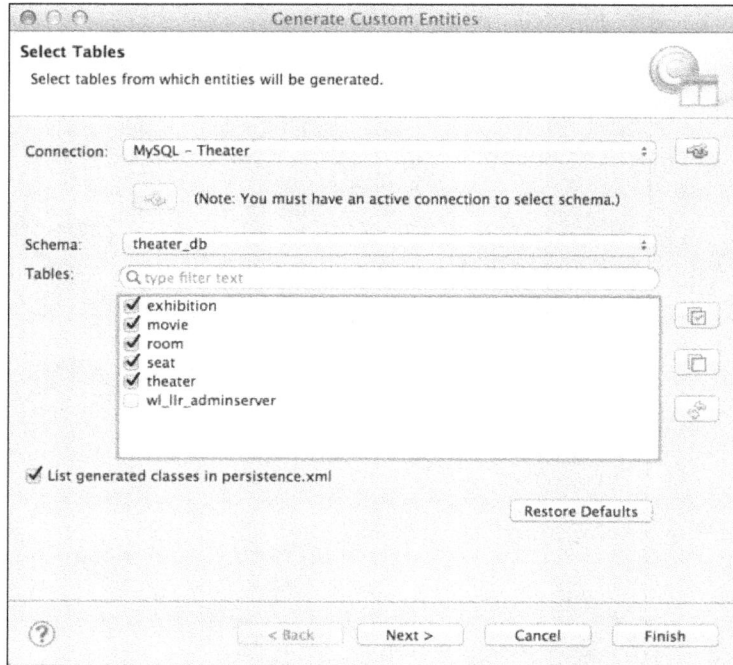

6. On the **Table Associations** screen, the associations are already in place because in this schema all the relationships are set at the database level with the declaration of **foreign keys**:

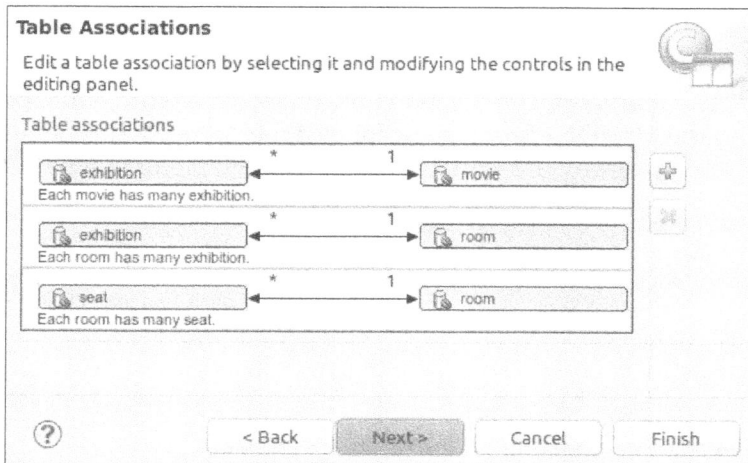

7. Click on **Next.**

8. Select **auto** for **Key generator, java.util.List** as **Collection properties type** and enter `com.packt.domain.theater` in the **Package** field:

Customize Default Entity Generation

Optionally customize aspects of entities that will be generated by default from database tables. A Java package should be specified.

Table mapping

Key generator:	auto
Sequence name:	

You can use the patterns $table and/or $pk in the sequence name. These patterns will be replaced by the table name and the primary key column name when a table mapping is generated.

Entity access:	⦿ Field ◯ Property
Associations fetch:	⦿ Default ◯ Eager ◯ Lazy
Collection properties type:	◯ java.util.Set ⦿ java.util.List

☐ Always generate optional JPA annotations and DDL parameters

Domain java class

Source folder:	TheaterBO/src	Browse...
Package:	com.packt.domain.theater	Browse...
Superclass:		Browse...
Interfaces:		Add...
		Remove

| ⑦ | < Back | Next > | Cancel | Finish |

> We are using **auto** for key generator to let the JPA layer decide which strategy to use when dealing with keys. Because the theater database schema is using MySQL's AUTO_INCREMENT feature to declare primary keys, it will use the **identity** approach, which lets the database engine deal with key generation.

9. Click on **Finish.**

At this point, your project should look like the following screenshot:

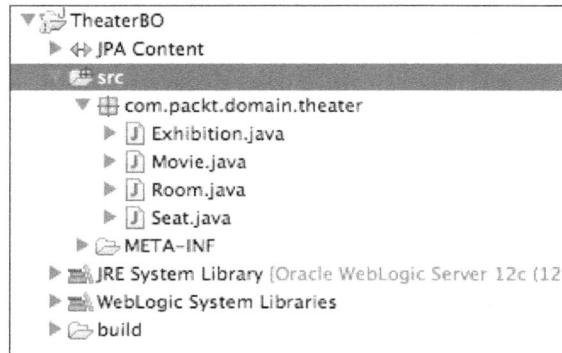

```
▼ 🗁 TheaterBO
  ▶ ⟨⟩ JPA Content
    📁 src
    ▼ ⊞ com.packt.domain.theater
      ▶ J Exhibition.java
      ▶ J Movie.java
      ▶ J Room.java
      ▶ J Seat.java
    ▶ 🗁 META-INF
  ▶ 📚 JRE System Library [Oracle WebLogic Server 12c (12.
  ▶ 📚 WebLogic System Libraries
  ▶ 🗁 build
```

Customizing the generated entities

The entities are in place, but we need to customize some of them in order to use as a base for a web service call and to avoid marshaling issues. In fact, we are going to show the usage of JAXB and JPA integration as shown in the following diagram – the data layer (materialized by the entities) is responsible for the conversion between object instances and XML or JSON using the corresponding framework:

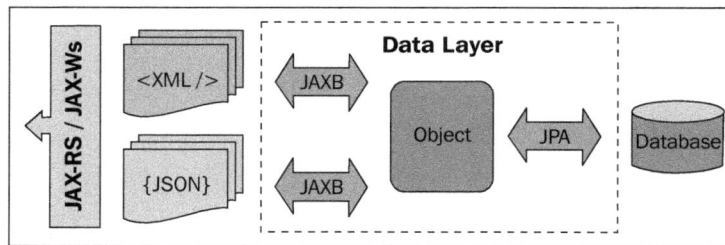

Creating named queries

In order to query for instances of this business entity, we are going to add a few named queries. We also have to mark the entity as an XML element, so it can be processed by JAXB.

First, let's add the named queries that will support our use case. So, open the Exhibition class and add this block of code after the @Entity decoration:

```
@NamedQueries({
    @NamedQuery(name=Exhibition.findAll,
        query="SELECT r FROM Exhibition r"),
```

```
@NamedQuery(name=Exhibition.findById,
    query="SELECT r FROM Exhibition r WHERE r.id = :id"),
@NamedQuery(name=Exhibition.findByMovie,
    query="SELECT r FROM Exhibition r WHERE
    r.movie.id = :movieId")
})
```

Also, add the names of the queries:

```
public final static String findAll = "Exhibition.findAll";
public final static String findById = "Exhibition.findById";
public final static String findByMovie = "Exhibition.findByMovie";
```

As we're going to expose this entity through a web service, we need to decorate the class with a JAXB annotation, `java.xml.bind.annotation.XmlRootElement`, so the engine can process the instance as a JAXB object when generating the web service's response. This must be done only to top-level entities of a request or response — for instance, even though the Movie entity will be a part of our response, we don't need to mark it. Just add the following line after `@Table`:

```
@XmlRootElement(name="Exhibition")
```

This annotation states that this class can be represented as an *XML* or *JSON* document through the use of JAXB and its binding providers, such as EclipseLink MOXy, the default JAXB provider of WebLogic Server 12c.

> The same concepts applied to RESTful services using JAX-RS on this chapter can easily be reused for SOAP-based services through JAX-WS, Java API for XML Web Services. In other words, entities annotated with `XmlRootElement` will produce XML documents through JAXB and these documents can be used as input or output for both SOAP and RESTful services.

After adding these customizations to the class, your code should look like this:

```
@Entity
@NamedQueries({
    @NamedQuery(name=Exhibition.findAll,
        query="SELECT r FROM Exhibition r"),
    @NamedQuery(name=Exhibition.findById,
        query="SELECT r FROM Exhibition r WHERE r.id = :id"),
    @NamedQuery(name=Exhibition.findByMovie,
        query="SELECT r FROM Exhibition r WHERE
        r.movie.id = :movieId")
    })
@XmlRootElement(name="Exhibition")
public class Exhibition implements Serializable {
```

```
public final static String findAll = "Exhibition.findAll";
public final static String findById = "Exhibition.findById";
public final static String findByMovie =
    " Exhibition.findByMovie";
...
```

Preventing cyclic references

We have to do a simple modification to two entities, Movie and Room, in order to prevent a very common issue with JAXB and XML parsing: **cyclic references** or **bidirectional relationships**. In standard JAXB this is not supported and one side of the relationship must be marked with @XmlTransient, but some JAXB implementations are also trying to solve this issue with extensions, such as EclipseLink MOXy.

Following the database model, for each Exhibition instance we have references to both Movie and Room via @ManyToOne relationships. And Movie and Room both have a list of all exhibitions pointing back to the Exhibition entity, a @OneToMany relationship. The object graph generated by default for a given Exhibition object and its references would look like this:

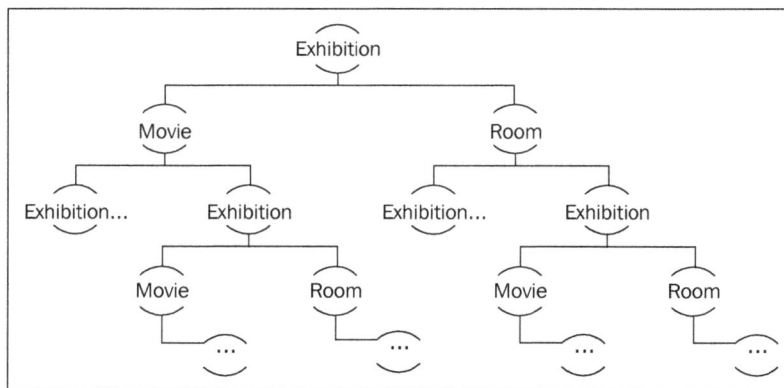

The solution for this situation is to mark the field and method you don't want JAXB to parse with the XmlTransient annotation, found in the javax.xml.bind.annotation package. So, in this specific case, we need to modify the Movie and Room classes to instruct JAXB to not go over their list of exhibitions. Update your code by decorating both the variable declaration and their getter methods with @XmlTransient:

```
@Entity
public class Movie implements Serializable {
    ...
```

```
    @XmlTransient
    @OneToMany(mappedBy="movie")
    private List<Exhibition> exhibitions;
...
    @XmlTransient
    public List<Exhibition> getExhibitions() {
        return this.exhibitions;
    }
    ...
```

And:

```
    @Entity
    public class Room implements Serializable {
        ...
    @XmlTransient
    @OneToMany(mappedBy = "room")
    private List<Exhibition> exhibitions;
        ...
    @XmlTransient
    public List<Exhibition> getExhibitions() {
        return this.exhibitions;
    }
        ...
```

We also need to execute the same procedure to adjust the relationship between
Seat and Room—when marshaling a Seat instance, JAXB must not include the
referenced Room instance. To do so, open the Seat class and mark the Room reference
with @XMLTransient, also add @XMLRootElement to the class declaration while you
are at it:

```
    @Entity
    @Table("Seat")
    @XmlRootElement(name="Seat")
    public class Seat implements Serializable {
        ...
    @XmlTransient
    @ManyToOne
    @JoinColumn(name = "roomRef")
    private Room room;
        ...
    @XmlTransient
    public Room getRoom() {
        return this.room;
    }
        ...
```

Formatting exhibitions' date and time

In order to show a user-friendly exhibition time on the query page, we are going to change the getDate method of the Exhibition class to join the date and time information (available as separate attributes, date and hour) and return the result. Also, the hour is saved in **military** format, so we need to break it down to hours and minutes before joining it to the date.

Open the source code of Exhibition and change the contents of getDate() from the following code:

```
public Date getDate() {
    return this.date;
}
```

To this:

```
public Date getDate() {
    Calendar cal = Calendar.getInstance();
    cal.setTime(this.date);
    cal.set(Calendar.HOUR_OF_DAY, this.hour / 100);
    cal.set(Calendar.MINUTE, this.hour % 100);

    return cal.getTime();
}
```

After these changes, the entities are good to go, we just need to create the proper descriptors before packaging the project for deployment.

Completing the persistence.xml file

The persistence.xml file needs some tweaking but nothing different from what you already did in *Chapter 3, Java EE Basics – Persistence, Query, and Presentation*, so we're not going into all the details here. Just remember that you need to update the JTA data source accordingly. Here is how your file should look like:

```
<?xml version="1.0" encoding="UTF-8"?>
<persistence version="2.0"
    xmlns="http://java.sun.com/xml/ns/persistence"
        xmlns:xsi="http://www.w3.org/2001/XMLSchema-instance"
    xsi:schemaLocation="http://java.sun.com/xml/ns/persistence
        http://java.sun.com/xml/ns/persistence/persistence_2_0.xsd">
    <persistence-unit name="TheaterBO" transaction-type="JTA">
        <jta-data-source>jdbc/tickets/theater</jta-data-source>
        <class>com.packt.domain.theater.Exhibition</class>
        <class>com.packt.domain.theater.Movie</class>
        <class>com.packt.domain.theater.Room</class>
```

```
        <class>com.packt.domain.theater.Seat</class>
    </persistence-unit>
</persistence>
```

Packaging the library

This project will be used as a library and shared between both web projects, `Store`
and `Theater`. In order to avoid having duplicated JAR files, we're going to deploy the
entity project as an **optional package** just like we have done with the `StoreBO` project
in *Chapter 3, Java EE Basics – Persistence, Query, and Presentation*. To do that, create a
`MANIFEST.MF` file inside the `src/META-INF` folder and add the following lines:

```
Manifest-Version: 1.0
Extension-Name: theaterBO
Specification-Version: 1.0
Implementation-Version: 1.0.0
```

After creating the `MANIFEST.MF` file, you can export the project to a JAR file using
Eclipse's Export wizard—it is a very simple procedure, but to avoid problems with
the manifest file, remember to mark the **Add Directory Entries** option, especially, the
Use existing manifest from workspace option pointing to the file you just created, as
shown in the following screenshot:

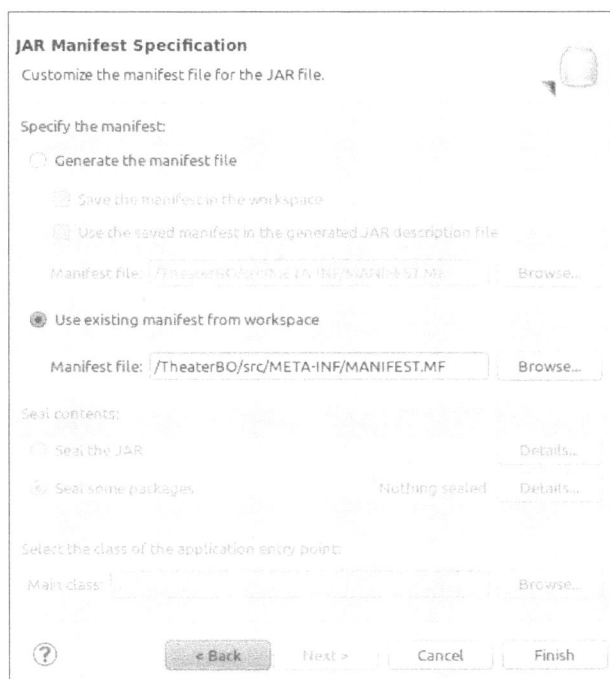

Make sure the packaged `MANIFEST.MF` file has exactly the same content and sequence as we created inside the project. Without the specific tags we added, and in that particular order, the deployment will work, but the reference by other projects will not.

> As an alternative to Eclipse's Export wizard we have created a `build.xml` **Ant** script that you can use to generate the JAR. You will find this script in the code bundle available at the Packt Publishing website, www.packtpub.com. A similar script was explained in *Chapter 3, Java EE Basics – Persistence, Query, and Presentation*.

To complete the optional package creation procedure, we need to publish it into the WebLogic Server. To do so, access the WebLogic Administration Console and perform the following steps:

1. Click on **Deployments** at **Domain Structure**.
2. Click on the **Install** button at the top of the **Deployments** list.
3. Click on the link **upload your file(s)** inside the **Note** phrase.
4. Click on the first **Choose File** button next to **Deployment Archive**.
5. Navigate to the folder where you saved the `TheaterBO.jar` file, select it, and click on **Open** and **Next** on the main page.
6. The **Path** field shows the complete path to our JAR file. Click on **Next**.
7. This page shows options to change the deployment strategy, but as the default settings are just fine, we don't need to change any of them, so just click on **Next**.
8. Click on **Finish** and conclude the deployment wizard.

> If you see only the library name without the version info, go back and check the `MANIFEST.MF` file of your package — the lines are certainly mixed up or not well formatted.

Creating the Theater web application

We are now going to create the web application that will stay in the movie theater, so the Store application, our central module, will interact with all the movie theaters through this application. Essentially, it will be responsible to validate and consume tickets, showing available movie exhibitions and seats.

A RESTful Web Service, as defined by JSR-311, will provide this interaction. The Java API that implements **Representational State Transfer (REST)** Web Services is **JAX-RS**. Oracle WebLogic 12c comes with **Jersey 1.9**, which is the JAX-RS reference implementation and also includes JSON APIs for processing and streaming data.

> Despite what many believe, JAX-RS was introduced in Java EE 5 but was only set as an official component in Java EE 6.

There is no official definition of what is a RESTful Web Service, unlike SOAP, which is completely specified by W3C and other organizations such as OASIS or WS-I. But a slight difference is that REST is an architectural style, while SOAP is a protocol. Also, even though RESTful Web Services are not completely specified, the technologies involved are—HTTP, URI, XML, or JSON.

The important concepts that define what a RESTful Web Service looks like are:

- **Resource**: Any meaningful concept or data structure that can be addressed. This resource is defined with Internet media types such as JSON or XML
- **Vocabulary**: REST uses an HTTP-based vocabulary as method names. GET, POST, PUT, and DELETE are the most common ones

Setting up the project

Here are the steps to create the Theater application:

1. Click on the **File** menu, then navigate to **New | Dynamic Web Project**.
2. On the **Dynamic Web Project** screen, enter `Theater` as the **Project name**.
3. The **Target runtime** should be **Oracle WebLogic Server 12c (12.1.2)** already. If not, select it.
4. Select **JavaServer Faces v2.1 Project** from the **Configuration** drop-down menu.
5. Click on **Next**.
6. Click on **Next** again—no need to change folder settings.
7. Change **Context root** to `theater` and click on **Next**.
8. On the **JSF Capabilities** screen, make sure you have the **Type** set to **"Disable Library Configuration"** and that the URL mapping patterns has ***.jsf** listed.
9. Click on **Finish**.

Now, add a reference to the PrimeFaces shared library by modifying the `weblogic.xml` descriptor inside the folder `WebContent/WEB-INF` and by including it on the build path of the project, just like we've done in *Chapter 3, Java EE Basics – Persistence, Query, and Presentation*. Your file should look like this:

```
<?xml version="1.0" encoding="UTF-8"?><wls:weblogic-web-app
xmlns:wls="http://xmlns.oracle.com/weblogic/weblogic-web-app"
xmlns:xsi="http://www.w3.org/2001/XMLSchema-instance"
xsi:schemaLocation="http://java.sun.com/xml/ns/javaee
http://java.sun.com/xml/ns/javaee/web-app_2_5.xsd
http://xmlns.oracle.com/weblogic/weblogic-web-app
http://xmlns.oracle.com/weblogic/weblogic-web-app/1.5/weblogic-
web-app.xsd">
    <wls:weblogic-version>12.1.2</wls:weblogic-version>
    <wls:context-root>theater</wls:context-root>
    <wls:library-ref>
        <wls:library-name>primefaces</wls:library-name>
        <wls:specification-version>3.5</wls:specification-version>
        <wls:exact-match>true</wls:exact-match>
    </wls:library-ref>
</wls:weblogic-web-app>
```

We also need to add a reference to optional package `TheaterBO` by editing the `MANIFEST.MF` file inside `WebContent/META-INF` and setting it as follows:

```
Manifest-Version: 1.0
Extension-List: theaterBO
theaterBO-Extension-Name: theaterBO
theaterBO-Specification-Version: 1.0
theaterBO-Implementation-Version: 1.0.0
```

The next step is to make the entities visible to OEPE's compiler:

1. Right-click on the **Theater** project, select **Properties**, then select **Java Build Path** entry from the tree, and click on the **Projects** tab.
2. Click on the **Add...** button.
3. Check the **TheaterBO** project and click on **OK.**
4. Click on **OK** again to close the **Properties** screen.

The last step is the configuration of the project's persistence layer:

1. Create a `META-INF` folder inside `/Java Resources/src` and make sure you can see the new folder from **Project Explorer.**
2. Open the `src/META-INF` folder of the project `TheaterBO`.
3. Copy the `persistence.xml` file from `TheaterBO` to the `META-INF` folder of project `Theater`.

Enabling JAX-RS

In order to enable JAX-RS in our web project:

1. Open the project's **Properties** window and go to the **Java Build Path** section.

2. Click on the **Libraries** tab and click on **Add External JARs…**.

3. Browse to the WebLogic 12c installation directory and go to the modules folder — `/$MW_HOME/oracle_common/modules`.

4. Select `jersey.core-1.17.1.jar` and `jersey.json-1.17.1.jar` files:

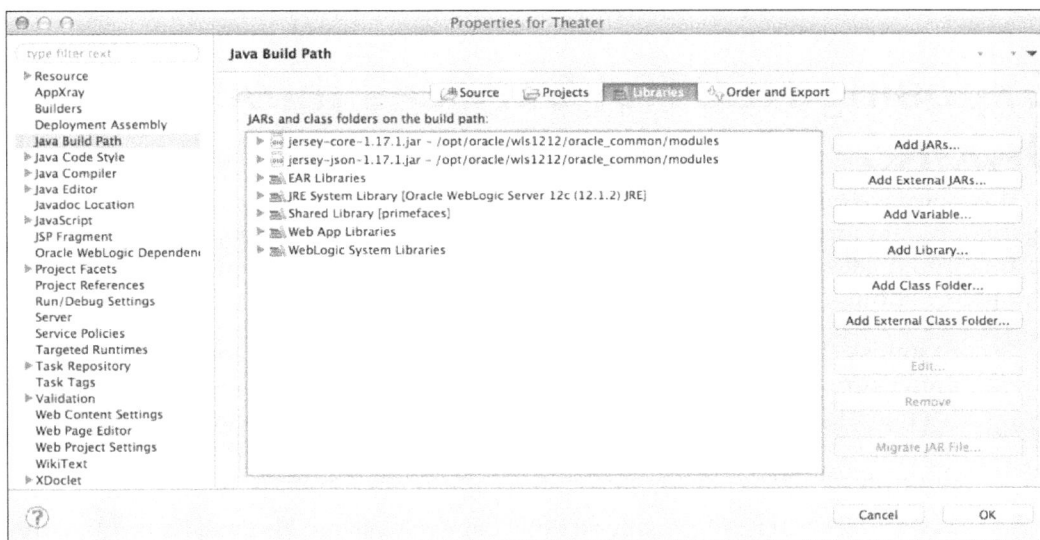

5. Click on **OK** to close the **Properties** window.

> Note that these files will not be included in the package when you generate or deploy the project. Just like JavaServer Faces (JSF), JAX-RS is part of WebLogic container and you don't need to configure or deploy any extra library on the server to enable JAX-RS support. We only need to add this setting during the development time in order to compile the project.

6. Open the `web.xml` file and add the following entries as the last ones inside the `web-app` tag:

```
<servlet>
    <servlet-name>JAX-RS Application</servlet-name>
    <servlet-class>
        com.sun.jersey.spi.container.servlet.ServletContainer
    </servlet-class>
```

```
      <load-on-startup>1</load-on-startup>
   </servlet>
   <servlet-mapping>
      <servlet-name>JAX-RS Application</servlet-name>
      <url-pattern>/api/*</url-pattern>
   </servlet-mapping>
```

These entries load the Jersey Servlet Container class and create the URL mapping that will host all RESTful services on the application, /api/*.

The Theater application is now completely set and ready for development.

Exposing RESTful Services through JAX-RS

At this point we need to create a **Stateless Session Bean** (EJB) that will query exhibition data through the JPA entities and return such information. Before getting into it, let's take a quick look at the types of beans supported by Java EE 6 and their definitions:

- **Stateless**: This is the same definition we find for EJB 2.x — components that aren't supposed to keep information between calls. The container keeps a bean pool, and any bean instance can serve an incoming request, being very lightweight to keep and having good scalability due to its ability to serve multiple clients.

- **Stateful**: When multiple interactions between system and user is needed, this kind of bean keeps consistent state through the conversation. As it holds data from a specific user, more instances have to be created to serve more users. Under heavy loads, it can degrade performance.

- **Message-driven**: The focus of this kind of bean is asynchronous processing — instead of calling its methods, we bound it to a **JMS Queue** or **JMS Topic** and publish messages to it, so it behaves like an event listener, the event being a JMS message.

- **Singleton**: New on EJB 3.1, the name is pretty clear about what this kind of functionality this bean offers. By default, all methods of this type of bean are thread-safe (synchronized) and transactional. You can tune this behavior with annotations **Lock** and **AccessTimeout**, or even disable the container's control with annotation **ConcurrencyManagement** with value BEAN.

> Another new feature related to beans is the **no-interface view**, which improves the **local client view** concept of EJB 3.0. Now, we don't have to create a separate interface to expose the methods of a bean—the public methods of a Session Bean are automatically exposed as its local business interface, making development easier. To use it, you either explicitly decorate your bean with @LocalBean or leave it without any interface-related decoration (@LocalBean, @Local, and @Remote) to implicitly use the no-interface strategy.

Let's get back to our code and create the stateless bean that is going to be exposed as a web service:

1. Create a Java class named ExhibitionBean.java under the package com.packt.theater.services.

2. Decorate the class with the Stateless annotation.

3. Add a reference to the persistence context through the PersistenceContext annotation:

    ```
    @PersistenceContext(unitName = "TheaterBO")
    private EntityManager em;
    ```

The session bean is now capable of interacting with the database through the persistence context we have declared and we can simply write Java methods to retrieve JPA objects, using named queries, for example. In the next section we're going to expose this stateless session bean as a RESTful service and how to write a REST client that will call this service from the Store application.

Coding the API

We're going to expose three basic functionalities as part of the RESTful API for the Theater application: list all exhibitions, list one exhibition, and retrieve an exhibition by movie. To support such operations, let's look at what must be done to the ExhibitionBean class:

1. Decorate the class declaration with a java.ws.rs.Path annotation. This annotation specifies the relative path for a resource or method that is going to be exposed through REST:

    ```
    @Stateless
    @Path("/exhibition")
    public class ExhibitionBean {
    ...
    ```

2. Create a Java method that is going to execute the named query that returns all exhibitions. This method of the API returns XML or JSON objects and that's what the decoration @Produces defines. We also use an HTTP verb, @GET, since this operation will not have any side-effect (it will not change any entity state on the server side):

```
@GET
@Produces({ MediaType.APPLICATION_XML,
    MediaType.APPLICATION_JSON })
public List<Exhibition> getAllExhibitions() {
    @SuppressWarnings("unchecked")
    List<Exhibition> result = em.createNamedQuery
        ("Exhibition.findAll")
        .getResultList();

    if (result.size() > 0)
        return result;
    else
        throw new WebApplicationException
            (Response.Status.NO_CONTENT);
}
```

> Notice that this method does not define a @Path tag, so it will be used as the default method for the class—a request to the base path, http://<server>:<port>/theater/api/exhibition, will be handled by this method.

3. Add another Java method that will receive an exhibition ID and return information about a single object. To consume a parameter JAX-RS uses the annotation PathParam and since this parameter will be part of the URL we need to use the Path annotation to differentiate from the default path of the service:

```
@GET
@Path("{id}")
@Produces({ MediaType.APPLICATION_XML, MediaType.APPLICATION_JSON
})
public Exhibition getExhibition(@PathParam("id") int id) {
    try {
        Exhibition entity = (Exhibition) em
            .createNamedQuery("Exhibition.findById")
            .setParameter("id", id)
            .getSingleResult();
        return entity;
    } catch (NoResultException nre) {
```

```
      throw new WebApplicationException
         (Response.Status.NOT_FOUND);
   }
}
```

> The following is how a request to this method must be done:
> `http://<server>:<port>/theater/api/exhibition/{id}`.

4. And now add the most important method of this service that will receive a movie ID and return a list of available exhibitions for that movie. In order to provide such functionality we will add another path for the method, /q, and pass the movie ID as a URL parameter that can be read through the annotation QueryParam of JAX-RS. The complete method is shown as follows:

```
@GET
@Path("/q")
@Produces({ MediaType.APPLICATION_XML,
           MediaType.APPLICATION_JSON })
public List<Exhibition> getAllExhibitionsByMovie
   (@QueryParam("movie") int movieId) {
      if (movieId > 0) {
         Query query = em.createNamedQuery
            (Exhibition.findByMovie);
         query.setParameter("movieId", movieId);

         @SuppressWarnings("unchecked")
         List<Exhibition> result = query.getResultList();

         if (result.size() > 0)
            return result;
         else
            throw new WebApplicationException
               (Response.Status.NOT_FOUND);
      }
      else
         throw new WebApplicationException
         (Response.Status.BAD_REQUEST);
```

> Note that if a request is made to `http://<server>:<port>/theater/api/exhibition/q` without a parameter or with a parameter but no value, a **BAD REQUEST error code (HTTP 400)** will be returned. Remember that HTTP status codes are heavily used for RESTful web services since they are a standard and have meaningful descriptions.

5. To deploy the application, open the **Servers** view accessing the menu **Window**, then navigate to **Show View | Servers**.

6. Right-click on the server name and click on the **Add and Remove...** entry from the context menu.

7. Select the **Theater** project from the **Available** list and click on **Add >**.

8. Click on the **Finish** button.

Testing the web service

After the successful deployment, test the application accessing the following URLs from a browser:

- `http://localhost:7001/theater/api/exhibition/`

- `http://localhost:7001/theater/api/exhibition/4`

- `http://localhost:7001/theater/api/exhibition/q?movie=5`

To complete the testing, we can call the service API from a command-line utility such as **cURL**, setting the **accept** HTTP header to `application/json`, which will change the web service's response, as shown in the following screenshot:

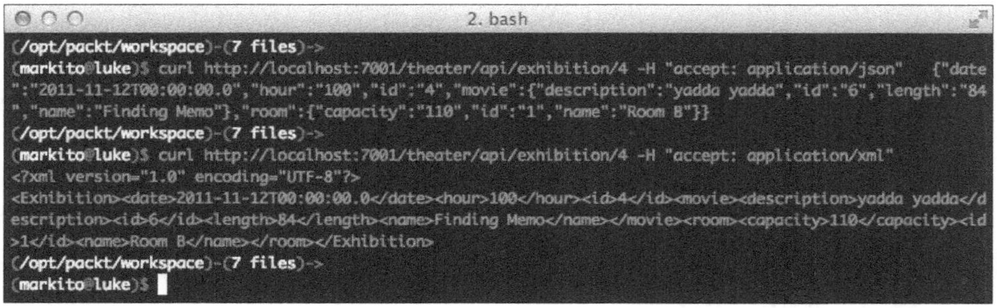

> To force a RESTful service support only one media type (only JSON or only XML, for example), you can modify the `Produces` annotation and set the appropriate media type. Actually the supported media types are listed in the Java docs of Jersey API at `https://jersey.java.net/apidocs/latest/jersey/index.html`.

You can check the RESTful APIs exposed by an application accessing the autogenerated **Web Application Description Language (WADL)** file at the API's root URL to get information about it. For the module we just coded, that address would be `http://localhost:7001/theater/api/application.wadl`:

The `application.wadl` file is generated by Jersey and contains all the basic information about the service such as operations, supported media types for each operation, HTTP verbs, and input/output data.

Creating the REST client

Now that there is a service that provides a list of movie exhibitions available on the Theater module, we need to update the Store module to consume this API and display the retrieved information on the query page. Here's a graphical representation of this functionality:

The JAX-RS RI defines a client API for RESTful Web Services clients and the base class for this is `com.sun.jersey.api.client.Client`. This is the main class we're going to use to develop our client in the next section.

Configuring JAX-RS client libraries and optional package

Before starting the creation of the client, we need to add some Jersey libraries to the project classpath since they provide the client API and JSON classes that we're going to use:

1. Open the **Properties for Store** window and go to the **Java Build Path** section.

2. Click on the **Libraries** tab and click on **Add External JARs...**.

3. Browse to the WebLogic 12c installation directory and go to the `modules` folder at `$MW_HOME/oracle_common/modules`.

4. Select files `jersey.core-1.17.1.jar`, `jersey.json-1.17.1.jar`, and `jersey.client-1.17.1.jar` and click on **OK**:

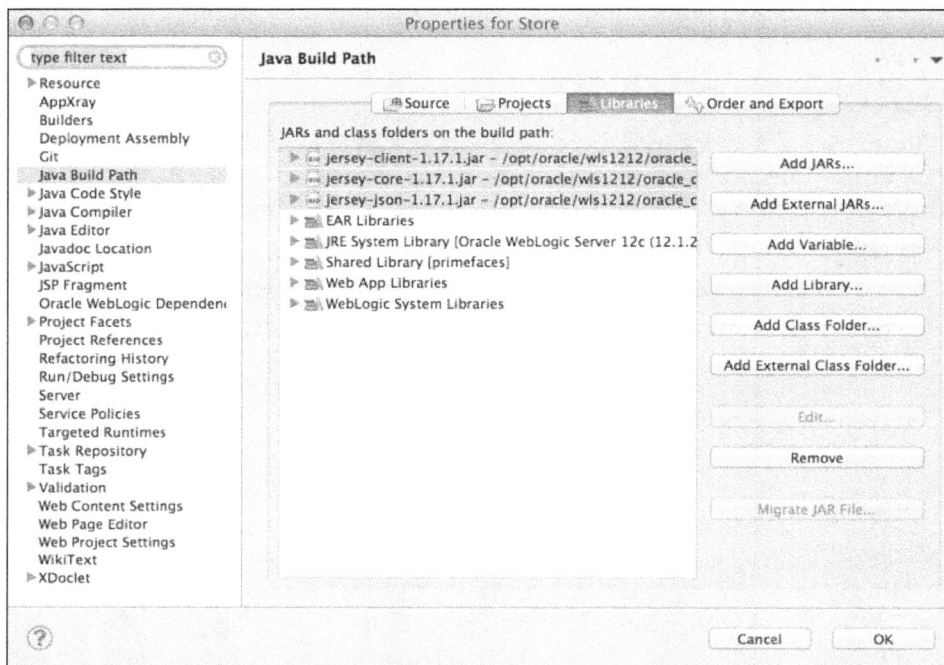

5. Click on **OK** to close the **Properties for Store** window.

Also, we need to add references to TheaterBO to properly manipulate the response of our REST Web Service. As we did with StoreBO in the previous chapter, we need to add a reference to the project for design-time compilation, and some tags to the project's `MANIFEST.MF` file to link them at runtime. Let's do so:

1. To add a project reference, right-click on the Store project and select **Properties**, then **Java Build Path** and finally **Projects**. Click on **Add...** and select the **TheaterBO** project.

2. Now, open the Store's project `MANIFEST.MF` file inside `WebContent/META-INF`, add a reference to the `Extension-List`, and then add the package details. Here's how your file should look after this step:

```
Manifest-Version: 1.0
Class-Path:
Extension-List: storeBO theaterBO
storeBO-Extension-Name: storeBO
storeBO-Specification-Version: 1.0
```

```
storeBO-Implementation-Version: 1.0.0
theaterBO-Extension-Name: theaterBO
theaterBO-Specification-Version: 1.0
theaterBO-Implementation-Version: 1.0.0
```

3. Save the file.

The Store project is now ready and you can start implementing the web service client.

Creating the web service consumer

Now that the Store project has the correct libraries, we can create the client that is going to consume the API exposed at `http://localhost:7001/theater/api/exhibition/q`. In order to achieve this, we must:

1. Create a named bean that is going to act as a proxy between our `SearchManager` bean and the Theater API.

2. Instantiate the JAX Client handler and retrieve an actual handler to call the remote methods, represented by a `WebResource` object.

3. Define and code the proxy method that is going to receive a movie ID from `SearchManager`, build the query, and execute it.

So, in the **Store** project, create a new Java class named `TheaterClient` under the package `com.packt.theater.client`, decorate it with `@Named` and add a method to retrieve a JAX-RS handler:

```
private WebResource getClient() {
    final Client client = Client.create();
    return client.resource(ENDPOINT);
}
```

The endpoint referenced above is going to be retrieved from a deployment descriptor, `web.xml`, using CDI. Add these lines just after the class declaration:

```
@Resource(lookup="theaterServiceEndpoint")
private String ENDPOINT;
```

Now, open your `web.xml` file and add this block at the end of the `web-app` tag:

```
<env-entry>
    <env-entry-name>theaterServiceEndpoint</env-entry-name>
    <env-entry-type>java.lang.String</env-entry-type>
    <env-entry-value>http://localhost:7001/theater/api
    </env-entry-value>
</env-entry>
```

> As we will simulate just one Theater module when running the projects, there's no need to worry about finding out the right recipient for a request (which theater), so we won't have such a logic in our project, that is, we will use a fixed endpoint address. In a real-world scenario, we should have several entries here, each pointing to a different partner.

The last step is to create a method, `getExhibitionByMovie`, that receives a movie ID as parameter and returns a list of exhibitions, executing the call to the REST Web Service exposed by the Theater module. Here's how the final code of the `TheaterClient` class should look like:

```
@Named
public class TheaterClient {
    @Resource(lookup="theaterServiceEndpoint")
    private String ENDPOINT;

    private WebResource getClient() {
        final Client client = Client.create();
        return client.resource(ENDPOINT);
    }

    public List<Exhibition> getExhibitionByMovie(int movieId) {
        if (null == ENDPOINT) {
            return null;
        }

        final List<Exhibition> exhibition = (List<Exhibition>)
            getClient()
            .path("exhibition")
            .path("q")
            .queryParam("movie", String.valueOf(movieId))
            .accept(MediaType.APPLICATION_XML)
            .get(ClientResponse.class)
            .getEntity(new GenericType<List<Exhibition>>() {});

        return exhibition;
    }
}
```

Now, we must change the `SearchManager` bean to call the brand new client proxy and add variables to deal with this new data.

Updating the SearchManager bean

The `SearchManager` class already has methods that list theaters (`getTheaters`) and movies (`getMovies`), and now we need to update the bean to include a method that will call `TheaterClient` and receive a list of available exhibitions of the selected movie:

1. Open class `SearchManager` and add two attributes, one to hold the list of exhibitions and another to hold the value of the selected entry from the exhibition drop-down menu (don't worry, it doesn't exist just yet, we're going to create it shortly), along with their respective getters and setters:

   ```
   private List<Exhibition> exhibitions;
   private int exhibition;
   ```

2. Inject an instance of `TheaterClient` into it, marking it as `transient` to avoid problems later when serializing the instance of `SearchManager`:

   ```
   @Inject
   private transient TheaterClient theaterClient;
   ```

3. Create a method that will handle any changes in the **Movie** drop-down menu, so every time you select a different movie, this method will be called and the list of exhibitions will be populated or refreshed:

   ```
   public void handleMovieChange() {
       if (movie != 0)
           exhibitions = new
               TheaterClient().getExhibitionByMovie(movie);
       else
           exhibitions = null;
   }
   ```

The complete class should look like this:

```
@Named("search")
@SessionScoped
public class SearchManager implements Serializable {
    private static final long serialVersionUID = 1L;

    @PersistenceContext(unitName="StoreBO")
    EntityManager em;

    @Inject
    private transient TheaterClient theaterClient;
```

```
    private List<Theater> theaters;
    private List<Movie> movies;
    private List<Exhibition> exhibitions;

    private int movie;
    private int theater;
    private int exhibition;

    // Change listener for Movie selectOneMenu
    public void handleMovieChange() {
        if (movie != 0) {
            exhibitions = theaterClient.getExhibitionByMovie(movie);
        } else {
            exhibitions = null;
        }
    }

    @SuppressWarnings("unchecked")
    public List<Theater> getTheaters() {
        if (theaters == null)
            theaters = em.createNamedQuery(Theater.findAll).
            getResultList();

        return theaters;
    }

    @SuppressWarnings("unchecked")
    public List<Movie> getMovies() {
        if (movies == null)
            movies = em.createNamedQuery(Movie.findAll).
            getResultList();

        return movies;
    }
}

// Other getters and setters omitted
```

Updating the query page

The web page that displays the search form needs to be updated with the exhibition dates retrieved from the Theater module. To accomplish this without refreshing the whole page, we will rely on some **Ajax (Asynchronous JavaScript and XML)** features provided by JavaServer Faces. This can be accomplished by firing an Ajax call when the user selects an entry from the Movies drop-down menu:

1. Open the `index.xhtml` file and add a form named `queryForm` between tags `p:fieldset` and `p:panelGrid`—this is needed so that the Ajax engine can capture events:

   ```
   <p:fieldset legend="Basic Query">
      <h:form id="queryForm">
         <p:panelGrid columns="2">
         ...
         </p:panelGrid>
      </h:form>
   ```

2. Add a `p:ajax` component inside the `p:selectOneMenu` tag that shows the movie list. This component needs to inform which method should be called (that is, the event listener), and which component must be updated upon event execution. The component should look like this:

   ```
   <p:selectOneMenu id="movie" value="#{search.movie}"
      style="width: 350px;">
      <f:selectItem itemLabel="Select one" itemValue="0" />
      <f:selectItems value="#{search.movies}" var="n"
         itemLabel="#{n.name}" itemValue="#{n.id}" />
      <p:ajax process="@this" update="exhibition"
         listener="#{search.handleMovieChange}" />
   </p:selectOneMenu>
   ```

3. Add another `p:selectOneMenu` tag to list the exhibitions. It's very important to set the ID of this component to `exhibition` since it's the value configured in the Ajax event listener in the previous step:

   ```
   <h:outputLabel for="exhibition" value="Exhibition:" />
   <p:selectOneMenu id="exhibition"
      value="#{search.exhibition}" style="width: 350px;">
      <f:selectItem itemLabel="Select one" itemValue="0" />
      <f:selectItems value="#{search.exhibitions}" var="n"
         itemLabel="#{n.date}" itemValue="#{n.id}"/>
   </p:selectOneMenu>
   ```

4. Save all files and redeploy (publish) the Store application.

The resulting page should look like this:

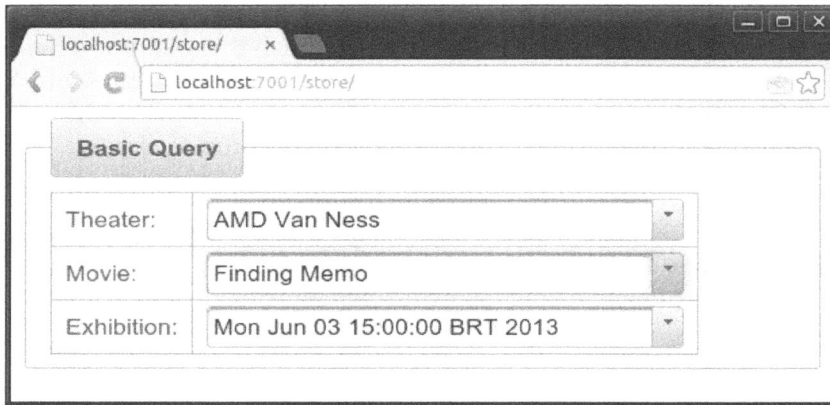

The **Exhibition** drop-down menu is being populated by the results returned by the `exhibition` RESTful web service, hosted by the Theater application. Every time the movie list changes, a new call is made and the exhibition list is refreshed. For a real-world scenario, many considerations would need to be taken into account, such as latency, caching, security, and other strategies. Some of these strategies will be explored in the following chapters.

Structuring the web application

Up to this point, the application has only one page and a simple form, which would not be acceptable as the interface provided for our fictional customers. To fix that we're going to add a few more pages and templates to make the application look better and leverage what we have already learned from the previous chapters and also by adding some JSF Facelets and PrimeFaces components.

Applying templates through Facelets

Let's create a template with the basic components of an application such as header, menu, main page, and so on. On OEPE, open the **Store** web project and perform the following actions:

1. Create a new folder under the `WEB-INF` directory named `templates`.

2. Now we need to create the basis for our template, which will basically consist of two files: `template.xhtml` and `top.xhtml`.

3. The main part of `template.xhtml` is to the define areas (variables) that will be replaced by other pages, using the inner structure declared at each of them. In our example, we have only two areas: `header` and `content`. They're defined by the `<ui:insert>` tag of Facelets as follows:

```
...
<p:layout fullPage="true">
    <p:layoutUnit position="north">
        <ui:insert name="header" >
            <ui:include src="top.xhtml" />
        </ui:insert>
    </p:layoutUnit>
    <p:layoutUnit position="south" style="border:0px">
        <p:notificationBar position="bottom" effect="slide"
            widgetVar="bar" styleClass="top" />
    </p:layoutUnit>
    <p:layoutUnit position="center" style="border:0px">
        <ui:insert name="content" >
            <ui:include src="index.xhtml" />
        </ui:insert>
    </p:layoutUnit>
</p:layout>
...
```

> The complete code of `template.xhtml` is part of the code bundle of this chapter, available at the Packt Publishing website, `www.packtpub.com`.

4. The `top.xhtml` file renders the menu for the application and eventually the logo and login information. This file is included by default in `template.xhtml`. Here is the relevant portion of code from this file:

```
...
<ui:composition>
<h:form>

    <h:graphicImage
        value="resources/images/movieStoreLogo.png"
        style="margin: 0px auto;margin-left:5%;" height="15%"
        width="15%" />

    <p:panelGrid columns="2" id="loginPanel"
        style="float: right; right:50%; margin-right:10%;
        padding:0px; font-size:10px; border:none;">
        <p:inputText id="loginUser">
```

```
            <p:watermark for="loginUser"
                value="user@mail.com" />
        </p:inputText>
        <p:password id="loginPass">
        </p:password>
        <div />
        <p:row>
            <p:commandButton value="Login" />
            <p:commandButton value="Sign up" />
        </p:row>
    </p:panelGrid>
    <p:megaMenu style="height:90%; font-size:12px;">
        <p:menuitem value="Home" url="/" />
        <p:menuitem value="Theaters"
            url="/theaters/theaters.jsf" />
        <p:menuitem value="Movies" url="/movies/movies.jsf"
            />

        <f:facet name="options">
            <p:inputText id="searchText"
                style="padding: 4px; margin:0px;
                font-size: 12px; margin-right:10px" />
            <p:watermark for="searchText" value="Search..." />
            <p:splitButton value="Search" actionListener="#"
                style="margin:0px; font-size: 10px;">
                <p:menuitem value="by Exhibition dates"
                    actionListener="#" />
                <p:menuitem value="by Movies"
                    actionListener="#" />
                <p:menuitem value="by Theaters"
                    actionListener="#" />
                <p:separator />
                <p:menuitem value="Advanced Search" url="#" />
            </p:splitButton>
        </f:facet>
    </p:megaMenu>

</h:form>
</ui:composition>
```

> The complete code of top.xhtml is part of the code bundle of this chapter, available at the Packt Publishing website, www.packtpub.com.

5. Open `index.xhtml` and replace the content of the `<body>` tag with the following code:

```
<ui:composition
    template="/WEB-INF/templates/template.xhtml">
    <ui:define name="title">Home</ui:define>
    <ui:define name="content">
        <h:form>
            <p:panel header="In Theaters">
                <p:ring id="basic" value="#{movie.movies}"
                    var="item">
                    <p:outputPanel style="text-align:center;"
                        layout="block">
                    #{item.name}
                    <p:rating />
                    </p:outputPanel>
                </p:ring>
            </p:panel>
        </h:form>
    </ui:define>
</ui:composition>
```

6. Save all files and publish the project. Access the index page and you will see the current application:

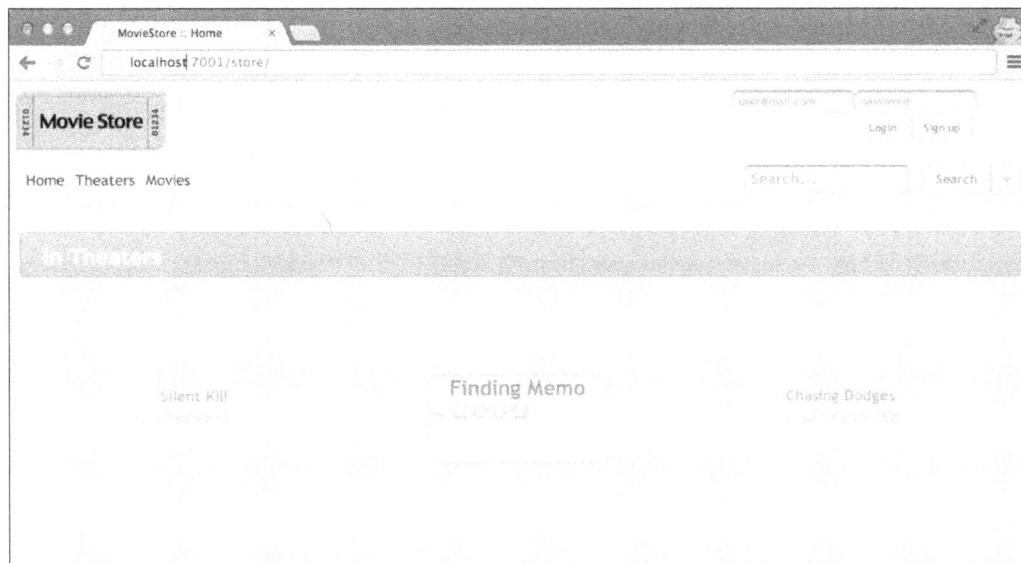

Some functionalities like the login or signup are not yet implemented and we will learn how to do so in the next chapters. But with the knowledge acquired from *Chapter 3, Java EE Basics – Persistence, Query, and Presentation*, and this chapter, we can create the Theater and Movie listing pages. To demonstrate, we're going to show how to create one for Theater and leave the creation of the Movie listing page as an exercise to the reader, although the complete code for all this is available at the Packt Publishing website, www.packtpub.com.

> Remember that **PrimeFaces** themes can be set or changed by modifying the value of primefaces.THEME context param on web.xml. The themes must be available to the application classpath, as we are bundling ours with the shared library.

Creating an entity listing page

We are going to build a generic example that will leverage our template and create a listing page for Theaters.

Start by creating an abstract class named AbstractRepository under the com.packt.store package. The important methods of the class are shown in the following code snippet:

```
...
public abstract class AbstractRepository<T> {
   private Class<T> entityClass;
   public AbstractRepository() { }
...
   public AbstractRepository(final Class<T> entityClass) {
      this.entityClass = entityClass;
   }

   protected abstract EntityManager getEntityManager();

   public T find(Object id) {
      return getEntityManager().find(entityClass, id);
   }

   public List<T> findAll() {
      CriteriaQuery<T> cq = (CriteriaQuery<T>)
         getEntityManager().getCriteriaBuilder().createQuery();
         cq.select(cq.from(entityClass));
         return getEntityManager()
            .createQuery(cq).getResultList();
   }
...
```

> The complete code of `AbstractRepository` is part of the code bundle of this chapter, available at the Packt Publishing website, `www.packtpub.com`.

Note that we have a method that lists all entities, `findAll()`, and another method that returns an entity given an ID, `find()`. These are basic methods that will be reused on several points throughout the application.

Now create a named CDI bean `TheaterManager` under `com.packt.store.theater` package that will be bound to the web page. This class will extend the abstract repository class by only implementing a very few necessary methods. The following is the complete code:

```
@Named("theater")
@RequestScoped
public class TheaterManager extends AbstractRepository<Theater> {

    private List<Theater> theaters;
    @PersistenceContext(unitName = "StoreBO")
    EntityManager em;

    public TheaterManager() {
        super(Theater.class);
    }

    @PostConstruct
    public void init() {
        theaters = this.findAll();
    }

    @Override
    protected EntityManager getEntityManager() {
        return em;
    }

    public List<Theater> getTheaters() {
        return theaters;
    }
}
```

Now the last part is the web page, so under `WebContent` create a new folder named `theaters`. In this folder, create a file named `theaters.xhtml`; it will just define the value of the content area of the template. Here is the example:

```
<ui:composition template="/WEB-INF/templates/template.xhtml">
<ui:define name="title">Theaters</ui:define>
<ui:define name="content">
    <p:panel header="Theaters">
       <h:form>
           <p:dataList value="#{theater.theaters}" var="item"
           itemType="none"
           paginator="true" rows="5" paginatorAlwaysVisible="false"
           paginatorPosition="bottom">
           <p:fieldset styleClass="fdsetNoBorder"
              legend="#{item.name}"
              toggleSpeed="500" style="margin:10px">
           <h:panelGrid columns="2" cellpadding="10">
           <h:outputText value="City: #{item.city}" />
           </h:panelGrid>
           </p:fieldset>
           </p:dataList>
       </h:form>
    </p:panel>
</ui:define>
</ui:composition>
. . .
```

Save all files and publish the project. Then access the index page of the Store application and click on the **Theaters** link on the menu. You should see a list of current theaters on the system, built by reusing the code and concepts we've learned so far:

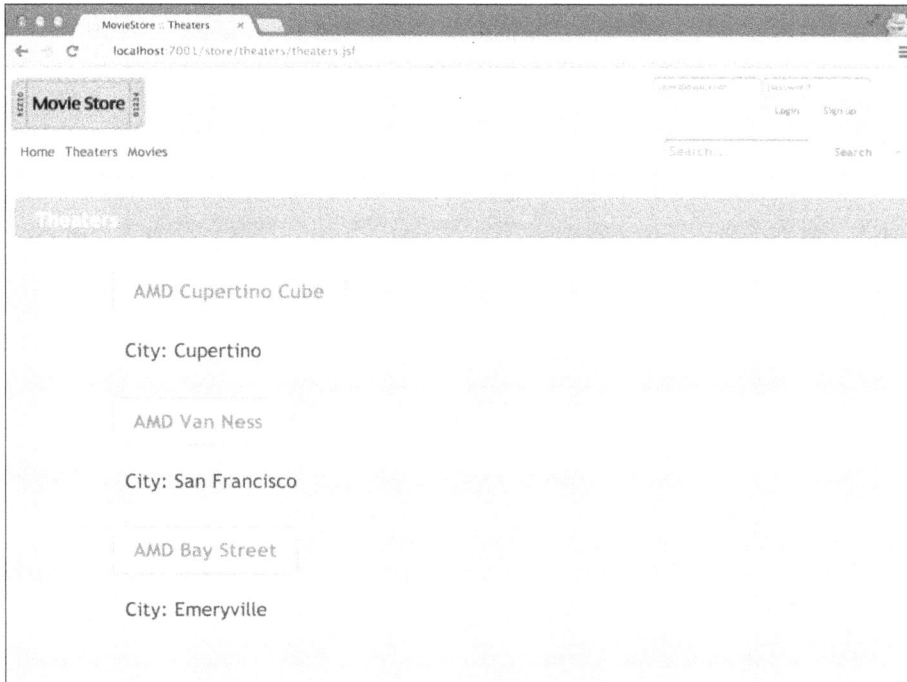

Now to create the same kind of listing page for movies will be very easy and we encourage the reader to do so. In the following chapters, we're going to assume that you have the application working and we're going to enhance it by adding extra features.

Web resources

- JSON (JavaScript Object Notation)
  - ○ `http://www.json.org/`

- Jersey 1.17 User Guide
  - ○ `https://jersey.java.net/documentation/1.17/index.html`

- Jersey site
  - ○ `http://jersey.java.net`

- Community Wiki for Project Jersey
  - `http://wikis.sun.com/display/Jersey/Main`

- Jersey 1.17 API Javadoc
  - `http://jersey.java.net/apidocs/latest/jersey/overview-summary.html`

- JSR-311 JAX-RS Specification
  - `http://jcp.org/en/jsr/summary?id=311`

- JSR-311 JAX-RS Project
  - `http://jsr311.java.net/`

- JSR-311 JAX-RS API Javadoc
  - `http://jsr311.java.net/nonav/javadoc/index.html`

- The Java EE 6 Tutorial—Building RESTful Web Services With JAX-RS
  - `http://download.oracle.com/javaee/6/tutorial/doc/giepu.html`

- Representational State Transfer (REST) in Architectural Styles and the Design of Network-based Software Architectures (Dissertation by Roy Fielding)
  - `http://www.ics.uci.edu/~fielding/pubs/dissertation/rest_arch_style.htm`

Summary

In this chapter we have learned how to create and expose an Enterprise Java Bean (EJB) as a RESTful web service through usage of JAX-RS annotations. We also created JPA entities and exposed those classes as XML and JSON objects through JAXB, composing the RESTful web service. Finally, we've updated the search page to consume the exposed API by showing how to create a RESTful client using Jersey's (JAX-RS RI) client API.

In the next chapter we're going to learn how to use JAX-WS to expose and invoke SOAP web services and how to create validations using the bean validation framework.

5
Singleton Bean, Validations, and SOAP Web Services

Now that we saw how to expose and consume web services using REST, let's see how to use another popular technology, **SOAP**, to achieve the same results.

> There's a wide (and sometimes wild) discussion about which one is better, and we aren't endorsing any of them by setting this specific order — the architectural factors and implications of such decisions are out of scope of this book.

Also, we already accessed the persistence layer provided by the server to connect and retrieve information from a database. In this chapter we will use this mechanism to insert data, detailing the transactional aspects involved, and will declare the bean validation rules to check the values being passed to the database.

Some of these functionalities will be encapsulated by a **singleton bean**, another new feature of Java EE 6 that makes the developer's life easier but brings a few details that must be considered to achieve the expected results.

Using bean validation

The bean validation specification, defined by **JSR 303**, is a new addition to Java EE 6 and sets a single validation framework — instead of declaring a set of validations for input mechanisms and another set in the model layer, now we can use a consistent group of constraints and apply them at both view and model levels.

A validation is composed of one or more constraints and can be applied to virtually any element — examples being a class, a method, an attribute, or even another constraint (a structure called **constraint composition**) depending on the scope of the constraint (its @Target decoration).

All validation constraints can be defined inside a validation.xml file or as annotations packaged with your application. We will focus on annotations as they are easier to read.

The rules defined in the validation.xml file have precedence over any constraint annotations a class may have.

About built-in constraints

The specification defines a fixed set of constraints as described in the following table:

Constraint	Description	Applies to
@AssertTrue	The value must be True: @AssertTrue Boolean isInitialized;	Boolean boolean
@AssertFalse	The value must be False: @AssertFalse Boolean isBlocked;	Boolean boolean
@Null	The value must be null: @Null String restrictions;	Everything but primitives
@NotNull	The value must not be null: @NotNull String productName;	Everything but primitives
@Min	The value must be equal to or higher than the specified minimum: @Min(21) Integer age;	BigDecimal and BigInteger byte, short, int, long, and their respective wrappers
@Max	The value must be equal to or lower than the specified maximum: @Max(10) short pendingProducts;	BigDecimal and BigInteger byte, short, int, long, and their respective wrappers

Constraint	Description	Applies to

@DecimalMin	The value must be equal to or greater than the specified value (represented as a string):
	
	`@DecimalMin("100.00")`
	`String insuranceTotal;`
		`BigDecimal` and `BigInteger`
		
		`String`
		
		`byte, short, int, long,` and their respective wrappers

@DecimalMax	The value must be lower than or equal to the specified value (represented as a string):
	
	`@DecimalMax("1000.00")`
	`BigDecimal allowance;`
		`BigDecimal` and `BigInteger`
		
		`String`
		
		`byte, short, int, long,` and their respective wrappers

@Digits	The value must comply to the maximum digits defined for both `integer` and `fraction` portions:
	
	`@Digits(integer=7,fraction=2)`
	`String grandTotal;`
		`BigDecimal` and `BigInteger`
		
		`String`
		
		`byte, short, int, long,` and their respective wrappers

@Size	The size of the object must be inside the range specified by the `min` and `max` values:
	
	`@Size(min=1, max=100)`
	`Map relationships;`
		`String`
		
		`Collection`
		
		`Map`
		
		`Array`

@Future	The value must be greater than the current date:
	
	`@Future`
	`Date exhibitionDate;`
		`Date`
		
		`Calendar`

@Past	The value must be lower than the current date:
	
	`@Past`
	`Date birthDate;`
		`Date`
		
		`Calendar`

@Pattern	The value must match the regular expression (follows Java conventions defined at `java.util.regex.Pattern`):
	
	`@Pattern(regexp="^[A-Z]+$")`
	`String capitalOnly;`
		`String`

Combining and grouping validation rules

All these built-in constraints — and custom constraints that we're about to create — can be combined to create complex validations; all we need to do is attach all the necessary constraints to a variable:

```
@NotNull
@Min(10)
@Digits(integer=5)
Long counter;
```

But you can't declare two annotations of the same type for the same object. When you need to do this, you must use the List format — actually, this is another annotation that extends all the built-in constraints — and pass an array of rules of the same type as its value:

```
@Pattern.List({ @Pattern(regexp="[a-z]*"),
                @Pattern(regexp="[A-Z]*")})
String name;
```

This is all good if you want to apply every single rule every time you check an object, and basically this is the expected behavior when applying validation to the user input via JSF.

But suppose you have a business entity that must be checked against specific rules depending on some entity's attribute. You can't create the validation set dynamically at runtime, which is when you have details about the object that must be checked. So, to solve this, you must use *validation groups*.

Every constraint exposes a groups attribute that can receive a list of Java interfaces, and this can be used to segregate rules. Notice that the definition of the interface is not used by the validation framework, only its name.

To illustrate the usage of groups, let's say we have a *customer* entity, and an individual can be a *regular* or a *premium* customer. This profile will define how many items can be set in the quantity attribute. To implement this scenario, we could use just three classes:

```
public class Customer {
  int quantity;

  public int getQuantity() {
        return quantity;
  }
  public void setQuantity(int quantity) {
```

```
        this.quantity = quantity;
    }
}

public class RegularCustomer extends Customer { }

public class PremiumCustomer extends Customer { }
```

As the *group* structure deals with interfaces, we need to attach the class definitions to the interfaces to be able to define the validation rules. So, let's create two empty interfaces and attach them to the classes we just created:

```
public interface Regular { }

public interface Premium { }

public class RegularCustomer implements Regular
                              extends Customer { }

public class PremiumCustomer implements Premium
                              extends Customer { }
```

We can now go back to the `customer` class and define the business constraints—a regular customer can add up to 10 items with no minimum value, and a premium customer can get up to 30 items but must get at least 10 items:

```
public class Customer {
    @Min.List({ @Min(value=10, groups={ Premium.class })})

    @Max.List({ @Max(value=10, groups={ Regular.class }),
                @Max(value=30, groups={ Premium.class })})
    int quantity;
```

To test the code, we're going to create a regular customer, instantiate a **validator** object—this object gives us a direct way to access the validation framework—and call the `validate` method to pass the customer and the interface whose rules must be checked:

```
import javax.validation.*;

Customer regular = new RegularCustomer();
regular.setQuantity(20);

ValidatorFactory vf = Validation.buildDefaultValidatorFactory();
Validator validator = vf.getValidator();
```

```
Set<ConstraintViolation<Customer>> violations =
                        validator.validate(regular, Regular.class);

for (ConstraintViolation<Customer> violation : violations) {
  System.out.println(violation.getMessage());
}
```

> Another decoration, @GroupSequence, can be used when you have
> overlapping groups and want to set a specific order to perform the
> checks. Remember that this annotation can only be attached to interfaces
> and classes.

Creating a custom constraint

If you need to declare validations that aren't covered by a specific built-in constraint
or a combination of them, you can create your own constraints.

> Another scenario where a custom constraint is a valid option is
> when you have a complex combination of built-in constraints that is
> frequently applied — creating a custom constraint to encapsulate it
> makes the developer's life easier, reduces the chance of an error, and
> improves code maintenance.

Here's an example of a custom constraint that just wraps two built-in constraints.
Apart from the @NotNull and @Pattern decorations that specifies the validation
rule, everything else just composes the minimum set of instructions needed to
define a constraint:

```
import java.lang.annotation.*;
import javax.validation.*;
import javax.validation.constraints.NotNull;
import javax.validation.constraints.Pattern;

@Constraint(validatedBy={})
@Retention(RetentionPolicy.RUNTIME)
@Target(ElementType.FIELD)

@NotNull
@Pattern(regexp = "[0-9]{1,3}.[0-9]{1,3}.[0-9]{1,3}.[0-9]{1,3}")
public @interface IP {
    String message() default "";
    Class<?>[] groups() default {};
    Class<? extends Payload>[] payload() default {};
}
```

> The regular expression declared here is a simplification of a real-world check—the number of groups and alternatives of a valid expression would not add to the point being illustrated, so we decided to use a simpler one.

The @Constraint decoration is the most important one because it defines this piece of code as a constraint to the container. As this custom constraint is just a composition of built-in constraints, an empty array is all we need to pass to validatedBy.

As constraints are checked at runtime, the @Retention decoration must be set to RUNTIME. The @Target decoration indicates which type of elements can be decorated with the custom constraint; for example, only fields (attributes) are allowed to have it, hence its FIELD value is decorated.

The message, groups, and payload methods are mandatory when defining a validation constraint. If you forget any of them, your code will compile and deploy, but when the WebLogic tries to check it at runtime, a javax.validation. ConstraintDefinitionException error will pop up.

You may have noticed that the message method has an empty string as its default value. This is because we don't have the actual code attached to this constraint—the built-in constraints will generate the output messages, so any text you enter here will not be used.

Coding a constraint validator

If your validation needs are more complex and some code is necessary, you can create one or more classes that implement the javax.validation. ConstraintValidator interface and list them in the validatedBy attribute in @Constraint.

In the class declaration, you must state which constraint this code will be bound to and to which type of data. Here's how the same IP validation would look like if we use Java code instead of the built-in constraints:

```
import javax.validation.ConstraintValidator;
import javax.validation.ConstraintValidatorContext;

public class IPValidator implements ConstraintValidator<IP, String>
{
    private IP constraint;

    // Lazy pattern, not designed for real situations
```

```
    private static String IP_PATTERN =
    "(?>[0-9]{1,3}.)(?>[0-9]{1,3}.)([0-9]{1,3}.)([0-9]{1,3}.)";

    @Override
    public void initialize(IP constraint) {
        this.constraint = constraint;
    }

    @Override
    public boolean isValid(String ipAddress,
      ConstraintValidatorContext cvc) {
        if (null == ipAddress)
            return false;

        return ipAddress.matches(IP_PATTERN);
    }
}
```

As our IP rule can only be applied to strings, the `validator` declaration reflects this decision as `ConstraintValidator<IP, String>`.

> You have to create a `Validator` class for each and every type of value it can be attached to, or you can declare a generic one, `<IP, Object>`, and check the value type at runtime inside its `isValid` method.

The `initialize` method receives the parameters set at the annotation, and this information can be stored to be used later by the `isValid` method; for example, to organize the sequence of checks based on the `groups` attribute.

Showing validation messages

When you attach constraints to bean attributes and these attributes are linked to a form, the validation phase is started upon the form's submission. If one or more of the constraints aren't met, the associated message(s) is returned to the view.

To exemplify this, let's attach a basic rule to the attributes of our `SearchManager` class in the project **Store**:

```
public class SearchManager {
    ...
    @Min(value = 1, message = "Please select a movie")
    private int movie;

    @Min(value = 1, message = "Please select a theater")
```

```
private int theater;

@Min(value = 1, message = "Please select an exhibition")
private int exhibition;
```

This set of constraints will guarantee that when the `search` method executes, the user selected an entry of each available dropdown: `theater`, `movie`, and `exhibition`.

We have a couple options to show the messages returned by JSF:

- JSF's **message component**, either attached to a field or as an independent area

- PrimeFaces's **Growl component**

> Consider using some of these restrictions on POJOs at `StoreBO` and `TheaterBO`. That way, you can easily apply some common restrictions for business objects. You can also save a layer hop to validate some of these restrictions that are actual database constraints, and every project that consumes these beans will share these basic validations. For instance, you can add the following validations to the `Ticket` class::
>
> ```
> ...
> @NotNull(message="Control numbers can't be null.")
> private String control;
>
> @NotNull(message="An exhibition must be assigned to the
> ticket.")
> private int exhibitionRef;
>
> @NotNull(message="Seat(s) must be assigned to the
> ticket.")
> private int seatRef;
> ...
> ```

Using the message component

You can attach a `message` component to each field of a form, so each one will show the messages related to its linked field. Just add an `h:message` tag with the name of the target component to its `for` attribute:

```
<h:message for="movie" />
```

To be able to submit the form and run validations, we need to add a **command button** inside `queryForm`, along with an HTML break to keep the screen aligned:

```
<p:commandButton id="query" update="queryForm" value="Search Seats"
action="#{search.query}"/>
<br />
```

Here's a snippet of the code from the `index.xhtml` file of the **Store** project showing how to use it:

```
<h:form id="queryForm">
    <p:panelGrid columns="3">
        <h:outputLabel for="movie" value="Movie:" />
    <p:selectOneMenu id="movie" value="#{search.movie}">
        . . .
    </p:selectOneMenu>
    <h:message for="movie" />
        . . .
    <p:commandButton id="query" update="queryForm" value="Search Seats"
action="#{search.query}"/>
    <br />
```

> Remember to target the `update` attribute of your command button, or else you're not going to see any messages.

The downside of this approach is that you have to code individual entries and obviously must consider them as screen components — to accommodate the message tags, we had to raise the number of columns of the `panelGrid` tag defined earlier. Conversely, when you have a screen with too many fields, using it brings better visual feedback to the user, despite the extra effort to format the page output.

The rendered screen with some validation messages would look similar to the following screenshot:

PrimeFaces also exposes a `message` component that works the same way as the JSF implementation; however, it shows an icon next to the message and applies a different style to the message's text, making it more graphically appealing.

You can also set a message area, which is not attached to a specific field, like this:

```
<h:form id="queryForm">
    <p:messages />
    ...
```

This is how the same messages would be shown using this component:

You can customize a component's style by adding your own stylesheet and overriding PrimeFaces' definitions. The appropriate tags you should change are detailed in the framework's documentation.

PrimeFaces's Growl

Growl is name of the notification system adopted by Apple's Mac OS X, and also the name of a PrimeFaces's component based on it that shows messages in an overlay.

In order to use the component, just add a reference to it inside your command's target update component—the form, in our example:

```
<h:form id="queryForm">
<p:growl showDetail="false"/>
```

And here's how the messages would be shown:

The `showDetail` attribute is set to `false` to avoid message repetition inside each box—each `FaceMessage` has a `summary` attribute and a `detail` attribute, and the bean validation framework sets both of them with the same value.

The book's example application will use PrimeFaces's Growl component.

Dealing with null and empty strings on JSF components

If you plan to use bean validations along with JSF, there's something you must remember; when you attach a bean element to a JSF text component such as `InputText`, the element is initialized with an empty string. So, if you mark such an element with a `@Null` or `@NotNull` constraint, the resulting check would be inaccurate.

To avoid this scenario, you must add a parameter to the application's `web.xml` file:

```
<context-param>
 <param-name>
   javax.faces.INTERPRET_EMPTY_STRING_SUBMITTED_VALUES_AS_NULL
 </param-name>
 <param-value>true</param-value>
</context-param>
```

By doing this, you're instructing the JSF engine that it must handle empty strings as null.

Singleton session beans

This new kind of bean helps developers create components that implement the pattern that gives its name — no need to declare class methods and attributes to create them anymore.

Its behavior is a crossover between stateless and stateful beans, as it holds its state between calls but isn't expected to keep the state consistent in case of a server shutdown. As just one instance of such a bean is available at any given time, the client state must not be kept by it for obvious reasons.

The application container guarantees that one bean instance is loaded per JVM. This means that each **Managed Server** — an instance of WebLogic Server — will load and keep only one instance of the class in memory. If your WebLogic domain has just one instance, the bean is truly singleton in the sense that only one instance will receive every single request. But, the most common scenario is to have a cluster of managed servers so you end up with several instances in memory, each receiving the requests generated by the JVM running it:

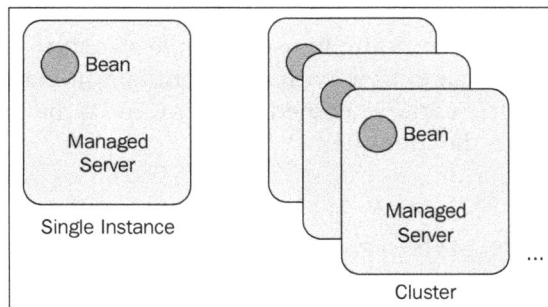

One strategy to ensure that just one bean instance is loaded onto the entire cluster is to target the application containing it to just one managed server.

> **Targeting** is the way you tell WebLogic Server where an application should run — this structure is used on other kinds of resources, such as Data Sources and JMS. You can target a component to specific servers or a cluster, which is a logical aggregation of servers.

But pinning an application to just one server raises a reliability-related issue. We now have a **Single Point of Failure (SPOF)**; if this WebLogic instance goes down for some reason, for example, system overload due to request saturation (also known as denial-of-service attacks), the singleton will no longer be available. Request saturation occurs when a massive amount of requests are targeted to a server on a scale that it can't handle, and eventually the server goes down.

Let's see how to use a singleton session bean to implement a business rule that must have controlled access.

> The scenario described here doesn't consider shared singleton session beans. If you have such a component packaged as a shared library referenced by multiple projects, each one will have an instance of the bean on its classloader. For such usage, a **singleton service** is a better approach as we're going to see in *Chapter 10, Scaling Up the Application.*

Implementing a singleton session bean

We're going to create a class that will generate control identifiers to attach to a ticket, so when a customer presents the ticket at the theater counter, there's a way to check its validity.

The most basic way to expose a class as a singleton is to decorate it with javax.ejb. Singleton. So, create a new class named ReservationCodeBean inside the package com.packt.util of the project **Store**, and mark it as a singleton.

To generate the identifier, we're going to use a simple structure where we concatenate the current date and time with a sequential number owned by the bean. For this, we need a numeric variable named counter and a method named generate that will create and return the identifier:

```
package com.packt.util;

import java.text.SimpleDateFormat;
import java.util.Date;
import javax.ejb.Singleton;

@Singleton
public class ReservationCodeBean {
  private int counter = 0;
  private SimpleDateFormat now =
              new SimpleDateFormat("yyyyMMdd-hhmmss");

  public String generate() {
    String control = String.format("%1$s-%2$06d",
              now.format(new Date()), ++counter);

    return control;
  }
}
```

A call to this method will return a string like 20130615-091654-000001.

For now, that's all we have to do in this class. We will get back to it later in this chapter, while finishing up the reservation process.

The next section details how the startup and shutdown sequences of singleton session beans can be defined.

Understanding how to use the startup annotation

A class annotation you can use with singleton beans is `javax.ejb.Startup`, which tells the container to call the method marked with `@PostConstruct` upon **activation** of the application—notice that this doesn't mean the application is **deployed** in the sense that it is already available to receive and process requests. To understand this, let's take a look at the graph showing the relevant states of an application inside the WebLogic Server:

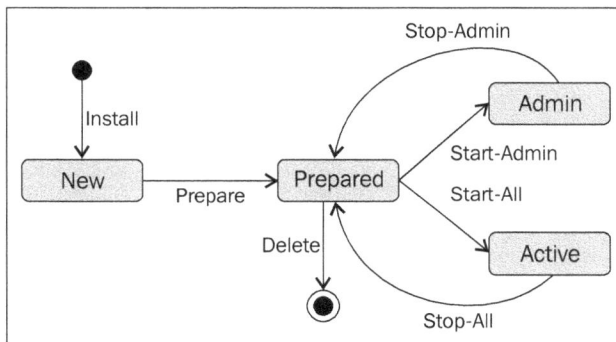

When you ask WebLogic to deploy a package, it is received by the deployer module and enters the **New** state. The **Prepared** state is reached when the application is distributed to all the servers that are going to host it, and all the servers accepted it, checked the package, and confirmed it as valid.

At this point, we can instruct the deployer to execute a full start, which is the commonly desired final state, or to serve only administrative requests; these are calls to the components using specific credentials so we can check whether everything is okay before releasing the application for general use.

This transition from **Prepared** to **Admin** or **Active** state is the point where the `@PostConstruct` methods of a class decorated with `@Startup` are called. Conversely, when a command to stop the application is issued, the `@PreDestroy` methods are called before the transition to the **Prepared** state.

> The examples used in this section refer to the components of our applications to make them easier to understand, but we don't need any of them to execute our business scenario.

Establishing a startup and shutdown sequence

You can attach singleton beans decorated with @Startup to another bean using the javax.ejb.DependsOn annotation, effectively creating a bean load sequence:

```
@Singleton
@DependsOn({"InitialBean" })
public class ReservationCodeBean {
...
```

When executing the shutdown procedure, the server calls the @PreDestroy methods following the reverse sequence so the dependencies are still available:

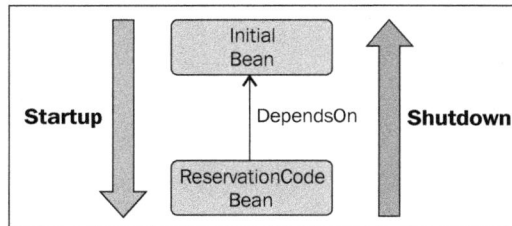

> If a cyclic reference happens to be introduced by @DependsOn, an error message carrying the exception weblogic.application. naming.ReferenceResolutionException will be presented upon deployment, stating the names of the offending beans.

This works fine if your bean depends on just one other bean, as described earlier. If you declare more than one bean, the container doesn't guarantee that the declaration sequence will be followed. Consider this dependency list:

```
@Singleton
@DependsOn({"InitialBean", "LoggingBean", "AuditBean" })
```

The beans will be loaded in no specific order; the only commitment made by the container is that it will load all the dependencies before the topmost bean, and that's it. If a predefined sequence is really needed, you must chain the dependencies; something similar to the following:

```
@Singleton
@DependsOn({ "InitialBean" })
```

```
public class ReservationCodeBean { ... }

@Singleton
@DependsOn({ "LoggingBean", "AuditBean" })
public class InitialBean { ... }
```

This is the only way to guarantee specific load and destroy sequences.

Dealing with concurrency when using singletons

The default behavior of a singleton session bean, which has synchronized access to all of its methods, is the consequence of default values set up by the container, and it may not fit every business need.

To understand what can be changed, here's how the code we just created would look like with explicit declaration of all concurrency-related tags that represent the default behavior:

```
@Singleton
@ConcurrencyManagement(ConcurrencyManagementType.CONTAINER)
@AccessTimeout(1000) // Default unit: milliseconds
public class ReservationCodeBean {
  ...
    @Lock(LockType.WRITE)
    public String getNextId() {
    ...
```

By setting the ConcurrencyManagement annotation to CONTAINER, the responsibility of the synchronization demarcation is transferred to the container. Also, the Lock annotation attached to each method is set to LockType.WRITE, which is the most restrictive strategy of locking—every call to the method is supposed to change its state, so all access must be serialized.

The most common scenario is to have a couple of methods that need a more restrictive lock. These are the ones that actually alter the bean's state; others that don't are methods that just read some data. If this is the case, decorate access methods with @Lock and the value, LockType.READ:

```
@Lock(LockType.WRITE)
public void updateData(String key, String value) {
  ...
}

@Lock(LockType.READ)
```

```
public String getData(String key) {
  return value;
}
```

By doing this, concurrent accesses to the read methods are allowed, improving the overall response time.

> Remember that even operations marked as LockType.READ are subject to contention — when a request to an operation marked with WRITE is received, the whole bean is locked to execute it.

The last related annotation is AccessTimeout, which controls how long a request must wait for the lock to release. If time is exceeded, the container raises a ConcurrentAccessTimeoutException exception.

> There is no default value to this parameter inside the WebLogic Server. If you don't explicitly declare @AccessTimeout, the more generic **JTA timeout** value is used. This is the maximum time a transaction can be held open by a request, and it applies to the whole container.

On the other end of the spectrum, if you set @ConcurrencyManagement as BEAN, the container leaves all of the responsibility of synchronization to the developer, who must resort to Java features in order to accomplish this — mark blocks with synchronized or volatile keywords, for instance, or use classes such as ConcurrentHashMap or ConcurrentLinkedQueue if the scenario allows it (as concurrent collections aren't always a viable alternative to synchronized blocks).

If you set the concurrency management to BEAN, none of the @Lock or @AccessTimeout declarations will be used by the container, and you won't get any errors when compiling or deploying it. So you may think that the annotations are effective but they are not, and you get no warnings about it, so be careful.

Singleton applied to web services

If you need to limit the consumption of a web service, one easy way to accomplish this is to annotate it with @Singleton; automatically, just one thread of each managed server will be allocated to process it.

Keep in mind that this is a rather radical solution. When you enable it, all consumers will have to wait for their turn to execute its target operation, so in practice, you're creating a queue. If the business process takes some time to finish and the queue is long, timeouts can happen, leading to undesired effects.

Persisting an object using JPA

Up to this point, we configured and used the persistence layer to connect and retrieve information from the database but have not tried to store data into it. This is a pretty straightforward procedure that involves the **Entity Manager** component—the same one we used in *Chapter 3, Java EE Basics – Persistence, Query, and Presentation,*—to read data from MySQL, and also a **transaction**, which is something we haven't seen yet.

The concept is pretty widespread nowadays, so there's no need to have painstaking explanations here but just a quick refresher. We use transactions to coordinate efforts on disparate resources—which obviously must support it—so we have a consistent unit of work. The **ACID** concept (atomicity, consistency, isolation, and durability) states the primary attributes that must be observed when a transaction is used:

- All or none of the participating resources are committed
- If an error happens, no resource is updated
- The changes being made inside a transaction aren't visible to resources outside of it
- If a transaction finishes as expected and is committed, the participating resources must ensure that the data will be persisted so that even when a failure occurs, its state is correctly kept

When using an application server such as WebLogic, we can access its transaction manager via the **Java Transaction API (JTA)**; by doing this, we have access to the resources mapped by the container that supports transactions, for example a **JMS queue**, a data source, a local EJB, or even a remote EJB (hosted at another WebLogic Server).

Understanding the available transaction contexts

If the code that must deal with a transaction happens to be inside an EJB, you can use **container-managed transactions** (**CMT**), meaning that you don't have to acquire and control the transaction manually—the container takes care of all boilerplate procedures involved in this process.

> For a complete list of transaction context availability in constructors and EJB interface methods such as `afterBegin()` or `ejbCreate()`, refer to the *Web resources* section at the end of this chapter for the *Programming JTA for Oracle WebLogic Server* entry.

On the other hand, you can take control of everything by disabling the container's transaction control and deal with the transaction manager, and an actual transaction, through code; this mode is called **bean-managed transaction (BMT)**.

You can declare which mode will be used by decorating the bean with the `TransactionManagement` annotation and setting its value to `TransactionManagementType.CONTAINER` or `TransactionManagementType.BEAN`.

CMT is the default setting when no explicit annotations are found by the application server.

Using container-managed transactions

So, if **container-managed transactions (CMT)** is the way to go, you don't need to use `@TransactionManagement` because it already is the default strategy.

For each method, you can use another annotation, `TransactionAttribute`, to tell the container how a transaction should be set up when a request to the method is made, if this is the case. You must set its value with an entry from the enum `TransactionAttributeType` that fits your requirement. Here's a list of possible values and a description of how each one works:

Value	Description
REQUIRED	If the caller already has a transaction context, the method participates in it. If not, a new transaction is created and finished upon completion of the method. This is the default value.
MANDATORY	If a transaction context is passed along by the caller, the method is executed using it. If not, an exception is raised.
NOT_SUPPORTED	The caller should not pass a transaction context. If a transaction happens to be present, the container suspends it and creates a new one. At the end of the execution, the *local transaction* is finished and the original one is resumed.
SUPPORTS	It has the same behavior as REQUIRED if a transaction context has been received, and same as NOT_SUPPORTED when no caller transaction is found.
NEVER	The method states that it will not accept or create a transaction. If the caller passes one, an exception is thrown.
REQUIRES_NEW	A new transaction context is always created. What is done inside this transaction is committed before passing the control back to the caller. If a context is present, the manager suspends it before passing the control to the method and resumes it after the method finishes.

To demonstrate the CMT feature, we're going to create and save a `Ticket` instance in the `generate` method of `ReservationCodeBean`, the one that generates the control number we will send as part of the SOAP web service call we're about to create:

1. Open the singleton session bean `ReservationCodeBean` from the **Store** project.

2. Inject an **Entity Manager** to get access to the persistence layer:

   ```
   @PersistenceContext(unitName = "StoreBO")
   private EntityManager em;
   ```

3. The controlled number returned by the `generate` method is sensitive information, so we're going to annotate it to create a new transaction each time it's called. This way, it doesn't participate in previously opened transactions, avoiding data tampering. Also, we're going to assign two parameters to the method's signature that is necessary to create the `Ticket` instance:

   ```
   @TransactionAttribute(TransactionAttributeType.REQUIRES_NEW)
   public String generate(int theaterRef, int exhibitionRef)
   ```

4. After the generation of the control number, we create and load an instance of the class `Ticket` with the necessary data:

   ```
   // Create an instance
   Ticket ticket = new Ticket();

   // Create Mandatory reference (Ticket --> Theater)
   Theater theater = new Theater();
   theater.setId(theaterRef);

   // Set
   ticket.setTheater(theater);
   ticket.setExhibitionRef(exhibitionRef);
   ticket.setControl(control);
   ```

5. We are all set; now we just need to instruct the entity manager to save the object:

   ```
   // Save
   em.persist(ticket);
   ```

6. The method still returns the generated control number, so there is no need to change the `return` instruction.

7. As soon as the method exits, the transaction is committed, and a new record in the table `Ticket` (inside the `store_db` database) is created.

> The @TransactionAttribute decoration is the single line of code that mentions a transaction, and even this one isn't mandatory for our use case.

Using bean-managed transactions

As said earlier, this mode leaves all of the responsibility of acquiring and releasing a transaction to the bean's code. There are some helpers that can be used to ease these procedures, but it is the developer's burden to code it all.

To reach the same outcome of the previous section, the code should look as follows:

1. The class must be decorated with TransactionManagement and the value BEAN:

    ```
    @Singleton
    @TransactionManagement(TransactionManagementType.BEAN)
    public class ReservationCodeBean {
        ...
    ```

2. As we are coding an EJB, we still can use CDI to get a persistence context:

    ```
    @PersistenceContext
    private EntityManager em;
    ```

3. We also need to inject a UserTransaction component so we can demarcate our transaction:

    ```
    @Resource
    private UserTransaction ut;
    ```

4. The load procedure for Theater and Ticket instances remains unchanged. When the data is ready to be saved, we must start a transaction, save the objects, and then commit the transaction. The catch block checks whether there is an active transaction that must be rolled back:

    ```
    // Save
    try {
        ut.begin();
        em.persist(ticket);
        ut.commit();
    } catch (Exception e) {
        try {
            if (Status.STATUS_ACTIVE == ut.getStatus()) {
                ut.rollback();
            }
        } catch (Exception rbe) {
    ```

```
                rbe.printStackTrace();
        }
    }
```

Not that much work, but you do have to put some extra effort when compared to CMT. The decision of using bean-managed transactions is usually taken when several business steps must be executed as a whole, but some of them must be committed even though the bigger transaction must be rolled back if an error occurs. Also, keep in mind that not participating in a global transaction can be both a strength and a weakness, depending on the business scenario you must implement.

> If a `javax.persistence.TransactionRequiredException` error pops up when you try to run your bean-managed transaction business method, go back and check the code. Most likely, you must have forgotten to acquire a transaction context.

Acquiring a transaction context manually

We discussed the usage of transactions inside the context of EJBs, but you can also acquire and use transactions where CDI isn't available. WebLogic exposes a helper class to make this process easier:

```
import weblogic.transaction.TransactionHelper;
...
TransactionHelper th = TransactionHelper.getTransactionHelper();
UserTransaction anotherUT = th.getUserTransaction();
```

The other pieces of code — opening and closing a transaction and saving an object — are exactly the same.

A brief intermission

Before we get into the SOAP web service implementation, we need to complement the applications to execute a seat query using the existing REST web service and display the results on the query page. Once this is done, we can pick up from there and develop our SOAP service. So, to get this done, follow these steps:

1. Open `ExhibitionBean` of the **Theater** project, add a method that will receive the exhibition ID chosen by the user, and return a list of seat types that are linked to that specific exhibition:

    ```
    @GET
    @Path("{id}/seats")
    @Produces({ MediaType.APPLICATION_XML, MediaType.APPLICATION_JSON })
    ```

```java
public List<Seat> getSeatsByExhibition(
                                @PathParam("id") int id) {
    String jpql = "SELECT s FROM Seat s, Exhibition e "
            + "WHERE (s.room.id = e.room.id) "
            + "AND (e.id = ?1)";

    if (id != 0) {
        Query query = em.createQuery(jpql);
        query.setParameter(1, id);

        @SuppressWarnings("unchecked")
        List<Seat> result = query.getResultList();

        if (result.size() > 0)
         return result;
        else
         throw new WebApplicationException(
                    Response.Status.NOT_FOUND);
    }

    throw new WebApplicationException(
                Response.Status.NO_CONTENT);
}
```

> The structure of this method is the same as another method of this class, getExhibition. We just need to change its path, the query, and the type being retrieved.
>
> A call to this API would look similar to the following: http://localhost:7001/theater/api/exhibition/4/seats.

2. Go to the **Store** project, and add a consumer for this new method in the TheaterClient class:

```java
public List<Seat> getSeatsByExhibition(int exhibitionId) {
    final List<Seat> seats = (List<Seat>) getClient()
        .path("exhibition")
        .path(String.valueOf(exhibitionId))
        .path("seats")
        .accept(MediaType.APPLICATION_XML)
        .get(ClientResponse.class)
        .getEntity(new GenericType<List<Seat>>() {});

    return seats;
}
```

> In *Chapter 4, Remote Access – Creating RESTful Services with JAX-RS*, we added annotations XMLRootElement and XMLTransient to the Seat class. As explained there, this must be done to avoid cyclic references when JAX-RS is creating the query response.

Again, this new method follows the same structure of the other method already in the class, getExhibitionsByMovie, so it's basically a copy and paste operation with a few tweaks to the code.

1. Now that we have both the service's provider and consumer, let's adjust the component connected to the JSF page, SearchManager, to expose this information to the page by adding the following code snippets:

```java
// Variable to hold the list of seats
private List<Seat> seats;
// current quantity of seats
private String[] quantities;

// Getter and setters
public void setSeats(List<Seat> seats) {
  this.seats = seats;
}

public List<Seat> getSeats() {
  return seats;
}

public String[] getQuantities() {
    return quantities;
  }

  public void setQuantities(String[] quantities) {
    this.quantities = quantities;
}

// The method that will call the reservation service
public void reserve() {
}

// Helper method to translate the seat type
private String getSeatDescription(int type) {
  switch (type) {
    case 1:
      return "Regular";
```

```
      case 2:
        return "Comfort";
      case 3:
        return "Disability";
      default:
        return "Unknown";
    }
  }
```

2. Also, in `SearchManager`, replace the contents of the method `query` with this single line that executes the call and sets the variable with the result:

```
public void query() {
    if (exhibition != 0) {
        seats =
            theaterClient.getSeatsByExhibition(exhibition);

        /*
         * Set the variable that holds the selection
         * done by the user to zero
         */
        quantities = new String[seats.size()];

        for (int i = 0; i < seats.size(); i++) {
            quantities[i] = "0";
        }
    } else {
        seats = null;
    }
}
```

3. The last step is to change our query page — that would be the `search.xhtml` (previously `index.xhtml`) file of the **Store** project — to show the information retrieved. We're going to add this block of code just below the `query` button:

```
<br/>
<p:spacer width="100" height="10" rendered="#{!empty search.
seats}" />
<p:spacer width="100" height="10" rendered="#{!empty search.
seats}" />

<h:outputLabel for="seats"
               value="Available seats:"
```

```
                        rendered="#{!empty search.seats}" />
<p:dataTable id="seats"
             var="seat"
             value="#{search.seats}"
             rowIndexVar="index"
             rendered="#{!empty search.seats}">
   <p:column headerText="Type">
      <h:outputText
       value="#{search.getSeatDescription(seat.type)}" />
   </p:column>
   <p:column headerText="Price">
      <h:outputText value="#{seat.price}">
         <f:convertNumber type="currency"
                          currencySymbol="" />
      </h:outputText>
   </p:column>
   <p:column headerText="Quantity">
     <p:spinner id="spinnerBasic"
                value="#{search.quantities[index]}"
                min="0" max="99"
                maxlength="2" size="3" />
   </p:column>
</p:dataTable>

<p:commandButton id="reserve" update="queryForm"
             value="Reserve Seats"
             action="#{ search.reserve}"
             rendered="#{!empty search.seats}" />
```

> The rendered attribute prevents components from being rendered
> on the screen when they aren't needed, so we use it to show the
> second part of the screen only after the user actually executes a query
> for available seats.

4. Save all the files, publish both **Store** and **Theater** projects and navigate to the search page, `http://localhost:7001/store/search.jsf`. Select the entries from the three dropdowns and click on **Search Seats**. A new table showing the types of seats available should appear after it:

Now that we have the seat query up and running, we can proceed to the next section where we're going to expose and consume a SOAP web service.

Web services and SOAP

The **Simple Object Access Protocol (SOAP)** is present in probably 97.32 percent (an educated guess) of all the web service-related products available today, although it isn't mandatory to assemble a service. As it plays such an important role to integrate systems, let's take a look at how this is accomplished using WebLogic Server 12c.

To illustrate the usage of SOAP, we will expose a service from the **Theater** project that makes a seat reservation. This web service will be consumed by the **Store** project once the user has decided which and how many of each seat type he/she wants for a specific exhibition.

The reservation web service

To create and expose a web service, we just need to annotate a POJO class with `javax.jws.WebService`. By default, all public methods of the class are automatically exposed as operations.

We're going to create a service in the **Theater** project that will receive a reservation request and pass it to the partner's system to register it. Then, we subtract the number of seats received from the available seats of the given exhibition.

The update of the `Exhibition` instance is going to be done inside a `UserTransaction` that we must manually acquire. Also, the `find` instruction to retrieve the instance using the persistence layer is going to be marked with the `PESSIMISTIC_WRITE` lock mode. So, only one instance of the web service is able to update the entity at a given moment (all others will wait for the release of the entry).

> The communication with the partner's system will not be implemented since our focus is on how to expose and consume a web service.

Let's implement the web service:

1. Create a new class named `ReservationBean` in the package `com.packt.theater.services` of the project **Theater**, and add a `javax.jws.WebService` annotation to the class definition:

    ```
    @WebService(serviceName="ReservationService",
                targetNamespace="http://com.packt.wls12c")
    public class ReservationBean {
    }
    ```

    > The `serviceName` parameter defines the name by which the service will be known, not exactly a revealing statement. But what happens when you don't declare it? Your service's name will be a contraction of the class name plus the suffix, `Service`. For our class, this would be `ReservationBeanService`.
    >
    > The default `targetnamespace` value is the class' package converted to a URL - `http://services.theater.packt.com/` using the same example.

2. We need just one operation that will receive the exhibition ID along with a list of seat types and quantities:

```
public String execute(@WebParam(name="exhibitionId")
                        int exhibitionId,
                      @WebParam(name = "reservationCode")
                        String reservationCode,
                      @WebParam(name="seats")
                        Map<Integer, Integer> seats) throws
ReservationException {
}
```

> The `WebParam` annotation is used here to give meaningful names to the parameters — when an explicit name attribute isn't declared, the parameters are called `arg0`, `arg1`, and so on. The `ReservationException` class is a simple POJO that extends the `Exception` class. We need a specific class like that in order to generate `SoapFault` messages when exceptions occur in the service. For more details, check the code bundle of this chapter.

3. As we're going to update an `Exhibition` instance, we need to inject a persistence context:

```
@PersistenceContext
EntityManager em;
```

4. At this operation, we should communicate with the partner's backend system to proceed with the seat reservation and update the related `Exhibition` instance to subtract the number of seats passed onto the request - the first step can't be implemented as there is no system to connect to, so here is the logic for the remaining steps:

```
// Find the total number of seats for this reservation
int seatsTotal = 0;

for (Iterator<Entry<Integer, Integer>> it =
        seats.entrySet().iterator(); it.hasNext();) {
        seatsTotal = seatsTotal + it.next().getValue();
}

// and subtract then from the Exhibition instance
UserTransaction ut = TransactionHelper.
        getTransactionHelper().
        getUserTransaction();

//
// The find method _must_ be inside the transaction!
//
```

```
try {
  ut.begin();

  Exhibition exhibition = em.find(Exhibition.class,
                  exhibitionId,
                  LockModeType.PESSIMISTIC_WRITE);

  if (null == exhibition) {
    throw new ReservationException("Exhibition not found");
  }

  exhibition.setAvailableSeats(
                  exhibition.getAvailableSeats() -
                  seatsTotal);
  ut.commit();
} catch (Exception e) {
  e.printStackTrace();
  throw new ReservationException();
}
return ReservationBean.OK;
```

> To keep things simple, we are considering the sum of all seats received, regardless of its kind. A real-world application must process this information accordingly.

5. Save the file and publish the **Theater** project. To check whether the service is ready for use, open your browser and go to `http://localhost:7001/theater/ReservationService?WSDL`. If you get the XML definition of the service, we're good to go.

> Another possible strategy to deal with the locking of an instance of `Exhibition` is to decorate the entity with `@Version` instead of retrieving it with the `PESSIMISTIC_WRITE` flag. This approach uses a table column to deal with concurrency. It can be more effective because we're instructing the entity to behave in a certain way instead of leaving the decision to the consumers, as is the case shown here.

Testing the service provider

WebLogic Server gives us a pretty useful utility to call services, the **WebLogic Universal Test Client (ws_utc)**. This is a web-based application that you can use to test services exposed by WebLogic as well as external endpoints.

This feature is only available when WebLogic Server is running in the **development mode**. We're not supposed to mess around with production servers, so when such environments are configured, its mode flag is set to **production** and a few *productivity* features are disabled.

To start it, type `http://localhost:7001/ws_utc/` in your browser, and after a message stating that the package is being deployed, a screen like this will show up:

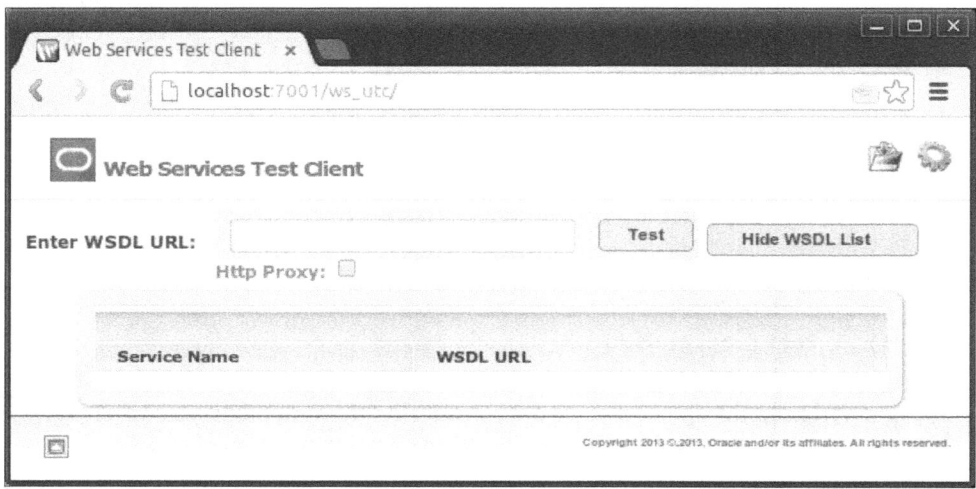

If you need to find the address of a web service exposed by WebLogic Server, you can open the administration console (`http://localhost:7001/console`), select **Deployments** in the navigation tree, and expand the desired package to see the list of available services under the **Web Services** group:

By clicking on a web service's name, you can access pages to check and configure several parameters such as security credentials and policies, and advanced features such as reliable messaging and buffering. Click on the **Testing** tab, and expand the box besides the service name to get the service's WSDL address:

Settings for ReservationService

| Overview | Configuration | Security | **Testing** | Monitoring |

Deployment Tests

Showing 1 to 1 of 1   Previous | Next

Name ⌃	Test Point	Comments
⊟ ReservationService		Test points for this WebService module.
/theater/ReservationService	?WSDL	WSDL page on server AdminServer

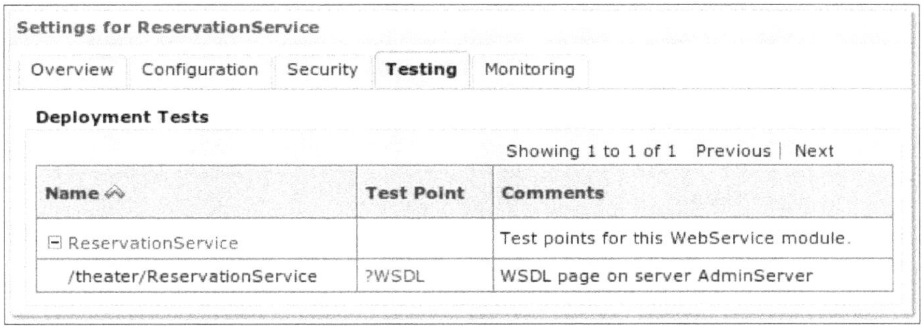

After you enter the service's WSDL address, the operations exposed by the service are listed. Click on the **Test** button of the operation you want to run:

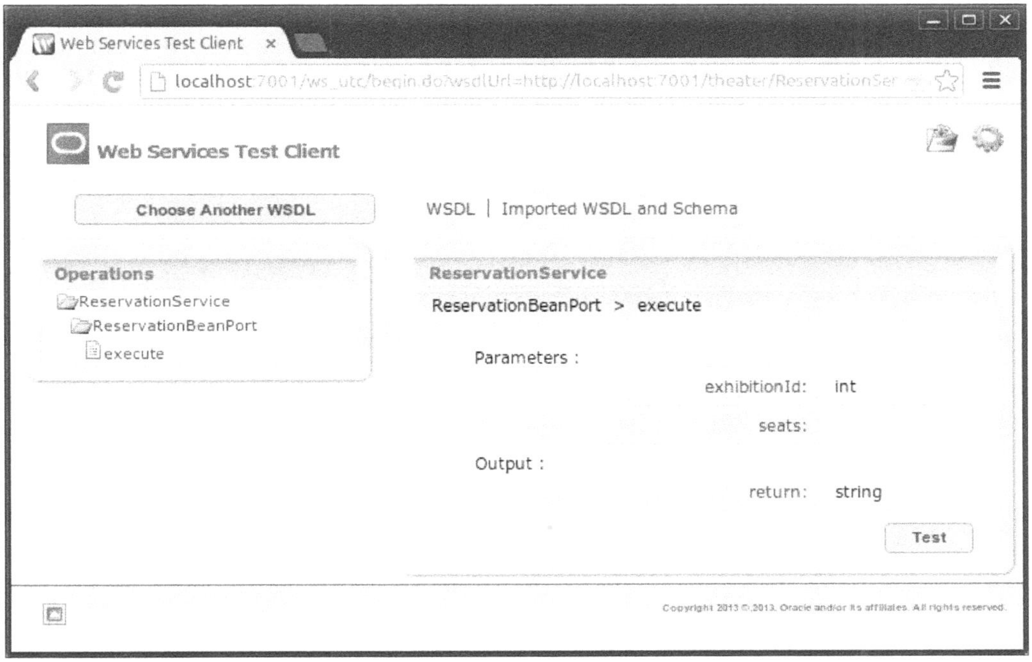

A new screen is loaded with a form mapping the entries from the request element. Click on the **Raw Message** button to switch to the textbox where we can edit an XML payload; here's a valid payload to use (change the values of the generated XML to match the following ones):

```
<soap:Envelope
        xmlns:soap="http://schemas.xmlsoap.org/soap/envelope/">
    <soap:Body>
        <ns1:execute xmlns:ns1="http://com.packt.wls12c">
            <exhibitionId>3</exhibitionId>
            <reservationCode>1234-1234-1234</reservationCode>
            <seats>
                <entry>
                    <key>1</key>
                    <value>5</value>
                </entry>
            </seats>
        </ns1:execute>
    </soap:Body>
</soap:Envelope>
```

Click on the **Invoke** button at the bottom of the screen; the **Test Results** block will be loaded right below the **Invoke** button, showing both request and response XML files. Check whether the **return** node in the **response** block is set to **ok**:

> In the **Settings** tab, you can change several aspects of a call; for instance, the credentials passed when an HTTP username token is required, or setting a callback address when the service provider processes the **WS-Addressing** entries.

To execute the same call again with the same payload, just click on the **Invoke** button one more time. To test other methods or to use another payload, click on the name of the desired operation in the **Operations** tree on the left-hand side of the screen:

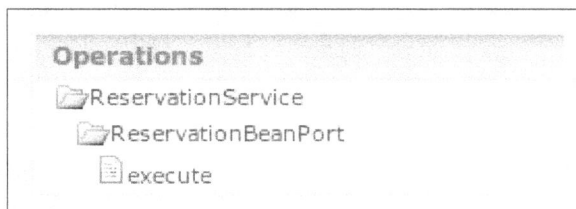

Consuming the service

We just checked that the service implementation is working as it should be, so now it's time to code the service call from our Store module. To do so, we must perform either of the following:

- Build a call by instantiating and loading the objects that represent the service and its payload. This is called a **dynamic invocation**.
- Create Java classes that act as a stub to the service provider. As this solution involves creating structures that must match the service's and having them pinned to our code—either by having the actual source added to the project or by packing the stub inside a JAR library—it is referred to as a **static invocation method**.

> There are external tools such as **Apache Axis**, but we will keep our scope to the features provided by WebLogic Server and the JDK.

The most common way to consume a web service is to create a stub for it. This way we don't have to manually create all the boilerplate code needed to map the service's operations, its data structures, and the actual invocation to the provider.

To create the classes, we can use the `wsimport` command-line tool provided by the JDK. This tool gives us the option to create a JAR file with the generated classes or to keep the code and insert it into our project. Let's use the latter option so you can check how it works by browsing the Java source.

Open a command prompt or terminal, and enter the following command — as a single line — with the necessary replacements for your environment:

```
/opt/packt/install/jdk1.7.0_21/bin/wsimport -keep         \
    -Xnocompile                                           \
    -p com.packt.util.gen                                 \
    -d /opt/packt/workspace/Store/src/                    \
    http://localhost:7001/theater/ReservationService?WSDL
```

The parameters in the preceding code tell the utility:

- To keep the sources instead of erasing them after compilation, use the `-keep` argument.
- That a specific package name must be used when creating the classes use the `-p` argument.
- The root directory where the files are to be written with the `-d` argument. As we are adding the source to our **Store** project, the value is the root source of the project, `/opt/packt/workspace/Store/src/`.
- That we don't need the compiled objects, hence the `-Xnocompile` option.

If you go to Eclipse and press *F5* to refresh the project, a new package `com.packt.util.gen` will appear. The `Execute` and `ExecuteResponse` classes are wrappers to the request and response payloads respectively. The `ReservationBean` class is the wrapper to the actual service provider, and `ReservationService` is the client we're going to use to code our call.

> Don't worry if you feel like this is too much information, because it is! All you need to know is that `ReservationService` is the proxy that must be used to call the service.

So, open the `SearchManager` class and make the following changes:

1. Start by adding a reference to the `ReservationService` class:

   ```
   private transient ReservationService reservationService;
   ```

2. Then, we need to make the WSDL location of our web service configurable and dynamic, just like we already did for the RESTful service. Add an entry in the `web.xml` file as follows:

   ```xml
   <env-entry>
       <env-entry-name>reservationServiceEndpoint</env-entry-name>
       <env-entry-type>java.lang.String</env-entry-type>
   ```

```
    <env-entry-value>
http://localhost:7001/theater/ReservationService?WSDL
    </env-entry-value>
</env-entry>
```

3. Then we can add a lookup for this resource entry through `@Resource`:

```
@Resource(lookup = "reservationServiceEndpoint")
private String RESERVATION_SVC_ENDPOINT;
```

4. And finally let's create an `init()` method marked with `@PostContruct` so it will be executed after all the injected resources are ready. In this method, we are going to set the service endpoint to the resource:

```
@PostConstruct
public void init() {
  try {
     reservationService = new ReservationService(
              new URL(RESERVATION_SVC_ENDPOINT));
  } catch (MalformedURLException e) {
    e.printStackTrace();
  }
}
```

5. Locate the `reserve` method in the same class and insert the code to load a `Seats` instance that we're going to pass as part of the request. The definition of this class is inside the `Execute` class file that maps the input structure of the operation:

```
public void reserve() {
    Seats seats = new Seats();

    List< com.packt.util.gen.Execute.Seats.Entry>
    entries = seats.getEntry();

    for (int i = 0; i < quantities.length; i++) {
        String quantity = quantities[i];

      if (0 < Integer.parseInt(quantity)) {
        Entry entry = new Entry();
        entry.setKey(this.seats.get(i).getType());
        entry.setValue(Integer.parseInt(quantity));
         entries.add(entry);
      }
    }
```

6. A control code must be generated and the reservation must be added to the central database. This is done by a call to the generate method of the class ReservationCodeBean, which also must be injected here:

```
@Inject
private transient ReservationCodeBean controlBean;

    ...
    public String reserve() {

    ...
    String reservationCode =
                    controlBean.generate(this.theater,
                                this.exhibition);
```

7. As an instance of ReservationService is created after the bean initialization, we just need to get the declared port—the concrete reference to the service's endpoint—and call the desired operation, execute. By doing this, we're actually consuming the service:

```
String response = reservationService.getReservationBeanPort().
                    execute(this.getExhibition(),
                            reservationCode, seats);
```

8. Now, check the response received from the service provider and whether the process returned an *ok* literal. We must show a confirmation message to the user and redirect them to the reservation page, so they can print a receipt that must be presented at the theater's booth to redeem the reservation. Simply add the following:

```
...
if (response.equals("ok")) {
  FacesContext context = FacesContext.getCurrentInstance();
  context.getExternalContext().getFlash().setKeepMessages
(true);

  FacesContext.getCurrentInstance().addMessage(
            null,
            new FacesMessage(
            "New reservation of " +
            quantities.length +
            " seats completed. Number is " +
            reservationCode));

  resetSearch();
  return "reservation?faces-redirect=true";
} else {
... // error treatment
```

9. The code in the last step adds a confirmation message, resets the search data, and redirects the user to the reservation page where the system keeps a history of all the reservations made by a customer. Note that at this point, we don't have an authenticated customer yet, so it's showing data from all of them. So let's create a `reservation.xhtml` page:

```
<ui:composition template="/WEB-INF/templates/template.xhtml">
  <ui:define name="title">Reservations</ui:define>
  <ui:define name="content">
    <h:form>
      <p:growl showDetail="false" />
      <p:panel id="tpanel" header="Reservations">
      <p:dataGrid columns="3" value="#{ticket.tickets}"
        emptyMessage="You have no reservations yet." var="item">
        <p:panelGrid style="font-size:12px" columns="2" id="div-
#{item.id}">
          <h:outputLabel for="control" value="Code:" />
          <h:outputText id="control" value="#{item.control}" />
          <h:outputLabel for="tname" value="Theater:" />
          <h:outputText id="tname" value="#{item.theater.name}" />
          <h:outputLabel for="exhib" value="Exhibition:" />
          <h:outputText id="exhib" value="#{exhibition.find(item.
exhibitionRef).date}">
            <f:convertDateTime pattern="MMM dd, yyyy hh:mm a" />
          </h:outputText>
        </p:panelGrid>
        <p:commandButton icon="ui-icon-print" style="font-
size:12px;" id="print"
          value="Print" type="button">
          <p:printer target="div-#{item.id}" />
        </p:commandButton>
      </p:dataGrid>
      </p:panel>
    </h:form>
  </ui:define>
</ui:composition>
```

10. The final step is to create the `resetSearch` method referenced by the `reserve` method:

```
public void resetSearch() {
  this.theater = 0;
  this.movie = 0;
  this.exhibition = 0;
  this.seats = null;
}
```

Now, save all the files, publish both **Theater** and **Store** projects to WebLogic Server, and execute the business scenario. Here's how the reservation page and the confirmation message would look like after a successful reservation:

From this page, a customer can see the history of reservations. Also, by clicking on the **Print** button, the selected reservation will be printed; the entries are ordered, and the newest ones are showed first.

If you want to check whether the web service ran as expected, check the contents of the `exhibition` table of the theater_db database — the `available_seats` column should have its value updated by the subtraction of the number of seats sent by the page. Also, each successful submission should create a new entry in the table `ticket` of the database `store_db`.

Web resources

The following are a list of web resources you can check:

- Principled Design of the Modern Web Architecture
  - http://www.ics.uci.edu/~taylor/documents/2002-REST-TOIT.pdf

- SOAP 1.2 specification
  - `http://www.w3.org/TR/soap12-part1/`
- Enterprise JavaBeans (EJBs)
  - `http://docs.oracle.com/middleware/1212/wls/INTRO/ejbs.htm`
- Be careful with singleton session bean
  - `http://www.jbesolutions.com/blog/?p=17`
- Tuning WebLogic Server EJBs
  - `http://docs.oracle.com/middleware/1212/wls/PERFM/ejb_tuning.htm`
- Bean validation specification website
  - `http://beanvalidation.org/`
- Bean validation with custom constraints and grouping
  - `http://workingonbits.com/2011/02/28/custom-constraints-with-bean-validation/`
- Programming JTA for Oracle WebLogic Server
  - `http://docs.oracle.com/middleware/1212/wls/WLJTA/index.html`
- Javadoc of TransactionAttributeType
  - `http://docs.oracle.com/javaee/6/api/javax/ejb/TransactionAttributeType.html`
- Developing web service clients
  - `http://docs.oracle.com/middleware/1212/wls/WSGET/jax-ws-client.htm`
- Developing RESTful web service clients
  - `http://docs.oracle.com/middleware/1212/wls/RESTF/develop-restful-client.htm`
- Developing advanced features of JAX-WS web services
  - `http://docs.oracle.com/middleware/1212/wls/WSGET/part_4.htm`
- Javadoc of Class TransactionHelper
  - `http://docs.oracle.com/middleware/1212/wls/WLAPI/weblogic/transaction/TransactionHelper.html`

Summary

In this chapter we covered the basic usage of the validation framework, its built-in validations, and how to expand it by creating custom constraints. We also covered how to insert records to a database using JPA and JTA along with considerations about transaction isolation and the different ways of dealing with a transaction. Furthermore, we looked at how to expose web services using SOAP; how to generate a web service client with WebLogic's utility, adding it to our business scenario; and how to implement and configure singleton session beans to control concurrency.

In the next chapter, we will take a tour of the event system available to Java EE applications, understanding and using events and interceptors, among other features.

6

Using Events, Interceptors, and Logging Services

In this chapter, we are going to briefly introduce two concepts of Java EE development: **interceptors** and **events**. We will also see how to integrate these concepts with WebLogic services. It's a common misunderstanding that these technologies are complex and difficult to use, but after working with examples of this chapter, it will become clear that they are powerful yet easy to use. Along the way, we will cover WebLogic Server's logging services, which shows us how to configure the framework, how to write messages to it, and how to read them using the administration console.

Understanding interceptors

Interceptors are defined as part of the EJB 3.1 specification (JSR 318), and are used to intercept Java method invocations and lifecycle events that may occur in **Enterprise Java Beans (EJB)** or **Named Beans** from **Context Dependency Injection (CDI)**.

The three main components of interceptors are as follows:

- **The Target class**: This class will be monitored or watched by the interceptor. The target class can hold the interceptor methods for itself.
- **The Interceptor class**: This interceptor class groups interceptor methods.
- **The Interceptor method**: This method will be invoked according to the lifecycle events.

As an example, a logging interceptor will be developed and integrated into the Store application. Following the hands-on approach of this book, we will see how to apply the main concepts through the given examples without going into a lot of details.

[✎ Check the *Web Resources* section to find more documentation about interceptors.]

Creating a log interceptor

A log interceptor is a common requirement in most Java EE projects as it's a simple yet very powerful solution because of its decoupled implementation and easy distribution among other projects if necessary. Here's a diagram that illustrates this solution:

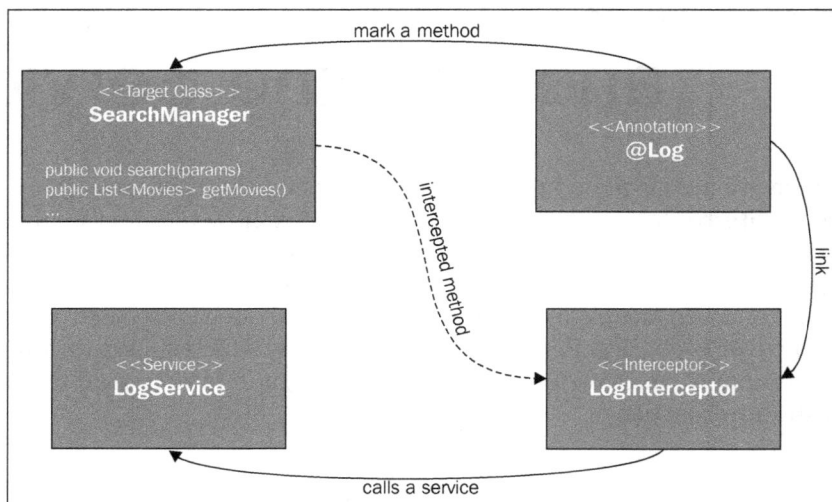

Log and LogInterceptor are the core of the log interceptor functionality; the former can be thought of as the interface of the interceptor, it being the annotation that will decorate the elements of SearchManager that must be logged, and the latter carries the actual implementation of our interceptor. The business rule is to simply call a method of class LogService, which will be responsible for creating the log entry.

Here's how to implement the log interceptor mechanism:

1. Create a new Java package named com.packt.store.log in the project **Store**.
2. Create a new enumeration named LogLevel inside this package. This enumeration will be responsible to match the level assigned to the annotation and the logging framework:

   ```
   package com.packt.store.log;

   public enum LogLevel {
   ```

```
// As defined at java.util.logging.Level
SEVERE, WARNING, INFO, CONFIG, FINE, FINER, FINEST;

public String toString() {
    return super.toString();
}
}
```

> We're going to create all objects of this section—LogLevel, Log, LogService, and LogInterceptor—into the same package, com.packt.store.log. This decision makes it easier to extract the logging functionality from the project and build an independent library in the future, if required.

3. Create a new annotation named Log. This annotation will be used to mark every method that must be logged, and it accepts the log level as a parameter according to the LogLevel enumeration created in the previous step:

```
package com.packt.store.log;

@Inherited
@InterceptorBinding
@Retention(RetentionPolicy.RUNTIME)
@Target({ElementType.METHOD, ElementType.TYPE})
public @interface Log {
    @Nonbinding
    LogLevel value() default LogLevel.FINEST;
}
```

> As this annotation will be attached to an interceptor, we have to add the @InterceptorBinding decoration here. When creating the interceptor, we will add a reference that points back to the Log annotation, creating the necessary relationship between them.
>
> Also, we can attach an annotation virtually to any Java element. This is dictated by the @Target decoration, where we can set any combination of the ElementType values such as ANNOTATION_TYPE, CONSTRUCTOR, FIELD, LOCAL_VARIABLE, METHOD, PACKAGE, PARAMETER, and TYPE (mapping classes, interfaces, and enums), each representing a specific element. The annotation being created can be attached to methods and classes or interface definitions.

4. Now we must create a new stateless session bean named `LogService` that is going to execute the actual logging:

```
@Stateless
public class LogService {
    // Receives the class name decorated with @Log
    public void log(final String clazz, final LogLevel level, final
String message) {
        // Logger from package java.util.logging
        Logger log = Logger.getLogger(clazz);
        log.log(Level.parse(level.toString()), message);
    }
}
```

5. Create a new class, `LogInterceptor`, to trap calls from classes or methods decorated with `@Log` and invoke the `LogService` class we just created — the main method must be marked with `@AroundInvoke` — and it is mandatory that it receives an `InvocationContext` instance and returns an `Object` element:

```
@Log
@Interceptor
public class LogInterceptor implements Serializable {
    private static final long serialVersionUID = 1L;

    @Inject
    LogService logger;

    @AroundInvoke
    public Object logMethod(InvocationContext ic) throws
    Exception
    {
        final Method method = ic.getMethod();

        // check if annotation is on class or method
        LogLevel logLevel = method.getAnnotation(Log.class)
        != null ?
        method.getAnnotation(Log.class).value()  :
        method.getDeclaringClass().getAnnotation(Log.class).value();

        // invoke LogService
        logger.log(ic.getClass().getCanonicalName(),
        logLevel, method.toString());
        return ic.proceed();
    }
}
```

As we defined earlier, the Log annotation can be attached to methods and classes or interfaces by its @Target decoration; we need to discover which one raised the interceptor to retrieve the correct LogLevel value.

When trying to get the annotation from the class shown in the method.getDeclaringClass().getAnnotation(Log.class) line, the engine will traverse through the class' hierarchy searching for the annotation, up to the Object class if necessary. This happens because we marked the Log annotation with @Inherited. Remember that this behavior only applies to the class's inheritance, not interfaces.

Finally, as we marked the value attribute of the Log annotation as @Nonbinding in step 3, all log levels will be handled by the same LogInterceptor function. If you remove the @Nonbinding line, the interceptor should be further qualified to handle a specific log level, for example @Log(LogLevel.INFO), so you would need to code several interceptors, one for each existing log level.

6. Modify the beans.xml (under /WEB-INF/) file to tell the container that our class must be loaded as an interceptor—currently, the file is empty, so add all the following lines:

```
<beans xmlns="http://java.sun.com/xml/ns/javaee"
       xmlns:xsi="http://www.w3.org/2001/XMLSchema-instance"
       xsi:schemaLocation="http://java.sun.com/xml/ns/javaee
http://java.sun.com/xml/ns/javaee/beans_1_0.xsd">
    <interceptors>
        <class>com.packt.store.log.LogInterceptor</class>
    </interceptors>
</beans>
```

7. Now decorate a business class or method with @Log in order to test what we've done. For example, apply it to the getTheaters() method in SearchManager from the project **Store**. Remember that it will be called every time you refresh the query page:

```
@Log(LogLevel.INFO)
public List<Theater> getTheaters() {
    ...
}
```

8. Make sure you have no errors in the project and deploy it to the current server by right-clicking on the server name and then clicking on the **Publish** entry.

9. Access the theater's page, `http://localhost:7001/theater/theaters.jsf`, refresh it a couple of times, and check the server output. If you have started your server from Eclipse, it should be under the **Console** tab:

```
Nov 12, 2012 4:53:13 PM com.packt.store.log.LogService log
INFO: public java.util.List com.packt.store.search.SearchManager.
getTheaters()
```

Let's take a quick overview of what we've accomplished so far; we created an interceptor and an annotation that will perform all common logging operations for any method or class marked with such an annotation. All log entries generated from the annotation will follow WebLogic's logging services configuration.

Interceptors and Aspect Oriented Programming

There are some equivalent concepts on these topics, but at the same time, they provide some critical functionalities, and these can make a completely different overall solution. In a sense, interceptors work like an event mechanism, but in reality, it's based on a paradigm called **Aspect Oriented Programming (AOP)**. Although AOP is a huge and complex topic and has several books that cover it in great detail, the examples shown in this chapter make a quick introduction to an important AOP concept: **method interception**.

> Consider AOP as a paradigm that makes it easier to apply crosscutting concerns (such as logging or auditing) as services to one or multiple objects. Of course, it's almost impossible to define the multiple contexts that AOP can help in just one phrase, but for the context of this book and for most real-world scenarios, this is good enough.

Using asynchronous methods

A basic programming concept called **synchronous execution** defines the way our code is processed by the computer, that is, line-by-line, one at a time, in a sequential fashion. So, when the main execution flow of a class calls a method, it must wait until its completion so that the next line can be processed.

> Of course, there are structures capable of processing different portions of a program in parallel, but from an external viewpoint, the execution happens in a sequential way, and that's how we think about it when writing code.

When you know that a specific portion of your code is going to take a little while to complete, and there are other things that could be done instead of just sitting and waiting for it, there are a few strategies that you could resort to in order to optimize the code. For example, starting a thread to run things in parallel, or posting a message to a JMS queue and breaking the flow into independent units are two possible solutions.

> If your code is running on an application server, you should know by now that thread spawning is a bad practice—only the server itself must create threads, so this solution doesn't apply to this specific scenario.

Another way to deal with such a requirement when using Java EE 6 is to create one or more **asynchronous methods** inside a stateless session bean by annotating either the whole class or specific methods with `javax.ejb.Asynchronous`.

> If the class is decorated with @Asynchronous, all its methods inherit the behavior.

When a method marked as asynchronous is called, the server usually spawns a thread to execute the called method—there are cases where the same thread can be used, for instance, if the calling method happens to end right after emitting the command to run the asynchronous method.

Either way, the general idea is that things are explicitly going to be processed in parallel, which is a departure from the synchronous execution paradigm. To see how it works, let's change the `LogService` method to be an asynchronous one; all we need to do is decorate the class or the method with `@Asynchronous`:

```
@Stateless
@Asynchronous
public class LogService {
    ...
```

As the call to its `log` method is the last step executed by the interceptor, and its processing is really quick, there is no real benefit in doing so. To make things more interesting, let's force a longer execution cycle by inserting a `sleep` method into the method of `LogService`:

```
public void log(final String clazz,final LogLevel level,final String
message) {
    Logger log = Logger.getLogger(clazz);
    log.log(Level.parse(level.toString()), message);
```

```
try {
    Thread.sleep(5000);
    log.log(Level.parse(level.toString()), "reached end of method");
} catch (InterruptedException e) {
    e.printStackTrace();
}
}
```

> Using `Thread.sleep()` when running inside an application server is another classic example of a *bad* practice, so keep away from this when creating real-world solutions.

Save all files, publish the **Store** project, and load the query page a couple of times. You will notice that the page is rendered without delay, as usual, and that the **reached end of method** message is displayed after a few seconds in the **Console** view. This is a pretty subtle scenario, so you can make it harsher by commenting out the @Asynchronous line and deploying the project again—this time when you refresh the browser, you will have to wait for 5 seconds before the page gets rendered.

Our example didn't need a return value from the asynchronous method, making it pretty simple to implement. If you need to get a value back from such methods, you must declare it using the `java.util.concurrent.Future` interface:

```
@Asynchronous
public Future<String> doSomething() {
    ...
}
```

The returned value must be changed to reflect the following:

```
return new AsyncResult<String>("ok");
```

> The `javax.ejb.AsyncResult` function is an implementation of the `Future` interface that can be used to return asynchronous results.

There are other features and considerations around asynchronous methods, such as ways to cancel a request being executed and to check if the asynchronous processing has finished, so the resulting value can be accessed. For more details, check the *Creating Asynchronous methods in EJB 3.1* reference at the end of this chapter.

Understanding WebLogic's logging service

Before we advance to the event system introduced in Java EE 6, let's take a look at the logging services provided by Oracle WebLogic Server.

By default, WebLogic Server creates two log files for each managed server:

- `access.log`: This is a standard HTTP access log, where requests to web resources of a specific server instance are registered with details such as HTTP return code, the resource path, response time, among others
- `<ServerName.log>`: This contains the log messages generated by the WebLogic services and deployed applications of that specific server instance

These files are generated in a default directory structure that follows the pattern `$DOMAIN_NAME/servers/<SERVER_NAME>/logs/`.

If you are running a WebLogic domain that spawns over more than one machine, you will find another log file named `<DomainName>.log` in the machine where the administration server is running. This file aggregates messages from all managed servers of that specific domain, creating a single point of observation for the whole domain.

> As a best practice, only messages with a higher level should be transferred to the domain log, avoiding overhead to access this file. Keep in mind that the messages written to the domain log are also found at the managed server's specific log file that generated them, so there's no need to redirect everything to the domain log.

Anatomy of a log message

Here's a typical entry of a log file:

```
####<Jul 15, 2013 8:32:54 PM BRT> <Alert> <WebLogicServer> <sandbox-
lap> <AdminServer> <[ACTIVE] ExecuteThread: '0' for queue: 'weblogic.
kernel.Default (self-tuning)'> <weblogic> <> <> <1373931174624> <BEA-
000396> <Server shutdown has been requested by weblogic.>
```

The description of each field is given in the following table:

Text	Description
####	Fixed, every log message starts with this sequence
`<Jul 15, 2013 8:32:54 PM BRT>`	Locale-formatted timestamp
`<Alert>`	Message severity
`<WebLogicServer>`	WebLogic subsystem — other examples are WorkManager, Security, EJB, and Management
`<sandbox-lap>`	Physical machine name
`<AdminServer>`	WebLogic Server name
`<[ACTIVE] ExecuteThread: '0' for queue: 'weblogic.kernel. Default (self-tuning)'>`	Thread ID
`<weblogic>`	User ID
`<>`	Transaction ID, or empty if not in a transaction context
`<>`	Diagnostic context ID, or empty if not applicable; it is used by the Diagnostics Framework to correlate messages of a specific request
`<1373931174624>`	Raw time in milliseconds
`<BEA-000396>`	Message ID
`<Server shutdown has been requested by weblogic.>`	Description of the event

> The Diagnostics Framework presents functionalities to monitor, collect, and analyze data from several components of WebLogic Server.

Redirecting standard output to a log file

The logging solution we've just created is currently using the Java SE logging engine — we can see our messages on the console's screen, but they aren't being written to any log file managed by WebLogic Server. It is this way because of the default configuration of Java SE, as we can see from the following snippet, taken from the `logging.properties` file used to run the server:

```
# "handlers" specifies a comma separated list of log Handler
# classes. These handlers will be installed during VM startup.
```

```
# Note that these classes must be on the system classpath.
# By default we only configure a ConsoleHandler, which will only
# show messages at the INFO and above levels.
handlers= java.util.logging.ConsoleHandler
```

> You can find this file at $JAVA_HOME/jre/lib/
> logging.properties.

So, as stated here, the default output destination used by Java SE is the console. There are a few ways to change this aspect:

- If you're using this Java SE installation solely to run WebLogic Server instances, you may go ahead and change this file, adding a specific WebLogic handler to the handlers line as follows:

    ```
    handlers= java.util.logging.ConsoleHandler,weblogic.logging.
    ServerLoggingHandler
    ```

- Tampering with Java SE files is not an option (it may be shared among other software, for instance); you can duplicate the default logging.properties file into another folder $DOMAIN_HOME being a suitable candidate, add the new handler, and instruct WebLogic to use this file at startup by adding this argument to the following command line:

    ```
    -Djava.util.logging.config.file=$DOMAIN_HOME/logging.properties
    ```

- You can use the administration console to set the redirection of the standard output (and error) to the log files. To do so, perform the following steps:

    1. In the left-hand side panel, expand **Environment** and select **Servers**.
    2. In the **Servers** table, click on the name of the server instance you want to configure.
    3. Select **Logging** and then **General**.

4. Find the **Advanced** section, expand it, and tick the **Redirect stdout logging enabled** checkbox:

```
Settings for AdminServer

  Configuration   Protocols   Logging   Debug   Monitoring   Control

  General   HTTP   Data Source

  Save

  Use this page to define the general logging settings for this server.

  Log file name:                    logs/AdminServer.log

  — Rotation —————————————

  Rotation type:                    By Size ▼

  Rotation file size:               500

  — ▽ Advanced ————————————

  Logging implementation:           JDK ▼

  ☐   Redirect stdout logging enabled

  ☐   Redirect stderr logging enabled
```

5. Click on **Save** to apply your changes.

If necessary, the console will show a message stating that the server must be restarted to acquire the new configuration.

> If you get no warnings asking to restart the server, then the configuration is already in use. This means that both WebLogic subsystems and any application deployed to that server is automatically using the new values, which is a very powerful feature for troubleshooting applications without intrusive actions such as modifying the application itself—just change the log level to start capturing more detailed messages!

Notice that there are a lot of other logging parameters that can be configured, and three of them are worth mentioning here:

- The **Rotation** group (found in the inner **General** tab): The rotation feature instructs WebLogic to create new log files based on the rules set on this group of parameters. It can be set to check for a size limit or create new files from time to time. By doing so, the server creates smaller files that we can easily handle. We can also limit the number of files retained in the machine to reduce the disk usage.

> If the partition where the log files are being written to reaches 100 percent of utilization, WebLogic Server will start behaving erratically. Always remember to check the disk usage; if possible, set up a monitoring solution such as Nagios to keep track of this and alert you when a critical level is reached.

- **Minimum severity to log** (also in the inner **General** tab): This entry sets the lower severity that should be logged by *all destinations*. This means that even if you set the domain level to debug, the messages will be actually written to the domain log only if this parameter is set to the same or lower level. It will work as a gatekeeper to avoid an overload of messages being sent to the loggers.
- **HTTP access log enabled** (found in the inner **HTTP** tab): When WebLogic Server is configured in a clustered environment, usually a load-balancing solution is set up to distribute requests between the WebLogic managed servers; the most common options are **Oracle HTTP Server** (**OHS**) or **Apache Web Server**. Both are standard web servers, and as such, they already register the requests sent to WebLogic in their own access logs. If this is the case, disable the WebLogic HTTP access log generation, saving processing power and I/O requests to more important tasks.

Integrating Log4J to WebLogic's logging services

If you already have an application that uses Log4J and want it to write messages to WebLogic's log files, you must add a new weblogic.logging.log4j. ServerLoggingAppender appender to your lo4j.properties configuration file.

This class works like a bridge between Log4J and WebLogic's logging framework, allowing the messages captured by the appender to be written to the server log files.

As WebLogic doesn't package a Log4J implementation, you must add its JAR to the domain by copying it to `$DOMAIN_HOME/tickets/lib`, along with another file, `wllog4j.jar`, which contains the WebLogic appender. This file can be found inside `$MW_HOME/wlserver/server/lib`. Restart the server, and it's done!

> If you're using a *nix system, you can create a symbolic link instead of copying the files — this is great to keep it consistent when a path changing these specific files must be applied to the server.

Remember that having a file inside `$MW_HOME/wlserver/server/lib` doesn't mean that the file is being loaded by the server when it starts up; it is just a central place to hold the libraries. To be loaded by a server, a library must be added to the classpath parameter of that server, or you can add it to the domain-wide `lib` folder, which guarantees that it will be available to all nodes of the domain on a specific machine.

Accessing and reading log files

If you have direct access to the server files, you can open and search them using a command-line tool such as tail or less, or even use a graphical viewer such as Notepad. But when you don't have direct access to them, you may use WebLogic's administration console to read their content by following the steps given here:

1. In the left-hand side pane of the administration console, expand **Diagnostics** and select **Log Files**.

2. In the **Log Files** table, select the option button next to the name of the log you want to check and click on **View**:

Log Files

View		Showing 1 to 7 of 7 Previous | Next

	Name △	Type	Server
○	DataSourceLog	Data Source Profile Log	AdminServer
○	DomainLog	Domain Log	AdminServer
○	EventsDataArchive	Instrumentation	AdminServer
○	HarvestedDataArchive	Metric Data	AdminServer
○	HTTPAccessLog	HTTP Access	AdminServer
○	JMSMessageLog/JMSServer-Tickets	JMS Log	AdminServer
●	ServerLog	Server Log	AdminServer

View		Showing 1 to 7 of 7 Previous | Next

The types displayed on this screen, which are mentioned at the start of the section, are **Domain Log**, **Server Log**, and **HTTP Access**. The others are resource-specific or linked to the diagnostics framework. Check the *Web resources* section at the end of this chapter for further reference.

3. The page displays the latest contents of the log file; the default setting shows up to 500 messages in reverse chronological order. The messages at the top of the window are the most recent messages that the server has generated.

Keep in mind that the log viewer does not display messages that have been converted into archived log files.

Events

The **Observer Pattern** is a very popular software design pattern in every object oriented programming language. The concept is that an object, **the subject**, will be monitored by one or more objects, **the observer(s)**, which will be notified when specific state changes happen on the subject. The state change is called an **event** and this pattern is at the core of most event-handling systems.

Events are part of Java SE since its very beginning and have always been standard in common UI frameworks such as AWT, Swing, and JavaFX. By contrast, Java EE never had a specific JSR to attend to such requirements until the JSR 299 (*Context and Dependency Injection for Java EE*) release that defines an event-handling mechanism which is completely integrated with Java EE and easy to use.

In order to show an example of this mechanism, we're going to create an auditing module for the **Store** application, which is very similar to what has been accomplished by the logging interceptor in the previous section, illustrating key concepts of event handling in Java EE 6.

Check the *Web Resources* section of this chapter to find more documentation on Events and CDI.

Defining audit events

Defining *auditing* can be very tricky, but in the context of our example, it means displaying additional information for a specific function or method call. In a sense, it will be very similar to a log entry, but for the sake of the example, the audit entry will have more information, such as method parameters and possibly the response of the method call. The solution is illustrated by the following diagram:

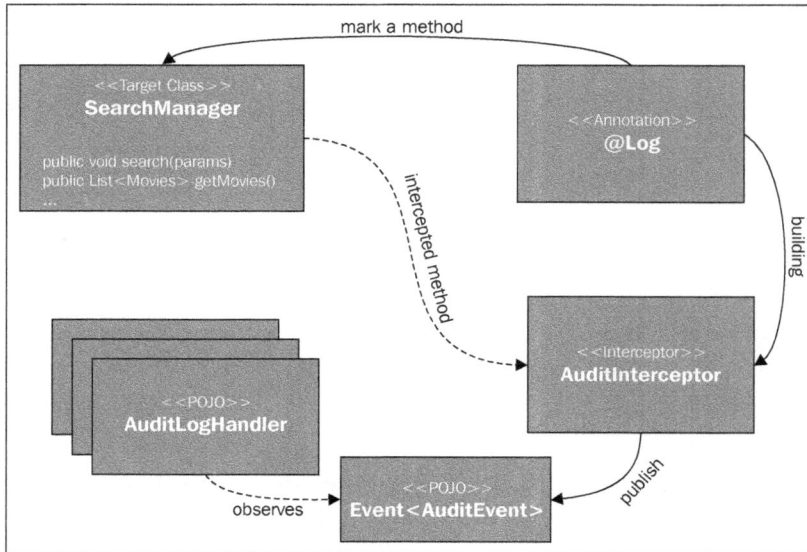

The details of the solution and how to create its components are given as follows:

1. Start by creating a new Java package named `com.packt.store.audit` in the **Store** project.

> Creating a single package that holds all the necessary classes for the solution will make it easier to extract and use it as a library in the future. All the further classes will be created in this package, unless explicitly said otherwise.

2. Create a new class named `AuditEvent`. This class defines the event data's structure:

```
package com.packt.store.audit;

public class AuditEvent {
    private final long timestamp = System.currentTimeMillis();
    private String message;
```

```
    private Object[] params = null;

    public AuditEvent(String message, Object[] params) {
        this.message = message;
        this.params = params;
    }

    public String toString() {
        StringBuilder sb = new StringBuilder();

        sb.append("[").append(new Date(timestamp)).append("] - ")
                            .append(message);

        if (getParams() != null) {
            sb.append("- Param value(s): ");

            for (Object o : params)
                sb.append(o).append(",");
                sb.deleteCharAt(sb.length() - 1);
            }
            return sb.toString();
        }
    // getters and setters
}
```

3. Create a new annotation named `Audit`. It will be the binder between the interceptor and our code, marking the classes or methods that must be audited. This is the same concept we saw when implementing the log interceptor:

```
package com.packt.store.audit;

//imports omitted for brevity

@Inherited
@InterceptorBinding
@Retention(RetentionPolicy.RUNTIME)
@Target({ElementType.METHOD, ElementType.TYPE})
public @interface Audit {
}
```

4. Let's create two more annotations, @Enter and @Exit, which will act as **event qualifiers**. A CDI qualifier is a special annotation that can be applied to a class or field to indicate the kind of bean we're working with. In our example, CDI qualifiers will differentiate the events and qualify them into two categories, representing the entry and exit points of a method:

```
package com.packt.store.audit;

//imports omitted for brevity

@Qualifier
@Retention(RetentionPolicy.RUNTIME)
@Target({ElementType.METHOD, ElementType.FIELD, ElementType.
PARAMETER, ElementType.TYPE})
public @interface Enter {
}

package com.packt.store.audit;

//imports omitted for brevity

@Qualifier
@Retention(RetentionPolicy.RUNTIME)
@Target({ElementType.METHOD, ElementType.FIELD, ElementType.
PARAMETER, ElementType.TYPE})
public @interface Exit {
}
```

> Remember to create each annotation into separate files.

5. Create a new class named `AuditHandler`. This class will simply print the audit message to the standard output, but a creative reader can actually implement anything here, such as publishing the message to a JMS queue or making a web service call. Note that we're using qualifiers to filter which event the methods should listen to:

```
package com.packt.store.audit;

// imports omitted for brevity

@Stateless
@Named
public class AuditHandler {
```

```
private static final String PREFIX = " [ AUDIT ] ";
private static final String ENTER = "[ Entering ]";
private static final String EXIT = "[ Exiting ]";

public void logEnter(@Observes @Enter AuditEvent event) {
    System.out.println(PREFIX + ENTER + event);
}
public void logExit(@Observes @Exit AuditEvent event) {
    System.out.println(PREFIX + EXIT + event);
}
}
```

6. Create a new class named `AuditInterceptor`, which will be the actual interceptor that traps the messages from the annotated classes or methods and forwards them as CDI events. The events are observed by `AuditHandler`, but there are no dependencies in compile or design time between the two classes:

```
package com.packt.store.audit;

//imports omitted for brevity

@Audit
@Interceptor
public class AuditInterceptor implements Serializable {
    private static final long serialVersionUID = 1L;

    @Inject @Enter
    // The Event referenced here is javax.enterprise.event.Event
    Event<AuditEvent> enterEvent;

    @Inject @Exit
    Event<AuditEvent> exitEvent;

    @AroundInvoke
    public Object auditMethod(InvocationContext ic) throws
Exception {
        enterEvent.fire(new AuditEvent(ic.getMethod().toString(),
                    (ic.getParameters().length > 0 ?
ic.getParameters() : null)));

        Object obj = ic.proceed();

        exitEvent.fire(new AuditEvent(ic.getMethod().toString(),
                    (ic.getParameters().length > 0 ?
```

```
                        ic.getParameters() : null)));

        return obj;
    }
}
```

> Note the usage of the @Enter and @Exit qualifiers in the event objects.
>
> If you compare this interceptor implementation to the one created for the logging mechanism, you will notice that it isn't calling the handler directly as we did before, it just publishes events that will be consumed by components that the interceptor doesn't have to know about. This is one benefit of this approach, decoupling the producers and consumers and creating a more flexible structure.

7. Modify the beans.xml file (under /WEB-INF/) to tell the container that the AuditInterceptor class must be loaded as an interceptor:

```
<beans xmlns="http://java.sun.com/xml/ns/javaee"
       xmlns:xsi="http://www.w3.org/2001/XMLSchema-instance"
       xsi:schemaLocation="http://java.sun.com/xml/ns/javaee
http://java.sun.com/xml/ns/javaee/beans_1_0.xsd">
    <interceptors>
        <class>com.packt.store.log.LogInterceptor</class>
        <class>com.packt.store.audit.AuditInterceptor</class>
    </interceptors>
</beans>
```

> Keep in mind that if you decorate an element with multiple interceptors, the sequence of execution will follow the order in which they were declared in the beans.xml file.

8. Save all files, making sure you have no missing imports or build errors in the project.

9. Open the SearchManager class and add the @Audit decorator to this class. This will perform the audit functionality on every method of the class:

```
@Named("search")
@SessionScoped
@Audit
public class SearchManager implements Serializable {
    ...
```

In a real-world scenario, auditing the whole class can bring a serious performance overhead, but to test and demonstrate our implementation, it's just fine. You may want to remove the annotation after testing it, as we will use this class frequently throughout the book.

10. Save and publish the **Store** application to the running server.

11. Browse to `http://localhost:7001/store/index.jsf` and check the output of the server to see the audit entries. If the server was started from Eclipse, you can see them on the **Console** tab:

```
<Nov 17, 2012 9:25:03 PM BRST> <Notice> <Stdout> <BEA-000000> <[
AUDIT ][ Exiting ][Sat Nov 17 21:25:03 BRST 2012] - public java.
util.List com.packt.store.search.SearchManager.getTheaters()>
<Nov 17, 2012 9:25:03 PM BRST> <Notice> <Stdout> <BEA-000000> <[
AUDIT ][ Exiting ][Sat Nov 17 21:25:03 BRST 2012] - public int
com.packt.store. search.SearchManager.getTheater()>
<Nov 17, 2012 9:25:03 PM BRST> <Notice> <Stdout> <BEA-000000> <[
AUDIT ][ Entering ][Sat Nov 17 21:25:03 BRST 2012] - public java.
util.List com.packt.store. search.SearchManager.getMovies()>
<Nov 17, 2012 9:25:03 PM BRST> <Notice> <Stdout> <BEA-000000> <[
AUDIT ][ Exiting ][Sat Nov 17 21:25:03 BRST 2012] - public java.
util.List com.packt.store. search.SearchManager.getMovies()>
<Nov 17, 2012 9:25:03 PM BRST> <Notice> <Stdout> <BEA-000000> <[
AUDIT ][ Entering ][Sat Nov 17 21:25:03 BRST 2012] - public int
com.packt.store. search.SearchManager.getMovie()>
<Nov 17, 2012 9:25:03 PM BRST> <Notice> <Stdout> <BEA-000000> <[
AUDIT ][ Exiting ][Sat Nov 17 21:25:03 BRST 2012] - public int
com.packt.store. search.SearchManager.getMovie()>
```

Let's review what we have done in this section. We created another interceptor in the **Store** application to handle audit entries based on a new annotation, `@Audit`, which can be applied to classes and methods. The interceptor uses CDI events to communicate with a simple handler, which, in this example, only writes a message to the standard output of WebLogic Server. These events can be listened to by multiple classes if needed, so based on what you've learned, you can create a JMS or a web service handler that can send specific audit messages to these components.

Note that the `AuditHandler` class in this example is an EJB, and that the processing of the `@Observer` decoration occurs by default in the same thread as the event publisher (our business class). In order to decouple the caller thread from the called object, we just need to add the `@Asynchronous` decoration to `AuditHandler`.

Web resources

The following are a few web resources that you can refer to:

- JavaBeans tutorial
    - ° `http://docs.oracle.com/javase/tutorial/javabeans/`

- JavaBeans specification
    - ° `http://www.oracle.com/technetwork/java/javase/documentation/spec-136004.html`

- Java logging overview
    - ° `http://docs.oracle.com/javase/7/docs/technotes/guides/logging/overview.html`

- Using logging services for application monitoring
    - ° `http://docs.oracle.com/middleware/1212/wls/LOGSV/index.html`

- Understanding WebLogic logging services
    - ° `http://docs.oracle.com/middleware/1212/wls/WLLOG/logging_services.htm`

- Configuring WebLogic logging services
    - ° `http://docs.oracle.com/middleware/1212/wls/WLLOG/config_logs.htm`

- Overview of the WLDF (Diagnostics Framework) architecture
    - ° `http://docs.oracle.com/middleware/1212/wls/WLDFC/architecture.htm`

- Monitoring WebLogic JDBC resources
    - ° `http://docs.oracle.com/middleware/1212/wls/JDBCA/monitor.htm`

- WebLogic log message format
    - ° `http://docs.oracle.com/middleware/1212/wls/WLLOG/logging_services.htm#i1180710`

- Annotations
    - ° `http://java.sun.com/docs/books/jls/`

- Java EE 6 tutorial – Interceptors
    - ° `http://docs.oracle.com/javaee/6/tutorial/doc/gkeed.html`
- Java EE 6 tutorial – CDI Events
    - ° `http://docs.oracle.com/javaee/6/tutorial/doc/gkhic.html`
- Creating asynchronous methods in EJB 3.1
    - ° `http://www.oracle.com/webfolder/technetwork/tutorials/ obe/java/asyncMethodOfEJB/AsyncMethodEJB.html`
- Observer pattern
    - ° `http://en.wikipedia.org/wiki/Observer_pattern`
- Interceptors Javadoc
    - ° `http://docs.oracle.com/javaee/6/api/javax/interceptor/ package-summary.html`

Summary

In this chapter, you've learned about Java EE interceptors by creating a logging annotation that can be attached to classes or methods, how to publish and observe events by using CDI, how to create and use asynchronous methods in EJB, and details about the logging services enabled by WebLogic Server.

In the next chapter, we're going to see how to connect remote clients to a WebLogic Server application by explaining and using several JMS features, including an offline message sender.

7
Remote Access with JMS

Until this point, we have only used modules deployed to WebLogic Server to exchange information, mostly relying on the HTTP protocol using RESTful or SOAP based web services, but there are scenarios when you need some other functionalities on your messaging layer, such as transparent persistence, ways to send messages to multiple clients, and recovery alternatives for lost messages. Well, there are numerous features that can be leveraged by servers and clients depending on specific messaging needs. In this chapter, we are going to focus on a situation when you don't have the necessary infrastructure — or business demand — to run an application server instance on both sides. When this is the case, we can create a standalone Java client and use some of the features made available by WebLogic to enable remote communication between the server and the standalone module, which in this context is called a **remote client**.

In this chapter we will:

- Understand the different modes of remote connection presented by WebLogic
- See the concepts of **Java Messaging Service** (**JMS**) and create components to expose a **JMS queue** at the server
- Create a standalone Java client that post messages to this queue and a message-driven bean that will consume them
- Introduce the **Store-and-Forward** (**SAF**) client feature of WebLogic Server that allows a client application to post messages to a queue even when a connection to the server isn't available.

WebLogic clients

Before we dive into the details of JMS, let's take a quick look at some of the **client modules** that are available for use when creating applications that access WebLogic Server's features but are attached to JVMs that aren't running a WebLogic Server instance. A **client module library** is just a JAR library that enables a set of WebLogic features such as access to EJBs, JMS components, and others. While developing an application that will access WebLogic, you must choose a client that's best for your scenario and distribute it along with your binaries.

In the following sections, we will see the most commonly adopted client libraries, along with their description.

Thin T3 client – wlthint3client.jar

T3 is the proprietary transport protocol used by WebLogic Server to carry data between its nodes, and can also be used by clients to communicate with the server. With this library attached to your project, you can execute the most common EJB-related actions such as JNDI lookup, transaction participation and queuing and consuming JMS messages.

This should be the preferred way to connect to a server, as it implements some features that greatly improve communication - for example, it keeps an open connection between two points by sending regular heartbeats, and uses packet multiplexing to increase network efficiency.

Only when you need very specific features, such as administrative operations (to shut down an instance, or deploy a package, for instance), or when the scope of features you need is very narrow (for example, just to post or consume a JMS message) should you resort to other client libraries.

RMI thin client – wlclient.jar

The RMI thin client doesn't use the T3 protocol, leaving all RMI-related work to the Java SE where the application is running, so you have a smaller set of functionalities than the one exposed by the **Thin T3 client** and a not-so-optimized channel of communication. The RMI-related work is done by the Java SE's **Java Remote Method Protocol (JRMP)** protocol.

The most common need that justifies the RMI client over the T3 one is when you have to use SSL over an HTTP channel to communicate with the server, as the T3 client doesn't support this configuration.

> If the requirement is to cryptograph all communication, you could use the T3S protocol variant, which opens an SSL-enabled T3 channel between the client and the server (where *client* can be a remote client or another server node).

JMS thin client – wljmsclient.jar

The JMS thin client is an add-on to the **RMI client**, `wlclient.jar`, which adds JMS features on top of it, again, using the JSE's RMI stack.

To use this client, you must add a reference to the `wljmsclient.jar` file. This library depends on another one, `wlclient.jar`, but you don't need to explicitly reference the latter as the former has a `classpath` link to it. By default, they are located at the same location inside the WebLogic Server installation - `/server/lib`, so the reference is automatically satisfied. If this is not the case, you must reference both manually.

JMS SAF client – wlsafclient.jar

When using a JMS remote client, a direct connection to WebLogic must be present in order to publish messages to a queue or topic; if this is not the case, the client application must deal with this scenario, probably storing the messages locally until the connection is available again, inserting an unnecessary development overhead.

To help developers deal with this problem, WebLogic Server has a feature called **Store-and-Forward (SAF)** that takes care of the messages when a connection is not available, and automatically transmits them when communication is back online.

> This behavior is the same as the WebLogic Server's **SAF agent** feature that allows a server to store and transfer messages between other servers even when the destination isn't available.

To enable this feature, the client must use a specific library, `wlsafclient.jar`; it is an add-on to the JMS thin client described earlier that enables the SAF client feature. So, in order to use it, you also have to package the `wljmsclient.jar` and `wlclient.jar` libraries along with your code. Again, the libraries have internal references to each other, so if you add a reference to `wlsafclient.jar` from its original folder, the dependencies are automatically satisfied.

We will see how to implement a SAF client later in this chapter.

JMS T3 SAF client – wlsaft3client.jar

The JMS T3 SAF client's role is exactly the same as that of the previous one, that is, the JMS SAF client, `wlsafclient.jar`, the difference being that it adds the SAF client features to the T3 thin client.

Full client – wlfullclient.jar

The full client has the most complete set of features you can wish for. It actually has most of the modules that compose the WebLogic Server packaged as a single library. There are some exceptions; for instance, the `cryptoj.jar` library has a self-integrity check that would fail if changed.

If you have any prior experience with WebLogic client development, you probably attached the `weblogic.jar` library to your client package. This library is still available, but the official recommendation is to generate and use the `wlfullclient.jar` file if none of the other clients fit your needs.

When you install WebLogic Server, this library doesn't exist, so you have to run a utility in order to create it:

1. Open a command prompt or terminal, and go to the folder `$MW_HOME/wlserver/server/lib`.

2. Run the following command:

   ```
   java -jar wljarbuilder.jar
   ```

3. After more than 4000 messages, the execution finishes and you have a brand new `wlfullclient.jar` file with 60 MB of binary code.

It is indeed a large file, so you may want to double-check your needs to see if any of the other clients works for you — if you need to create an applet, for instance, this client is most definitely not the best way to go, due to its size. To its advantage, the full client is more scalable than its little brothers and covers more WebLogic features, although you will seldom need all its power.

JMX client – wljmxclient.jar

The JMX client is the last client module and is a very specific one as it is targeted to clients that want to access WebLogic's **MBeans**. MBeans are components that expose information about the application server and its components and allow the consumer to change some of them.

An MBean is a Java framework to expose components that can be used to manage Java platform resources. To give you an idea of the potential of this client, think about what you can accomplish using WebLogic's administration console. There's a lot of functionality there, right? The console is just a frontend to the same MBeans we can access and manage using JMX.

Here's a sample code showing how to use this client library to open a connection to a WebLogic instance, and to query the name and state of the servers of the domain it connected to:

```java
void run() throws Exception {
  JMXConnector connector;
  MBeanServerConnection conn;

  // Create the appropriate context parameters
  Hashtable<String, String> env = new Hashtable<>();

  env.put(JMXConnectorFactory.PROTOCOL_PROVIDER_PACKAGES,
                            "weblogic.management.remote");
  env.put(Context.SECURITY_PRINCIPAL, "weblogic");
  env.put(Context.SECURITY_CREDENTIALS, "welcome1");

  // Create a JMX connection
  JMXServiceURL url = new JMXServiceURL("t3",
        "localhost",
        7001,
        "/jndi/weblogic.management.mbeanservers.domainruntime");

    // Open the connection
    connector = JMXConnectorFactory.connect(url, env);
    conn = connector.getMBeanServerConnection();

    // Query and print objects
    ObjectName drs = new ObjectName(
      "com.bea:Name=DomainRuntimeService," +
      "Type=weblogic.management.mbeanservers.domainruntime." +
      "DomainRuntimeServiceMBean");

    ObjectName[] servers = (ObjectName[]) conn.getAttribute(drs,
                                    "ServerRuntimes");

  for(ObjectName server: servers) {
      System.out.print("Instance " +
                    conn.getAttribute(server, "Name"));
      System.out.println(" is " +
```

```
                                conn.getAttribute(server,"State"));
    }

    // Shutdown
    connector.close();
}
```

Most of the code deals with the opening of a properly configured connection to the server, then we query MBean objects and its values using the `getAttribute` method, and finally close the connection. Remember that T3 uses heartbeats to keep a connection alive, so it's a good practice to always release it at the end of your process.

As it happens with the JMS client module, this one also needs the `wlclient.jar` library explicitly referenced or available in the same folder of `wljmxclient.jar` in order to function properly.

> For a complete list of features and limitations of each client, check the *Web resources* section.

Java Messaging Service (JMS) and WebLogic

Now that we are familiar with some of the most common ways to connect to a WebLogic Server, let's take a look at one of the features enabled by them, the **Java Message Service (JMS)** module.

JMS is a Java API that makes the sharing of information between systems or modules possible by sending and receiving messages in an asynchronous way.

WebLogic Server's JMS implementation is compliant with JMS 1.1, and its provider exposes both the message models that are defined by the specification, **point-to-point** and **publish/subscribe**, which translate to **queue** and **topic** components. The basic difference between them is that a message sent to a queue is consumed by only one listener, no matter how many of them are attached to the queue. By contrast, a topic delivers a message to all its subscribers (the clients attached to it) whether they are online or not, depending on their configuration.

When using WebLogic's JMS, you must first create the destination queue or topic you are planning to use. This may sound a little obvious, but there are tools that automate these procedures and make them transparent for you, hence the statement.

Also, WebLogic's JMS implementation demands you to create and configure several other components in a specific order so that you can create your queue or topic. The following is a diagram that represents the most common components an application uses:

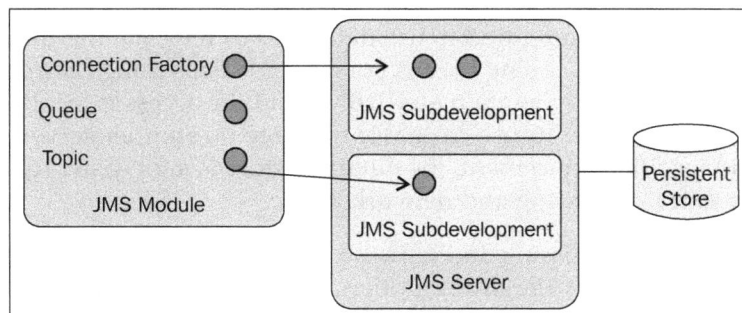

The components shown in the preceding diagram are discussed in the further sections. The following is a quick description of these components:

- A **persistent store** holds the messages waiting for delivery inside a file or database, instead of keeping all messages in memory.

- A **JMS module** is a logical container for components, such as queues, topics, and connection factories, which can be used by an application.

- A **JMS server** makes a bridge between JMS components and the underlying deployment structure, defining attributes such as which persistent store must be used by the components, if any, and logging parameters.

- A **JMS subdeployment** groups components from a JMS module into deployable units that can be targeted to a specific JMS server.

- A **JMS queue** will receive messages to be consumed by our application.

After checking the details of each component and how to create them, we will code the remote client project to post messages and the MDB that will consume the messages.

The business scenario that we will use to illustrate these functionalities is this: when our partner (the theater) needs to send new exhibition dates and times to our **Theater** module, it will do so using the remote client we're about to write. This client will receive information about the new exhibition as command-line arguments and post them to the queue that we're going to create in a later section. Finally, in the **Theater** module, a **Message Driven Bean** (**MDB**) will receive it and persist the new entity using the server's persistence layer.

The persistent store

WebLogic's persistent store is a service that provides physical storage to several other services and features such as JTA, the Timer EJB, and several components of the JMS system module.

A persistent store can be configured to use databases or files, having the same set of features for both options. Using files as persistence keeps things simple, as you don't need to configure and maintain an RDBMS and the access is local, but it may be harder to migrate the file store — to enable the store on another server — in case of failure. For this specific requirement, the database store is a lot easier to deal with, but you'll have extra processing and network traffic.

As a file store has less processing and network overhead when compared to a database store, it's generally the fastest option. Of course, this will depend on the hardware you have available — a SATA HDD is no match to a **network attached storage** (**NAS**) connected via a fiber channel, or to a high-performance system hosting your database.

> Using a shared NAS to keep the persistent stores from all servers can be a timesaver when you have to migrate a file store from one WebLogic instance to another, since all nodes have access to the same NAS.

So while defining one over the other, we have to consider all requirements and constraints of the project. Available hardware, expected network usage, databases, and disaster-recovery expectations are the basic items to be checked.

When you use WebLogic's JMS module, there are situations where a persistent store is mandatory, but this is not the case when you only need to enable a JMS queue — the behavior will be exactly the same, but instead of saving the messages to a file or database, they will be kept in memory. That said, there are a couple of things you need to know:

- Depending on the volume and size of your messages and the throughput of the consumers, you may get into a **resource starvation** scenario, that is, if the heap size of your JVMs isn't enough to hold all messages, the garbage collector starts to kick in frequently, leading to CPU peaks. Eventually, your system enters an overload condition, it can't recover itself, and you have to bounce it.

- Once you restart the server, as the messages exist solely in memory, they are gone for good. A sudden power outage also can make you lose them all.

The book's business scenario doesn't specify if we should tolerate loss of messages, so let's assume that we can't afford it. If a new exhibition entry is lost, the customer will not see it, and our partners aren't going to be happy with this, so better be safe than sorry, right?

The following steps are necessary to create a file-based persistent store:

1. Open the administration console by going to `http://localhost:7001/ console`, then log in, and click on the **Services** entry in the navigation tree, and then on the subentry, click on **Persistent Stores**.

2. Click on the **New** button at the top of the list of persistent stores and then select **Create FileStore** from the menu.

3. Set the value of **Name** to `FileStore-Tickets`, leave the value of **Target** as it is — we don't have any other configured instances — and set the **Directory** field to `./ticketFS`.

Create a New File Store

| OK | Cancel |

File Store Properties

The following properties will be used to identify your new file store.

* Indicates required fields

What would you like to name your new file store?

* **Name:**   FileStore-Tickets

Select a server instance for this file store.

Target: AdminServer ▼

The pathname to the directory on the file system where the file store is kept.
This directory must exist on your system, so be sure to create it before completing this tab.

Directory: ./ticketsFS

| OK | Cancel |

> You can specify either an absolute path or a relative one in the **Directory** field. The root for the relative path that we used in the preceding steps will be the domain folder `/opt/packt/domains/ tickets` if you're following the structure defined in this book.

4. Click on **OK** to finish the wizard and create the resource.

Starting with Version 12.1.2 of WebLogic, we can now target a persistent store to a cluster; that means that we don't need to create one persistent store for each server of a cluster, and associate one and only one JMS server to each store. When a persistent store is targeted to a cluster, WebLogic creates its file inside every managed server folder, making this procedure an easy task.

If you want to use a database store, there are a couple of things to remember:

- You must first create a **data source** that will be attached to the persistent store. This data source can't use an XA driver, and you can't enable the **Supports Global Transactions** flag of the non-XA data source you create.

- Just one table named WLStore is needed. If the system detects that the table doesn't exist upon startup, it tries to create it. If the user configured at the data source doesn't have the necessary permissions, the operation fails and the store will not be available.

If this is the case (the connection user doesn't have the permission to create objects), locate the com.bea.core.store.jdbc_3.0.0.0.jar file available in the modules subfolder of your WebLogic installation. Open it, get the script that corresponds to your database server at path /weblogic/store/io/jdbc/ddl, adjust the name of the table to WLStore, and run it with the necessary credentials.

Remember that you must give read and write permissions to the configured data source user on this table.

The JMS server

This component is a container for destination-related resources and acts as a link between them and the underlying environment; for example, the persistence store we just created must be linked to a JMS server, so when we send messages to our queue, it can use this configuration and persist the messages, if this is the case.

This component is also responsible for maintaining the state of durable subscribers, and is the unit used by the server migration feature to migrate data from a failed managed server to another one, avoiding loss of messages.

Until Version 12.1.1, a JMS server should be pinned to a specific managed server for increasing the administrative management. Since Version 12.1.2, JMS servers (and persistent stores, as already mentioned) can be targeted to a cluster, making the process of creating and starting new managed servers a breeze.

Let's create a JMS server to use with our code:

1. In the administration console, click on the **Services** entry in the navigation tree, then expand the **Messaging** entry, and click on **JMS Servers**.

2. Click on the **New** button just above the list of **JMS Servers**.

3. Enter `JMSServer-Tickets` as Name, select `FileStore-Tickets` as **Persistent Store**, and click on **Next**.

> If you click on the **Finish** button on this screen, your server will remain untargeted, and even though it's apparently OK, you will not be able to use it later.

4. Select the only entry available, **AdminServer**, as the target for the JMS Server, and then click on **Finish**.

The JMS module

A JMS module is a logical group of JMS components such as queues, topics, and connection factories. It's inside a module that these components are defined, but we must target the *component* to make it available and active—just existing inside a module doesn't mean it can be used.

There are two kinds of JMS modules:

- **The system module**: The modules created from the administration console or related technologies—by accessing MBeans through code or scripts, for instance—are named system modules. The components created inside them are visible to all applications targeted to the same WebLogic servers and can be shared by them.

- **The application module**: The declaration of such a module is done as a deployable package—all definitions go inside deployment descriptors, which are XML files—processed at deployment time. The package can be installed as a **standalone module**, which enables other applications to access the resources declared by it, or as a **packaged module** that exposes the components only to other modules deployed along with it—for instance, a EAR with a JMS module that declares a JMS queue and an EJB module with an MDB that consumes it. The components created by an application module aren't accessible via the administration console.

The general recommendation concerning which kind of module you should use is this: always choose the **system module** option. Although the appeal of flexibility given by the application module looks nice, it comes with a cost—no JMX management—that simply doesn't justify it.

> Keep in mind that if you choose to create an application module, you still need to create components outside it—at least the JMS Servers—and if persistence is needed, the persistence stores also must be created through the administration console or a script.

If component isolation is a strong requirement, you can resort to the security model provided by WebLogic to accomplish this. We discuss this topic in *Chapter 8, Adding Security*.

We're going to create a system module to use in our projects:

1. In the administration console, click on the **Services** entry in the navigation tree, then expand the **Messaging** entry, and click on **JMS Modules**.

2. Click on the **New** button just above the list of **JMS Modules**.

3. Enter JMSModule-Tickets as **Name** and click on **Next**, leaving the other fields empty.

4. Click on the checkbox beside the **AdminServer** entry to deploy the module to this server and click on **Next**.

5. Leave the checkbox next to the question **Would you like to add resources to this JMS system module?** unchecked, and click on **Finish**.

Just one more resource must be created before we can finally declare our queue.

The JMS subdeployment

The JMS subdeployment component works as the link between the logical group where it exists (a JMS module) and one or more physical destinations (JMS servers). You can have several subdeployments inside a JMS module, each targeting one or more different JMS servers, which by its turn can be targeted to different WebLogic servers.

> Although using a subdeployment can be an optional step when dealing with JMS resources, doing so is a best practice that helps management by targeting groups of components at once. Also, there are resources that must be explicitly bound to a subdeployment, such as the queue that we're going to set up shortly.

So, before we create a queue, we must have a subdeployment to be its target. This is how we define one:

1. In the administration console, click on the **Services** entry in the navigation tree, then expand the **Messaging** entry, and click on **JMS Modules**.

2. Click on the name of the module we just created, **JMSModule-Tickets**.

3. When the **Settings** page shows up, click on the **Subdeployments** tab at the top of the page.

4. Click on the **New** button, type `PersistentSD` in the **Name** field, and click on **Next**.

5. Bind the component to the **JMSServer-Tickets** JMS server and click on **Finish**.

> If you're wondering why you saw both WebLogic's **AdminServer** and **JMSServer-Tickets** JMS server on the target step, this is because there are JMS components that don't need to be explicitly bounded to a JMS server to be available, for instance the connection factories. Queues don't fall in this category. You can create a queue and target it to a subdeployment that points to a WebLogic Server, and no errors or warnings will be shown, but the resource will never be available.
>
> So, as a best practice, always target your subdeployments to JMS Servers.

The JMS queue

A **JMS queue** is the channel between a message producer and a consumer in a point-to-point model. A few things about its behavior and configuration:

- A message is delivered at the most to one consumer, even when multiple consumers are listening to the same queue.

- You can set the duration for which a message must be held waiting for consumption before it gets discarded. This is referred to as the **time-to-live limit**.

- If a queue receives a message but there are no consumer(s) listening to it, the message is held in the queue. It waits for a consumer to show up until the configured time-to-live limit expires.

- You can set the **expiration policy** value of a queue with one of the following:

  - **Redirect**: The message is posted to another queue previously created and pointed by at the **Error Destination** parameter of the original one

  - **Log**: The message is written to the JMS Server's log file. In order to be effective, you must also tick the **Enable Message Logging** checkbox inside the **Logging** tab of your queue

  - **Discard**: The message is just dropped. This is the default behavior

> If you attach a message-driven bean to a queue, by default its `onMessage` method is called by the container in the context of a transaction. So if something goes wrong and the method throws an exception, the message is kept in the queue, and its **redelivery policies** are processed, that is, the redelivery limit is checked, and if not reached, the message is made available to consumers after the redelivery delay interval.

To create the queue that will receive new exhibition instances, follow these steps:

1. In the administration console, click on the **Services** entry on the navigation tree, then expand the **Messaging** entry, and click on **JMS Modules**.

2. Click on the name of our module, `JMSModule-Tickets`.

3. Click on the **New** button, select the **Queue** option on the next page, and click on **Next**.

4. Enter `ExhibitionQueue` as **Name** and `jms.tickets.exhibition` as **JNDI Name**, then click on **Next**.

5. In the **Subdeployments** dropdown, select the **PersistentSD** entry and click on **Finish**.

You are now back on the JMS module's settings page, with the queue you just created listed in the **Summary of Resources** table. There are lots of other parameters and configurations that we can change, such as quotas and limits, security constraints, and logging, but the creation wizard only asks for the basic set of information it needs to do its job. If you want to, go ahead and click on the queue name to explore the available options.

We don't need to alter any of them, so at this point, we're all set to start posting messages to the queue.

The JMS connection factory

Another kind of resource you can create inside a JMS module is the **JMS connection factory**. When you post a message to a queue, several aspects of the produced message are read from the connection, such as the message's priority, transactional behavior, and persistence configuration.

One of the most important flags of a connection factory dictates if the resource is able to participate in global transactions, or in other words, if it's an **XA-enabled** resource. If the posting or consumption of a queue or topic is one step inside a complex business function that must be committed or rolled back as a single unit, then you must use an XA connection factory. You do so by checking the **XA Connection Factory Enabled** option presented by its creation wizard.

When a WebLogic domain is configured, two default JMS connection factories are created, and they can be retrieved using these **JNDI names**:

- `weblogic.jms.ConnectionFactory`
- `weblogic.jms.XAConnectionFactory`

The configurations of both are basically the same, except for one pretty obvious detail: `XAConnectionFactory` is an XA-enabled resource. All other parameters have the same default values you get when you create your own JMS connection factory.

As the piece of code we're about to write has very basic demands, we don't need to create a specific JMS connection factory. Instead, we will use the non-XA default connection factory, `weblogic.jms.ConnectionFactory`. The only step in our business scenario is to post a single message, so support for distributed transactions isn't necessary.

> When developing a real project, always create your own JMS connection factories. This way, you can control your factories by changing its parameters, which is something you can't do when using WebLogic's default ones. Even if you could, as they're global resources, other applications may use them, so you would influence their behavior as well.

Posting messages from a standalone client

The necessary code to write messages to a WebLogic Server queue doesn't have to use any WebLogic specific classes, just plain regular `javax.jms.*` and `javax.naming.*` components.

There are some classes and interfaces provided by WebLogic that help us access WebLogic-specific features, but as they address very specialized scenarios, chances are you're not going to use them very often. They are inside the `weblogic.jms.extensions` package, and you can find their Javadoc at `http://docs.oracle.com/middleware/1212/wls/WLAPI/weblogic/jms/extensions/package-summary.html`.

As said earlier in this chapter, the business functionality we're going to implement will act as a bridge between the partner's system and the **Theater** module deployed at their installations, and will receive information about new exhibition dates that must be uploaded to our module.

To accomplish this, we will create a standalone Java project named `RemoteClient` and add a Java class that will read the command-line arguments that represent the new exhibition, pack them inside an `Exhibition` class instance, and post it to a message queue.

Creating the project

The following are the steps to set up the environment that our code needs:

1. Open Eclipse IDE, select menu entries **File, New...**, and **Project...**. Then, type `Java` in the **Wizards** text field, click on the **Java Project** entry, and then on the **Next** button.

2. Type `RemoteClient` as **Project Name**, make sure you're using JDK 1.7 in the **JRE** group (change it if necessary), and click on **Next**.

3. Click on the **Libraries** tab and then on the **Add External JARs...** button.

4. Navigate to `/$MW_HOME/wlserver/server/lib` and select the `wlthint3client.jar` file.

5. As we're going to instantiate the `Exhibition` class, we also need to add a reference to its package, `TheaterBO.jar`, in the same way. Click on the **Add External JARs...** button, then navigate to the location where you saved the `TheaterBO.jar` file that is deployed as a shared library.

> If you don't remember where the deployed `TheatherBO.jar` file is, open WebLogic's administration console, go to the **Deployments** page, and click on the **theaterBO(1.0,1.0.0)** entry. The **Overview** tab will be loaded, and the **Path** line will tell you where to find it.

6. Click on **Finish**. You may choose to open the Java perspective.

Coding the message producer

As there are no specific needs regarding the message producer, we will write the code inside the `main` method of our class.

1. Create a package named `com.packt.client` inside the **RemoteClient** project, and add a class named `Enqueue` inside this package.

2. We will declare the address and component names as static constants inside the class as follows:

```
static final String WLS_ADDRESS =
                "t3://localhost:7001";
```

```
static final String WLS_CTX_FACTORY =
                "weblogic.jndi.WLInitialContextFactory";
static final String JMS_QUEUE_FACTORY =
                "weblogic.jms.ConnectionFactory";
static final String JMS_QUEUE_NAME =
                "jms.tickets.exhibition";
```

3. Create the public main method that is going to hold all the logic; also, it is going to throw the superclass `Exception`, so we save a few try/catch blocks:

```
public static void main(String args[]) throws Exception {
}
```

4. We first need to acquire a remote connection to WebLogic Server. You may need to change the username and password to be able to connect to your server:

```
Context ct;
Hashtable<String, String> env = new Hashtable<>();

env.put(Context.PROVIDER_URL, WLS_ADDRESS);
env.put(Context.INITIAL_CONTEXT_FACTORY,
                                WLS_CTX_FACTORY);
env.put(Context.SECURITY_PRINCIPAL, "weblogic");
env.put(Context.SECURITY_CREDENTIALS, "welcome1");

// Get a server connection
ct = new InitialContext(env);
```

5. Now we create and load instances of `Movie`, `Room`, and `Exhibition` using command-line arguments as attribute values:

```
/*
 * Argument sequence and format:
 *    0: Movie Id
 *    1: Room Id
 *    2: Exhibition date - MM.DD.YYYY
 *    3: Exhibition time - HHMM
 */
Movie movie = new Movie();
movie.setId(Integer.parseInt(args[0]));

Room room = new Room();
room.setId(Integer.parseInt(args[1]));

Exhibition exhibition = new Exhibition();
```

```
exhibition.setMovie(movie);
exhibition.setRoom(room);
exhibition.setDate(new SimpleDateFormat("MM.dd.yyyy").
                              parse(args[2]));
exhibition.setHour(Integer.parseInt(args[3]));
```

6. These are the declarations of all JMS components we will need, all from the package `javax.jms`:

```
QueueConnectionFactory qcf;
QueueConnection qc = null;
QueueSession qs = null;
QueueSender sender = null;

Queue queue;
ObjectMessage msg;
```

7. And here we grab the necessary JMS resources, create a sender, and post the message. This whole block is wrapped inside a try/catch block that's supposed to deal with any problems that may arise. At the end, there's a `finally` block to close the JMS resources, as they don't support Java 7's **try-with-resources** feature yet:

```
try {
    // Set up JMS components
    qcf = (QueueConnectionFactory) ct.lookup(JMS_QUEUE_FACTORY);
    qc = qcf.createQueueConnection();
    qs = qc.createQueueSession(false,
                              Session.AUTO_ACKNOWLEDGE);

    // Get a handle to the JMS queue
    queue = (javax.jms.Queue) ct.lookup(JMS_QUEUE_NAME);

    // Create ...
    msg = qs.createObjectMessage();
    msg.setObject(exhibition);

    // ... and send the message
    sender = qs.createSender(queue);
    sender.send(msg);
} catch(Exception e) {
    e.printStackTrace();
} finally {
    // Doesn't support try-with-resources yet...
    try { sender.close(); } catch (Exception e) { }
```

```
        try { qc.close(); } catch (Exception e) { }
        try { qs.close(); } catch (Exception e) { }
        try { ct.close(); } catch (Exception e) { }
    }
```

8. Save everything and check and correct any compilation errors.

> You will see an error mark at the top of the class. If you hover the
> mouse over it, the message **The type javax.persistence.TemporalType**
> **cannot be resolved. It is indirectly referenced from required .class**
> **files** will pop up. This class is used by the `TheaterBO` package, but
> as we aren't dealing with the persistence layer here, we can ignore the
> error. Compilation and execution will run as expected.

The code is ready to generate messages. Let's post a few entries!

Queuing messages

We're going to execute the client from Eclipse, so we need to create a
run configuration:

1. Just run the class for the first time and Eclipse will create a configuration
    for you: right-click on the class' name, then select **Run As** and then
    Java Application. An exception will be displayed, as we don't have any
    command-line arguments yet—just ignore it.

2. Right-click on the class name again, and then select **Run As** and the **Run**
    Configurations... option in the context menu.

3. In the **Run Configurations** window, find the Java Application entry at the list
    to the left, and then click on at the subentry with our class' name, `Enqueue`.

4. Click on at the **Arguments** tab, and enter the `5 1 01.01.2013 1400`
    sequence in the **Program arguments** box.

> The sequence of the parameters represents the movie ID, room ID,
> and exhibition's date, in the format `MM.DD.YYYY` and time.

5. Click on **Run**. If the execution finishes without errors, your message will
    most likely be waiting for consumption at the queue.

As we still don't have a consumer attached to the queue, you can check it and see that there are messages waiting for delivery:

1. Access WebLogic's administration console, and on the navigation tree click on **Services**, **Messaging**, and then **JMS Modules**.

2. Click on the name of our module, **JMSModule-Tickets**, and then on the queue's name, **ExhibitionQueue**.

3. Click on the **Monitoring** tab and you can check how many consumers the queue has, the number of current and total messages, along with other data:

Settings for ExhibitionQueue

| Configuration | **Monitoring** | Control | Security | Subdeployment | Notes |

A JMS destination identifies a queue (Point-To-Point) or a topic (Pub/Sub) that is targeted to a JMS server.

This page summarizes the active JMS destinations that have been created for this JMS module.

▷ **Customize this table**

Destinations (Filtered - More Columns Exist)

Show Messages   Showing 1 to 1 of 1 Previous | Next

	Name ⌃	Consumers Current	Messages Current	Messages Pending	Bytes Pending
☐	JMSModule-Tickets!ExhibitionQueue	0	1	0	0

Show Messages

> The **Messages Pending** column shows the messages that cannot be consumed because they are still part of a receive transaction. The **Messages Current** column shows how many messages are available to the consumers, and **Messages Total** indicates how many messages have been received by this queue.

4. You can drill down and see the messages by checking the box next to the name and then clicking on the **Show Messages** button:

Summary of JMS Messages

This page summarizes the available messages for a stand-alone queue, a distributed queue, or a topic durable subscriber. Use this page to view message details, create new messages, delete selected messages, move messages to another destination, export message contents in XML format to another file, import XML formatted message contents from another file, or drain all the messages from a destination.

Click on a message to view its contents.

Message Selector:		Apply

▷ **Customize this table**

JMS Messages (Filtered - More Columns Exist)

| New | Delete ∨ | Move ∨ | Import | Export ∨ | | Showing 1 to 4 of 4 Previous | Next |

☐	ID ⌂	Time Stamp	State String	JMS Delivery Mode	Message Size	Priority
☐	ID: <122815.1354449275601.0>	Sun Dec 02 09:54:35 BRST 2012	visible	Persistent	517	5

Notice the buttons just above the message table. Other than checking the messages already in the queue, you can:

- Create new messages from the administration console.

- Delete selected messages or all messages from the queue.

- Move some or all the messages from this queue to another one.

- Import and export messages to and from XML files with a specific format. These functionalities don't work with object messages unless the classes inside the payload are available from the server classpath.

As we post object messages, if you click on the message ID, a screen with the warning **Unable to view message, reason = java.class.ClassNotFoundException: com.packt.domain.theater.Exhibition** shows up. You must add the class' package to WebLogic's classpath, and the easiest way to accomplish this is to drop the `TheaterBO.jar` file for our example into the `/lib` folder of the target domain, `$ DOMAIN_HOME/tickets`, and restart the server.

This is how the detail screen should look like if you do this:

JMS Message Detail

Message ID:	ID:<122815.1354449275601.0>	Delivery Mode:	Persistent
Type:	(No value specified)	Correlation ID:	(No value specified)
Timestamp:	Sun Dec 02 09:54:35 BRST 2012	Expiration:	Sun Dec 02 09:56:15 BRST 2012
Priority:	5	Redelivered:	false
Delivery Time:	(No value specified)	Redelivery Limit:	-1

Properties:

key	value	type
JMSXDeliveryCount	0	java.lang.Integer

Text:

```
ObjectMessage[ID:
<122815.1354449275601.0>,com.packt.domain.theater.Exhibition@f76b02]
```

When you already have a consumer that is attached to a queue and needs to check the messages coming through it, you can stop the queue's **consumption**. Also, you can pause the **production** and/or **insertion** of messages of a given queue, for instance, to avoid an overload situation. Let's define these administration-related terms:

- **Production**: This is used for posting messages into the queue. When it's paused, no producer can post messages.

- **Insertion**: This does the same as the previous flag, but also blocks messages that are in flight, for instance, messages that are waiting to be inserted in the queue because its quota has been reached, or messages with a **delivery time** header that hasn't been reached yet.

- **Consumption**: The messages are received and put in the queue as usual, but the engine doesn't notify any consumers about them, so there's no message delivery.

> These pauses — production, insertion, and consumption — are held until the server goes down. If you restart a WebLogic node, all states are set back to *enabled*, or more specifically, to the default value for each state, which you can configure in the **Configuration** tab, the **General** inner tab, and the **Advanced** group of a destination component.

Here's the screen where we can pause or resume the production and/or consumption of our queue:

Settings for ExhibitionQueue

| Configuration | Monitoring | **Control** | Security | Subdeployment | Notes |

A JMS destination identifies a queue (Point-To-Point) or a topic (Pub/Sub) that is targeted to a JMS server.

This page summarizes the active JMS destinations that have been created for this JMS module.

▷ **Customize this table**

Destinations

| Production ∨ | Consumption ∨ | Insertion ∨ | | Showing 1 to 1 of 1   Previous \| Next |

✔	**Name** ⌃	**ProductionPaused**	**ConsumptionPaused**	**InsertionPaused**
✔	JMSModule-Tickets!ExhibitionQueue	false	false	false

Production ∨	Consumption ∨	Insertion ∨
	Pause	
	Resume	

Now that we confirmed that there's a message or two waiting in the queue, let's code a bean to consume them.

Consuming messages with an MDB

The last thing we must do to complete our business scenario is to retrieve the posted messages from the queue and create a new exhibition line in the database by using the persistence layer. To do so, follow these steps:

1. Right-click on the **Theater** project's name, select **New…** in the top of the context menu, and then select **Other…**.

2. Type `Message` in the search field, select the **Message-Driven Bean (EJB 3.x)** entry, and click on **Next**.

3. Configure the fields as shown in the following screenshot:

4. Click on **Finish**.

As a message carries an instance of class Exhibition, we will just extract and pass it to a persistence manager that will save the entity in following manner:

1. Add a reference to inject the default persistence context:

```
@PersistenceContext
EntityManager em;
```

2. In the onMessage method, we retrieve the object from the message and persist it. As the object is already an instance of exhibition, we didn't have to cast it, but let's do it for clarity and to print a message to the console:

```
ObjectMessage om = (ObjectMessage) message;

try {
    Exhibition ex = (Exhibition) om.getObject();

    // Print the object received to the console
StringBuilder msg = new StringBuilder();
        msg.append(ex.getMovie().getId())
        .append(", ")
```

```
                         .append(ex.getRoom().getId())
                         .append(", ")
                         .append(ex.getDate())
                         .append(", ")
                         .append(ex.getHour());

                    logger.info(msg.toString());

                em.persist(ex);

         } catch (JMSException e) {
             e.printStackTrace();
         }
```

3. Save the file; now go to the **Servers** tab and release the changes to the server by clicking on **Publish**.

If everything went OK, you should see messages similar to the following in the **Console** tab, along with the normal output from the server:

```
5, 1, Tue Jan 01 00:00:00 BRST 2013, 1400
5, 1, Tue Jan 01 00:00:00 BRST 2013, 1400
```

You can also check for new records in the exhibition table of the database theater_db.

This covers the common usage of JMS queues, showing how to produce and consume messages. Let's check some parameters that we can set when using WebLogic Server to deal with JMS consumers.

Configuring thread limits for MDBs

When using WebLogic's JMS system, there's a rather long list of parameters that are specific to this application server and control several aspects of our components, such as caching, security, and thread usage.

Some of these elements can be attached to a bean with annotations, some can only be declared inside a specific descriptor file, and some are available both ways. The following is a list of WebLogic-specific elements that you can apply to a bean only through a descriptor file, weblogic-ejb-jar.xml:

- dispatch-policy: This element attaches the MDB to a **work manager**, which is a way to share computational resources among WebLogic components.

- `initial-beans-in-free-pool`: This element tells the bean system how many beans should be created and put in the pool when the application is started. When WebLogic creates a message-driven bean, 16 instances are created. These can be seen in the **Consumers Current** column on the administration's queue monitoring screen.

- `max-beans-in-free-pool`: This parameter sets the limit of instances that can be held in a bean pool. The default value, 1000, is a pretty high number, if you consider that it applies to only one MDB.

- `security-role-assignment`: When you secure a bean, a role is attached to it, and this element maps the *virtual* role to the WebLogic's security layer. This topic will be explored in *Chapter 8, Adding Security*.

> For a complete list of elements declared by annotations and deployment descriptors, check the product's online documentation at http://docs.oracle.com/middleware/1212/wls/EJBPG/ejb_jar_ref.htm.

As we know beforehand that our `ExhibitionConsumer` bean isn't required to deal with heavy loads, we can set a lighter configuration to it by attaching both `initial-beans-in-free-pool` and `max-beans-in-free-pool` elements to it.

In order to accomplish this, we need to create a `weblogic-ejb-jar.xml` descriptor file inside the **Theater** project:

1. Right-click on the **Project Explorer** tab and click on **New**, then on **Other...**.

2. Type `Weblogic` in the search field, select **Oracle Weblogic EJB Module Descriptor**, and click on **Next**.

3. Navigate to the `Theater/WebContent/WEB-INF` folder and click on **Finish**.

> Some OEPE features haven't been updated to comply with the JEE 6 specification; hence a warning appears stating that the descriptor file must be placed inside an EJB Project. You can ignore this warning.

Now you can edit the file's source and add the following lines of code inside the existing `weblogic-ejb-jar` tag — remember to change it to allow the insertion of children:

```
<wls:weblogic-enterprise-bean>
  <wls:ejb-name>ExhibitionConsumer</wls:ejb-name>
  <wls:message-driven-descriptor>
    <wls:pool>
      <wls:max-beans-in-free-pool>3</wls:max-beans-in-free-pool>
```

```
    <wls:initial-beans-in-free-pool>1</wls:initial-beans-in-
      free-pool>
    </wls:pool>
  </wls:message-driven-descriptor>
</wls:weblogic-enterprise-bean>
```

> You could use the **Design** view to edit the file, but as this feature hasn't been updated yet, it will report errors that aren't actually there, so it may confuse you more than help.

Actually, there's a way to attach these two elements as annotations: we could use the `weblogic.ejbgen.MessageDriven` decorator, which is WebLogic-specific and explicitly exposes configuration elements, as opposed to `javax.ejb.MessageDriven` where we have to declare them as a list of `ActivationConfigProperty` annotations.

Our bean definition would look like something similar to the following code:

```
@weblogic.ejbgen.MessageDriven (
        ejbName = "ExhibitionConsumer",
        destinationJndiName = "jms.tickets.exhibition",
        destinationType = "javax.jms.Queue",
        initialBeansInFreePool = "1",
        maxBeansInFreePool = "3")
```

Thing is, as it happens with the **EJB Module Descriptor** wizard, the wizard associated with **EJBGen**—WebLogic's proprietary extension to EJB—doesn't acknowledge that we can create a bean inside a web project. That's because the **EJBGen module** is still bounded to *EJB Version 2.1*, so we can't use this feature in our projects.

The Store-and-Forward client feature

Since Version 9.2, Weblogic Server has this neat feature called the Store-and-Forward (SAF) client, which enables a JMS remote client to keep messages locally whenever a connection problem occurs with the server. When the connection is re-established, the messages are delivered.

From a developer's viewpoint, this behavior is *almost* transparent—our code will complete the procedure without any errors, as if the message were actually delivered to its destination queue. This is a great feature to use when network outages are frequent, or even when you only have a specific time window to communicate with the server—instead of dealing with all the batching details from inside your code, you just delegate this responsibility to the JMS transport.

Also, the changes you have to apply to your code in order to enable the SAF client are pretty simple. The following is a typical set of parameters that we must declare in order to acquire a server connection and use a JMS queue:

```
Context.INITIAL_CONTEXT_FACTORY=weblogic.jndi.WLInitialContextFactory
Context.SECURITY_PRINCIPAL=weblogic
Context.SECURITY_CREDENTIALS=welcome1
Context.PROVIDER_URL=t3://localhost:7001

QUEUE_CONNECTION_FACTORY=jms/yourQueueConnectionFactory
QUEUE_NAME=jms/yourQueue
```

> The preceding lines aren't the actual code, just key/value pairs showing parameters that are usually declared (or read from a properties file) to open a remote connection and acquire a queue.

To enable the JMS SAF client, we basically use the same set of parameters by dropping one and changing the other three:

```
Context.INITIAL_CONTEXT_FACTORY=
                    weblogic.jms.safclient.jndi.InitialContextFactoryImpl
Context.SECURITY_CREDENTIALS=packt
Context.PROVIDER_URL=file:/opt/packt/etc/SAFClient.xml

QUEUE_CONNECTION_FACTORY=jms/yourQueueConnectionFactory
QUEUE_NAME=jms/yourQueue
```

The following is a description of the changes:

- The PROVIDER_URL parameter must point to a configuration file generated by a command-line utility, ClientSAFGenerate. We're going to set up this file just after this block.

- The INITIAL_CONTEXT_FACTORY parameter must point to a class named weblogic.jms.safclient.jndi.InitialContextFactoryImpl that knows how to parse the file provided by Context.PROVIDER_URL.

- The SECURITY_PRINCIPAL parameter declares the username necessary to establish a connection to the server. When using the SAF client, though, this information is inside the XML file referred by PROVIDER_URL, so we don't need to use it when acquiring the server connection.

- The SECURITY_CREDENTIALS parameter usually holds the user's password that will open the connection. When using the SAF client, this credential is also put inside the XML file, but we still need this entry — it will hold a password key that the engine must use to decrypt the password inside the configuration file.

We don't need to change anything else in the code other than these set of parameters, so the portion of code that deals with acquiring a handle to the JMS queue and posts a message to it remains unchanged.

> When using the SAF client, there's one caveat that you must be aware of: the messages you post will always reach the local repository first, and then they will be delivered to the appropriate server. By default, the SAF client holds the message for *20 seconds* before trying to send it to the server.
>
> So, if your client isn't designed to stay in memory, for instance, listening to a TCP port for incoming messages, you must tweak this configuration to avoid having all messages kept at the local store. We will see how to do it shortly.

One final observation: the SAF client doesn't participate in **distributed transactions** (XA). If your design has this kind of requirement, you can either use the SAF client knowing that it runs local transactions (it doesn't influence any XA transactions that may be in course) or not use it at all.

The following is the sequence of steps we must execute in order to enable the SAF client:

1. Create the configuration file that points to the queue(s) we want to use.
2. Encrypt the connection password.
3. Edit the configuration file and add the encrypted password.
4. Add a reference to the SAF client in our code.

Let's do it.

Creating the configuration file

Almost all the information that the SAF client needs to connect to a server is located inside a configuration file created by the ClientSAFGenerate utility. Here's how we create it:

1. Open a terminal or a command prompt, and run the domain configuration script, setDomainEnv.sh (on Windows, setDomainEnv.cmd), to set up the environment—you can find it inside the bin folder of your domain:

```
$ cd $DOMAIN_HOME/tickets/bin
$ source ./setDomainEnv.sh
```

2. Now, go to /config/jms inside the domain—WebLogic Server creates one file for each JMS system module that you declare and saves them inside the subfolder of your domain:

```
$ cd ../config/jms
$ ls -w1
jmsmodule-tickets-jms.xml
```

3. Issue the following command to create the configuration file, adjusting the parameters according to your installation (check whether the output folder exists before running the command):

```
$ java weblogic.jms.extensions.ClientSAFGenerate
          -url t3://localhost:7001
          -username weblogic
          -moduleFile jmsmodule-tickets-jms.xml
          -outputFile /opt/packt/etc/SAFClient.xml
```

> If you need to map more than one JMS module, use the same command but add a -existingClientFile parameter pointing to the already created configuration file to append the new values, and keep everything else as is.

Leave the terminal open, we will use it again later. The utility doesn't connect to the server to gather information, as the URL and username parameters could imply— they are used to create the appropriate entries in the configuration file—so take extra care when typing them.

If everything went well, the /opt/packt/etc/SAFClient.xml file has been created with a reference to our destination queue and information about the connection:

```
<saf-imported-destinations name="jmsmodule-tickets">
  <saf-queue name="ExhibitionQueue">
    <remote-jndi-name>jms.tickets.exhibition</remote-jndi-name>
    <local-jndi-name>jms.tickets.exhibition</local-jndi-name>
  </saf-queue>
  <saf-remote-context>RemoteContext0</saf-remote-context>
</saf-imported-destinations>
<saf-remote-context name="RemoteContext0">
  <saf-login-context>
    <loginURL>t3://localhost:7001</loginURL>
    <username>weblogic</username>
  </saf-login-context>
</saf-remote-context>
</weblogic-client-jms>
```

> If you're using a cluster, you may want to set the `loginURL` entry to address all your WebLogic servers — for instance, `t3://node1:7001,node2:7011`, and so on. If the first node is down for some reason, the client tries to reach the next one and then the next, until a connection is established.

Encrypting the connection password

We must encrypt the connection password inside the configuration file, but the utility that generates it doesn't accept a password parameter, so we must create it using another application:

1. At the same terminal opened in the previous section, run this command:

    ```
    java -Dweblogic.management.allowPasswordEcho=true
         weblogic.jms.extensions.ClientSAFEncrypt
    ```

2. It will ask you to enter **Password Key** — this is a password that we will pass to the SAF client so it can decrypt the connection password. Enter a value — we will use `packt` — and hit *Enter*.

3. Now, in the **Password** prompt, enter the user's actual password — `welcome1` if you're following the book standard — and hit *Enter*.

4. The encrypted password will be shown; copy it so we can place the whole tag inside the configuration file:

    ```
    <password-encrypted>{Algorithm}AES/CBC/PKCS5Padding{Salt}
    OMDCZlaTWng={IV}KCcjtoVJqxYeQXvmKukpmg=={Data}
    Sm1TYOAlERODdHKHqKvGwaNU/YZuJXIhn/THV9+yel8=</password-encrypted>
    ```

5. You can encrypt other passwords or type `quit` to exit the utility. As we have just one value, go ahead and finish it.

Adjusting the configuration file

There are three things we must add to the configuration file, `SAFClient.xml`, so open it with a text editor and proceed with the following changes:

1. Paste the whole `password-encrypted` generated tag just below the `username` tag:

    ```
    <saf-remote-context name="RemoteContext0">
      <saf-login-context>
        <loginURL>t3://localhost:7001</loginURL>
        <username>weblogic</username>
    ```

```
<password-encrypted>{Algorithm} ... </password-encrypted>
  </saf-login-context>
</saf-remote-context>
```

2. As we adopted one of the default WebLogic's JMS connection factory, we need to add its declaration to the configuration file, just before the `saf-imported-destinations` tag:

```
<connection-factory name="wls.default">
  <jndi-name>weblogic.jms.ConnectionFactory</jndi-name>
  <transaction-params>
    <xa-connection-factory-enabled>false
        </xa-connection-factory-enabled>
  </transaction-params>
</connection-factory>
```

> When you create your own JMS connection factories, they exist inside a JMS module, as you may remember. As the `ClientSAFGenerate` utility maps a JMS module, you won't have to execute this extra step to add a JMS connection factory to the configuration file.

3. As our remote client has a very short lifespan, we must change SAF's posting delay to `0`, so as soon as a message is sent from our code, it will try to deliver the message to the server. To do it, add this block of tags after the `connection-factory` block we just inserted:

```
<saf-agent>
 <default-retry-delay-base>0</default-retry-delay-base>
</saf-agent>
```

4. Save and close the file.

We just have to change a few lines of code of our `Enqueue` class to be able to use the SAF client feature.

Adjusting the code

As said earlier, we need to change three connection parameters: `provider_url`, the user password, A.K.A `security credentials`, and the JNDI connection factory. The following are the current relevant lines of code:

```
static final String WLS_ADDRESS =
          "t3://localhost:7001";
static final String WLS_CTX_FACTORY =
```

```
             "weblogic.jndi.WLInitialContextFactory";

   env.put(Context.SECURITY_CREDENTIALS, "welcome1");
```

They must be changed to something similar to the following code:

```
// Points to the configuration file
static final String WLS_ADDRESS =
             "file:/opt/packt/etc/SAFClient.xml";

// Must have this exact value - it's the SAF Context Factory
static final String WLS_CTX_FACTORY =
             "weblogic.jms.safclient.jndi.InitialContextFactoryImpl";

// The password you use to encrypt the login password
env.put(Context.SECURITY_CREDENTIALS, "packt");
```

Also, we can comment the line that attaches a user to the context, as this information is already in the configuration file:

```
// env.put(Context.SECURITY_PRINCIPAL, "weblogic");
```

> If you want, you can leave the line as it is, but remember that this information is not considered. The SAF client expects to find a username tag in the configuration file, and an exception will be thrown if this condition isn't satisfied.

We now have to add the **SAF T3 client** library to the project's classpath:

1. Open the **Project Properties** window for the project **RemoteClient**.
2. Click on **Java Build Path** present in the list to the left.
3. Click on the **Libraries** tab, then on **Add External JARs...**.
4. Navigate to the server library folder, the same folder where you found the `wlthint3client.jar` library, select and click on `wlsaft3client.jar`, and then click on **Enter**.
5. Click on **OK** in the **Project Properties** window.

And we're good to go.

Testing the SAF client

This is the easiest part, just run the remote client a couple of times!

When the application is started, you will see a group of messages in the console stating that the SAF client has been initialized:

```
<Thu Dec 13 12:05:56 BRST 2012> <Info> <Store> <WL-280008> <Opening
the persistent file store "SAFSTORE0V" for recovery: directory=/
opt/packt/etc/stores/default requestedWritePolicy="Direct-Write"
fileLockingEnabled=true driver="NIO".>
<Thu Dec 13 12:05:57 BRST 2012> <Info> <Store> <WL-280009>
<The persistent file store "SAFSTORE0V" (91256ed7-83b7-
4b9d-a9c5-61831fe5bb74) has been opened: blockSize=512
actualWritePolicy="Direct-Write(single-handle-buffered)"
explicitIOEnforced=false records=11.>
<Thu Dec 13 12:05:58 BRST 2012> <Info> <Messaging> <WL-282003> <The
messaging kernel ClientSAFAgent0 will use up to 318,155,434 bytes of
memory before paging begins.>
<Thu Dec 13 12:05:58 BRST 2012> <Info> <Messaging> <WL-282001>
<The messaging kernel ClientSAFAgent0 is beginning recovery of its
persistent state.>
<Thu Dec 13 12:05:58 BRST 2012> <Info> <Messaging> <WL-282002> <The
messaging kernel ClientSAFAgent0 has recovered 0 persistent messages.>
<Thu Dec 13 12:05:58 BRST 2012> <Info> <Messaging> <WL-282003> <The
messaging kernel ClientSAFAgent0 will use up to 318,155,434 bytes of
memory before paging begins.>
```

Then, after a few seconds, another message will be printed stating that the client acquired a connection to the server:

```
Agent "ClientSAFAgent0" got connected to RemoteContext0 while
processing messages for ExhibitionQueue
```

To test the feature, you can stop WebLogic Server and post a few messages, then start it and run the remote client one more time. When you do this, the client will print recurrent error messages, but that's fine. Notice that one of the console messages prints the number of JMS messages being held by the SAF client:

```
<WL-282002> <The messaging kernel ClientSAFAgent0 has recovered 4
persistent messages.>
```

Web resources

The following are few web resources that you can refer to:

- Overview of standalone clients
  - `http://docs.oracle.com/middleware/1212/wls/SACLT/basics.htm`

- WebLogic JMS Thin Client
  - `http://docs.oracle.com/middleware/1212/wls/SACLT/wlthint3client.htm`

- WebLogic Server MBean reference
  - `http://docs.oracle.com/middleware/1212/wls/WLMBR/index.html`

- Understanding WebLogic JMS
  - `http://docs.oracle.com/middleware/1212/wls/JMSPG/fund.htm`

- JMS 1.1 specification
  - `http://www.oracle.com/technetwork/java/docs-136352.html`

- API reference: package `weblogic.jms.extensions`
  - `http://docs.oracle.com/middleware/1212/wls/WLAPI/weblogic/jms/extensions/package-summary.html`

- Programming standalone clients for Oracle WebLogic Server
  - `http://docs.oracle.com/middleware/1212/wls/SACLT/index.html`

- Reliably sending messages using the JMS SAF Client
  - `http://docs.oracle.com/middleware/1212/wls/SACLT/saf_client.htm`

- Weblogic EJBGen reference
  - `http://docs.oracle.com/middleware/1212/wls/EJBPG/ejbgen.htm`

- Using batching with message-driven beans
  - `http://docs.oracle.com/middleware/1212/wls/WLMDB/batching.htm`

Summary

At this point, you have knowledge of several client libraries that you can attach to your remote code when dealing with WebLogic, the concepts that involve creation and usage of JMS resources and how to actually create these components, post, and consume messages to a JMS queue, and the possibilities that the SAF client enables when you need to make a remote client more resilient to unexpected events such as network outages.

In the next chapter, we will explore some of the security-related features WebLogic Server gives us, such as using an LDAP server as a repository for user provisioning, authentication, and authorization.

8
Adding Security

Security is one of the most important aspects of any application, so we dedicated an entire chapter to this topic; even so, it would be presumptuous to say that this chapter covers all details regarding the subject; instead, the approach will be to bring some of the most common situations of security on Java EE and describe how to implement them through Oracle WebLogic features.

We will explore the security concerns associated with the EJB and Web containers of Java EE. In this context, you can specify the security constraints basically in two ways:

- **Declarative**: Through the use of descriptors, annotations, and XML files
- **Programmatic**: Hardcoded in an application component or Java class

It's also important to clarify some terminology and define what and how some of these terms will be used through this chapter. The most important ones are:

- **Authentication**: Authentication is a word that derives from the word *genuine* or *real* in Greek, according to Wikipedia. In the Java EE platform, it's the act to prove that a specific user is who he claims to be through the use of passwords, tokens, or certificates, according to what was specified as an **authentication method** for this server or container.

- **Authorization**: Authorization is very different from authentication because although you have proved who you are (through authentication), you may not have permission to do what you intend on the system and your action will mostly be denied, or not authorized.

- **Subjects and principals**: After a successful authentication process, the authorized user will receive an identity that is basically defined as a set of principals, which can be bound to other users or groups in the system. This set is a formal definition of a **subject** and will be stored and re-used every time the container needs to check the user identity and its permissions.

Other important terms used by security are **data integrity**, **auditing**, **quality of service**, and **confidentiality**. Also, some may define authentication and authorization as **access control** rules, and that most of the security constraints to protect data can be achieved through **cryptography**, **hashing**, and other advanced techniques.

Most of these concepts are implemented and can be applied using standard Java APIs and some specifics can depend on proprietary implementation of the Java EE container. The Java platform provides APIs for access control through the **Java Authentication and Authorization Service (JAAS)** and cryptography through the **Java Cryptography Extension (JCE)**. These two APIs will be used in this chapter to implement the security requirements for our application.

These concepts are discussed in much more detail in the Java EE Tutorial's *Security* chapter and the *Java Authentication and Authorization Service* reference guide; both links can be found in the *Web resources* section of this chapter.

Exploring Java SE and Java EE security

In Java, we have distinct security frameworks for Java SE and Java EE. Java SE uses policy files and JAAS, but Java EE offers declarative security through deployment descriptors such as web.xml, ejb-jar.xml; annotations; and transport security through **HTTP Basic/Form authentication**, **SSL**, **SAML**, and others.

A key difference between both security frameworks is that, by default, the Java SE security framework doesn't propagate security context across different JVMs. This concept is almost a native requirement for secure Java EE applications, which needs to propagate security contexts, principals, and subjects across several layers, applications, or even physical machines (clusters) in order to provide high availability and failover for security concepts such as authentication or authorization.

In order to minimize such problems, the **Java Authentication Service Provider Interface for Containers (JASPIC)** specification extended the JAAS model, implementing message authentication mechanisms that can be integrated into containers or runtimes. However, keep in mind that the applications still have to use some proprietary descriptors or libraries to perform more complex security tasks, and this varies for each application server.

WebLogic security

Oracle WebLogic supports and fully implements both Java SE and EE security models using JDK APIs such as JASPIC, JAAS, JSSE, or JCE for remote and even internal authentication. So, if the client is an EJB, a servlet, or an applet, the same mechanisms will be used to authenticate and authorize its execution.

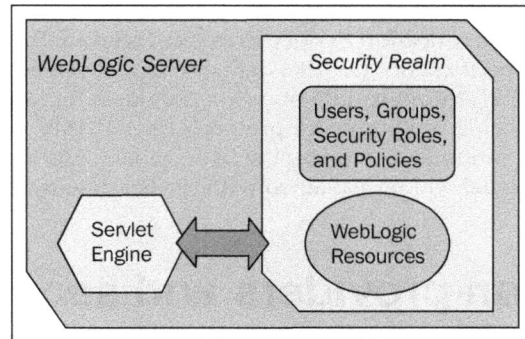

The authentication can be performed through these models:

- **Username/Password**: The most traditional model, which requires a user ID and password to authorize and provide access to a protected resource. It can be enhanced to use a certificate (SSL) or HTTPS to provide transport-level security.

- **Certificate**: During HTTPS/SSL requests, the client can verify whether the digital certificate is authentic and if the **Secure Socket Layer** (**SSL**) connection was established. WebLogic also supports two-way SSL authentication through a specific authentication provider (provided both client and server present a valid certificate).

- **Digest**: This is a very sophisticated method to authenticate and prevent replay attacks. When the client sends a request to the server, this model will return a **token** or challenge to inform the client it supports that mechanism. Then, the client must generate a hash that usually is a complement of password, **nonce** (an arbitrary number that can be used only one time), and timestamp. The server also stores a small cache of used passwords, so older requests are rejected since the hash will not match or would be already used by a successful authentication.

- **Perimeter**: Perimeter authentication relies on external systems or agents exchanging tokens with a WebLogic domain's **Identity Assertion**. Common examples of such a mechanism are **Simple and Protected GSS-API Negotiation Mechanism** (**SPNEGO**), **Security Assertion Markup Language** (**SAML**), or even **Virtual Private Networks** (**VPNs**). These authentication methods are much more complex and out of the scope of this book.

> The **Java Authentication Service Provider Interface for Containers**
> (**JASPIC**) specification (JSR 196) defines a model or a **Service Provider**
> **Interface** (**SPI**) through authentication providers for Java EE application
> servers, which is applicable for protocols (SOAP, JMS, and HTTP) and
> processing runtimes, extending the JAAS model. The authentication
> provider model will be explained with further details in the next section.

Authentication providers and security realms

Authentication can be performed using the methods described in the previous
section, and we can even combine them; for instance, using a digital certificate to
establish an SSL connection and passing a valid username/password credential
through it. An authentication provider can be configured based on these types:

- An embedded LDAP server – this is the default WebLogic authentication
  provider
- An external LDAP server – this supports any LDAP v2/v3 server, including
  some proprietary implementations
- An external database system (DBMS) – this supports any database system
  already supported as a WebLogic JDBC data source
- A simple text file – this is not recommended for a production environment

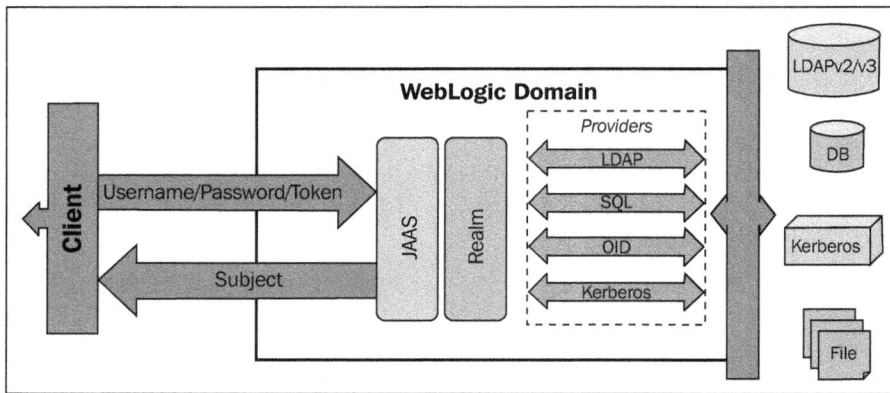

As already mentioned, WebLogic follows the **JAAS** security model and as a result
of a successful authentication on any of these providers, the return will be a **Subject**
with the appropriate principals according to what is set on the user profile in the
data store (an LDAP or database server, for instance).

Authentication providers have a special and very important attribute named `Control Flag`. WebLogic uses this attribute in case it has multiple authentication providers, which loads permissions from different stores (so it can check if, for example, a user exists in all providers and give it the appropriate identity and permissions). Another common scenario is when we have multiple stores and they can act as redundant options. So WebLogic will attempt to load the permissions using the default provider and then, if it's not available, move to the second on the list. The possible values for this attribute are:

- `REQUIRED`: This value is always called, irrespective of the authentication passing or failing; the authentication process will continue down the list of providers.
- `REQUISITE`: The authentication must pass this provider, irrespective of the authentication passing or failing; the next providers will be executed, but they can fail if this one succeeds.
- `SUFFICIENT`: This value is not always required, but if it succeeds, other providers will not be executed. If it fails, authentication will continue down the list of providers.
- `OPTIONAL`: The user can fail on this provider without further implications. However, if all providers are set to `OPTIONAL`, at least one of the providers must succeed.

WebLogic can have multiple **security realms**; however, you can have only one realm active for a domain. In the security realm, you can specify multiple authentication providers, and at least one of them must be active. Each authentication provider holds a LoginModule that performs the actual authentication, and if the realm uses multiple authentication providers, they will store multiple principals for the same subject.

It's also possible to implement **custom authentication** providers (with `LoginModule`) when the default authentication providers of WebLogic don't meet the security requirements of your application. Such custom providers are out of the scope of this book, but a link with an example can be found in the *Web resources* section of this chapter.

Using an external LDAP server

In our use case, we are going to set up an authentication provider to integrate with an external **OpenLDAP** server. This will provide the key functionalities we need to secure our web application and illustrate with an example a common requirement of most enterprise applications.

> The setup of the OpenLDAP server and the initial load of users were performed in *Chapter 2, Setting Up the Environment*. You can check using some of the command-line utilities provided by OpenLDAP. For example, ldapsearch -H ldap://localhost:389 -D "cn=Manager,dc=example,dc=com" -W.

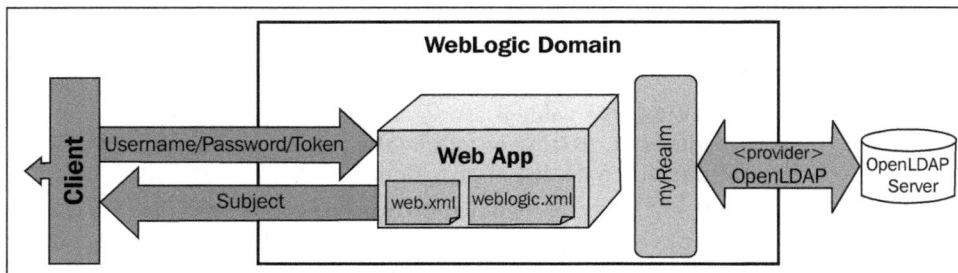

As the preceding diagram shows, our web application client will send username and password information, which will be processed by the WebLogic server against the active security realm; named **myrealm** by default. As we are using a standard Java EE web application, the **web.xml** deployment descriptor will be used to specify a few things:

- **Security constraint**: What should be protected and by which role
- **Login configuration**: Which authentication method will be utilized and (depending on the type) where the user will be redirected to authenticate in case of any errors
- **Security roles**: Declares the available roles for this application

But, as said, we still have to declare some security settings that are specific to the WebLogic implementation, and here is where a proprietary deployment descriptor comes in handy to connect the missing dots. We have to use the weblogic.xml file to specify the **security roles assignments**. It is a match between a security role declared in the web.xml file and the principals (users, groups, or other roles) available in the WebLogic Server security realm.

Besides the settings on the application, it's necessary to set up the authentication provider and adjust the proper connection settings to the OpenLDAP server. The configuration will be executed through the WebLogic console, but you can also use WLST scripts.

Configuring an OpenLDAP authentication provider

To configure a new authentication provider, follow these steps:

1. Open the **Security Realms** page from the navigation tree and click on **myrealm**.

2. In the **Settings** section for the **myrealm** page, click on the **Providers** tab. The page will list **DefaultAuthenticator** and **DefaultIdentityAsserter**, which are used by WebLogic natively in a standard installation.

	DefaultAuthenticator	WebLogic Authentication Provider
	DefaultIdentityAsserter	WebLogic Identity Assertion provider

New   Delete   Reorder

3. Click on **New**, and on the creation page use these values:
   - **Name**: StoreLDAP
   - **Type**: OpenLDAPAuthenticator

4. Click on **OK**.

5. You should see the **Authentication Providers** page again with the provider we've just created. Click on **StoreLDAP**.

	DefaultAuthenticator	WebLogic Authentication Provider
	DefaultIdentityAsserter	WebLogic Identity Assertion provider
	StoreLDAP	Provider that performs LDAP authentication

New   Delete   Reorder

6. In the **Settings** section for the **StoreLDAP** page, change the control flag value to **SUFFICIENT**. Click on **Save** after this change.

7. Still under the **Configuration** tab, select the **Provider Specific** tab.

8. If you kept the default values specified in *Chapter 2*, *Setting Up the Application*, to set up an OpenLDAP server, apply the following settings. Otherwise, replace them with your specified values. Also, if a property is not specifically changed, you can keep the default value.
   - **Host**: localhost
   - **Port**: 389
   - **Principal**: cn=Manager,dc=example,dc=com

- ○ **Credential**: welcome1
- ○ **Confirm Credential**: welcome1
- ○ **User Base DN**: ou=people, dc=example, dc=com
- ○ **User From Name Filter**: (&(cn=%u)(objectclass=inetOrgPerson))
- ○ **User Object Class**: inetOrgPerson
- ○ **Group Base DN**: ou=groups, dc=example, dc=com
- ○ **Group From Name Filter**: (&(cn=%g)(objectclass=groupOfNames))
- ○ **Static Group Object Class**: groupOfNames
- ○ **Static Member DN Attribute**: member
- ○ **Static Group DN from Member DN Filter**: (&(member=%M)(objectclass=groupOfNames))

Click on **Save** after you finish.

9. After saving, WebLogic will warn you that a restart is required for the changes to take effect. So restart your server.

> All security-related changes on WebLogic will have one of two possible characteristics: they're effective immediately, meaning you don't need to activate a change session, or may require a restart to take effect. Keep this in mind when doing any security changes, since this can help you troubleshoot your modifications. In general, the WebLogic console will mark items that require a restart with a yellow triangle and display a message after saving, indicating the need for a restart.

10. Now browse back to the **Providers** list page (**Security Realms | myrealm | Providers**). Click on the **Reorder** button. The order presented on this page is the exact order that authentication providers will be executed in at runtime. Change the ordering so that **StoreLDAP** is the first on the list. Click on **OK** when done.

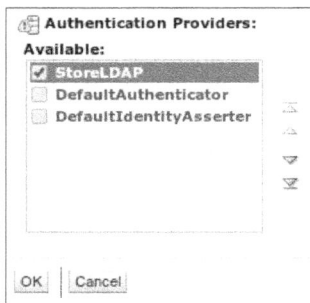

This concludes the OpenLDAP configuration on WebLogic. Now we have to do a few changes on the application's configuration in order to specify the security constraints, roles, and groups.

To double check if your configuration is correct, go to the **myrealm** page again and click on the **Users & Groups** tab. You should see a list of the available users on all providers, as well as a list of all groups. You can identify the source of each entry by checking the **Provider** column.

Consider using the **Record** feature of the WebLogic console in order to save the configuration steps in a WLST script. This can be re-used when setting up other environments and also save some time if you need to reinstall your own.

To start recording, click on the **Record** button on the WebLogic console toolbar at the top of the console.

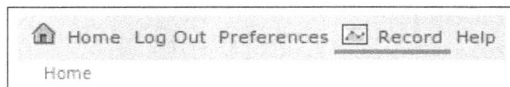

Click on the button again to finish the recording, and WebLogic will display a message with the name and directory of the WLST script just recorded.

Securing the web application

Now that the authentication provider is set, we have to modify the deployment descriptors of the application to set the security properties and create a login page to let users authenticate themselves.

Modifying the web.xml descriptor file

We first need to set the security constraints by editing web.xml:

1. Open the WEB-INF/web.xml file of the **Store** web application.
2. Paste the following lines right after the servlet-mapping tag:

```
<security-constraint>
  <web-resource-collection>
    <web-resource-name>protected</web-resource-name>
    <url-pattern>/reservation.jsf</url-pattern>
  </web-resource-collection>
  <auth-constraint>
    <role-name>User</role-name>
  </auth-constraint>
</security-constraint>
<login-config>
  <auth-method>FORM</auth-method>
  <form-login-config>
    <form-login-page>/login.jsf</form-login-page>
    <form-error-page>/login.jsf</form-error-page>
```

```
    </form-login-config>
  </login-config>
  <security-role>
    <role-name>User</role-name>
  </security-role>
```

Here's the explanation of each block of the preceding code snippet:

- The `security-constraint` tag defines where security will be applied. You need to declare a combination of HTTP methods, URL patterns, and role constraints. In our use case, we're protecting a specific URL pattern, `/reservation.jsf`, and telling that only users with an abstract role named `User` can proceed as per the `auth-constraint` tag. We say *abstract* because these roles don't actually have to match the roles at WebLogic Server. This match will be done later with another deployment descriptor, `weblogic.xml`.

> By default, all HTTP methods will be blocked since we're not explicitly specifying which ones must be secured. Here is how the same security constraint would look like protecting only POST and GET requests:
>
> ```
> <url-pattern>/reservation.jsf</url-pattern>
> <http-method>POST</http-method>
> <http-method>GET</http-method>
> ```

- The `login-config` tag plays a very important role in the security process: it defines the authentication method, which in our case is FORM, and then points to where the the login and error pages will be available. These are the pages that users will be redirected to, to perform a login or in case any error occurs. It can also enforce SSL access by specifying the `transport-guarantee` tag, which can be NONE, CONFIDENTIAL, or INTEGRAL.

> A brief description of the available authentication methods is as follows:
>
> **BASIC**: HTTP 1.0/1.1 basic authentication; a browser-controlled pop up will be displayed to input username/password.
>
> **FORM**: A custom web page will be used to perform the authentication through an HTML `<form>`. JSF or JSP pages are valid examples.
>
> **CLIENT-CERT**: Uses digital certificates to authenticate.
>
> **DIGEST**: An advanced version of the HTTP basic authentication that leverages MD5 hashing.

- The `security-role` tag is used to declare all abstract roles available for the web application. If we have some specific resources (constraints) for administrators and customers (groups) of the application, these rules must be declared here. Remember that you can name it anything you want, but later the value will be used in the `weblogic.xml` descriptor to match the abstract role and a real group in the LDAP server.

Modifying the weblogic.xml descriptor file

After setting `web.xml`, we need to tie the roles declared there and the principals in the WebLogic server, or, to be more precise, on the OpenLDAP server.

1. Open the `WEB-INF/weblogic.xml` file of the **Store** web application.

2. Add the following lines right after the `</wls:library-ref>` tag:

```
<wls:security-role-assignment>
    <wls:role-name>User</wls:role-name>
    <wls:externally-defined />
</wls:security-role-assignment>
```

3. Save the file.

Simple, isn't it? Now let's see the explanation in detail.

The `security-role-assignment` tag can be used to define the match of abstract roles of a web application and the actual roles of WebLogic authentication providers. So a valid example could be as follows:

```
<wls:security-role-assignment>
    <wls:role-name>User</wls:role-name>
    <wls:principal-name>weblogic</wls:principal-name>
</wls:security-role-assignment
```

This would actually let only the WebLogic user (yes, the WebLogic administrator user; not recommended but vastly used) be a valid one for the application. Alternatively, you could point to any group available to the WebLogic security realm. Instead, with the externally defined element, we are pointing to a role that we need to set up from the WebLogic console. This extra step will provide a lot of flexibility since any group, users, or conditions that this role may map are defined from the WebLogic console, allowing us to modify the mapping without having to redeploy the application.

Creating and mapping a global role

In order to accomplish this step, follow these instructions:

1. Log in to the WebLogic console and click on **Security Realms** and then **myrealm**.

2. Click on the **Roles and Policies** tab.

3. On the **Roles** table, expand the **Global Roles** tree and click on **Roles**.

Settings for myrealm

| Configuration | Users and Groups | **Roles and Policies** | Credential Mappings | Providers | Migration |

Realm Roles   Realm Policies

Use this table to view, add, modify or remove global or scoped security roles for this security realm. Global roles ar
Global Roles node. Scoped roles are listed in the Name column under the individual resources that they secure.

Notes:

- This table does not list scoped roles for JNDI resources or Work Context resources. To see these s
  JNDI node or Work Context object.
- If you imported security roles for EJBs or Web applications from deployment descriptors using the
  activate changes to access the roles.

Roles

Edit Role

Name ⌃	Resource Type
⊞ Deployments	
⊞ Domain	
⊟ Global Roles	
⊞ Roles	
⊞ JCOM	

4. On the **Global Roles** page, click on **New**.

5. Use the following information:
   - **Name**: User
   - **Provider Name**: XACMLRoleMapper

   When done, click on **OK**.

6. Then, back on the **Global Roles** page, click on the **User** role we just created.

7. At the **Edit Global Role** page, you will see a couple of buttons that can let you compose a set of rules that defines what this role actually maps. Click on **Add Conditions**.

Role Conditions :

| Add Conditions | Combine | Uncombine | Move Up | Move Down | Remove | Negate |

No Policy Specified

| Add Conditions | Combine | Uncombine | Move Up | Move Down | Remove | Negate |

8. On the predicate list, select **Group** and click on **Next**.

9. In the **Group Argument Name** textbox, type in `users`. This is the name of the group from the OpenLDAP server that holds all common users of our application. Click on **Add** and then on **Finish**.

10. The **Role Conditions** section should look as shown in the following screenshot. If everything looks good, click on **Save**.

Role Conditions :

| Add Conditions | Combine | Uncombine | Move Up | Move Down | Remove | Negate |

☐ **Group : users**

| Add Conditions | Combine | Uncombine | Move Up | Move Down | Remove | Negate |

Save

> It's also possible to create scoped roles instead of global ones. They will
> be tied specifically to an instance of a WebLogic resource, such as EJB
> methods or a specific branch of the JNDI tree. In case of conflicts, the
> role of the narrower scope will override the broader.

Creating the login form

The only missing part now is the login form. In the `web.xml` file, we've specified a login and an error page that will be used by the web container to perform the authentication process or redirect in case of errors. A managed bean will be created to perform the actual authentication using the `HttpServlet` API and the `login()` method, available in Java EE 6. Let's get started.

1. In the **Store** project, create a new JSF file named `login.xhtml`. The page will contain a web form with username and password fields with the proper binding to the managed bean.

2. Replace the body content of the page with the following code:

```
<ui:define name="content">
<center>
  <p:panel header="Login" style="width: 450px;" >
   <h:form>
     <p:growl id="messages" autoUpdate="true"
      closable="true" />
     <p:panelGrid columns="2"
                   rendered="#{request.userPrincipal ==
                   null}"
                   style="border:0">
       <p:outputLabel value="E-mail" for="email" />
       <p:inputText id="email" required="true"
                    value="#{login.customer.email}"
                    label="E-mail" />
       <p:outputLabel value="Password" for="password" />
       <p:password id="password" required="true"
                    value="#{login.customer.password}"
                    label="Password" />
       <p:commandButton value="Login"
                        action="#{login.login}" />
    </p:panelGrid>

  <h:panelGrid rendered="#{request.userPrincipal !=
   null}">
    <h:outputLabel value="#{request.userPrincipal}" />
    <p:commandButton value="Logout"
                     action="#{login.logout}" />
  </h:panelGrid>
 </h:form>
</p:panel>
</center>
</ui:define>
```

> Note the usage of the `rendered` property in some components. This allows the page to dynamically decide if the component must be rendered or not.

3. Create a new package named `com.packt.store.security`.

4. Still in the security package, create a class and name it `LoginBean`.

5. Copy and paste the following code. The code defines the `login()` and `logout()` methods referenced by the `login.xhtml` page that will be used to process the authentication.

```
@Named
@RequestScoped
public class LoginBean implements Serializable {
  private static final long serialVersionUID = 1L;

  private Customer customer = new Customer();

  private FacesContext context =
                      FacesContext.getCurrentInstance();
  private HttpServletRequest request =
  (HttpServletRequest)
                      context.getExternalContext().getRequest();

  public String login() {
    try {
      request.login(customer.getEmail(), customer.getPassword());
      addSuccessMessage(String.format("Welcome back,
      %s!", customer.getEmail()));

      return "index?faces-redirect=true";
    } catch (ServletException ex) {
      ex.printStackTrace();
      addErrorMessage("Wrong username or password,
      please try again.");
      return "login?faces-redirect=true";
    }
  }

  public String logout() throws ServletException {
    request.logout();
    addSuccessMessage("You have logged out.");

    return "login?faces-redirect=true";
  }
  ... // getters and setters
```

> Note that `addSuccessMessage()` and `addErrorMessage()` are just helper methods to create `FacesMessages` in the current `FacesContext`. Their code is part of the code bundle.

6. Save and close your open files and deploy the application. Your login form should look similar to the following screenshot:

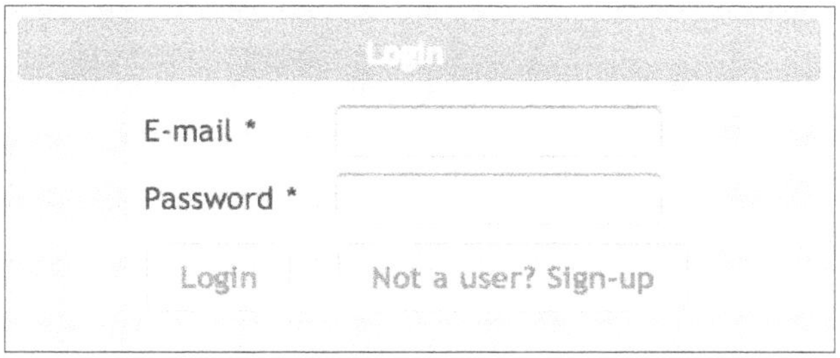

Testing the login procedure

As we have explicitly protected only the `reservation.jsf` page in `web.xml`, to test you just need to hit the URL `http://localhost:7001/store/reservation.jsf`. You will be redirected to the **Login** page and requested to input credentials of a valid user from LDAP. If any error occurs, you will be kept at the **Login** page and an error message will be displayed. On a successful login, the application will load the main page and you should see the principal name on the page header.

In order to check the security details of your web application using the WebLogic console, follow these steps:

1. In the left-hand side menu, click on **Deployments** and then select the **Store** application from the deployment list.

2. The **Settings** section for the **Store** application page will be displayed. Click on the **Security** tab. This tab shows various security settings but some of them are not available because this application is using the **DD Only** security model. So only the **Roles**, **Policies**, and **Security** settings declared by the web.xml and weblogic.xml deployment descriptors are valid, but this page is a good place to check if what has been set in the descriptors looks good.

3. To see a list of protected URLs in the web application, click on the **URL Patterns** tab and then **Policies**. But remember that you can't modify it from the console; that can be done only through deployment descriptors.

Settings for Store

| Overview | Deployment Plan | Configuration | **Security** | Targets | Control | Testing | Monitoring | Notes |

| Application Scope | **URL Patterns** | JASPIC |

| Roles | **Policies** |

This page summarizes the security policies that secure specific URL patterns in this stand-alone web application.

If you are using the DD Only or Custom Roles security model for this deployment, then you cannot use the Adminis

▷ **Customize this table**

Stand-Alone Web Application URL Patterns

URL Pattern 〰	Provider Name
/reservation.jsf	XACMLAuthorizer

Protecting WebLogic resources

WebLogic lets you define a set of rules to protect resources on the application or even on the server. These rules are called **security policies** and they leverage the WebLogic security framework using Authentication Providers, Users, and Groups. This model is extended by introducing conditions, which not only defines who can access a resource but also when; sometimes, a combination of other conditions can be used to let the user access the resources. Some examples of these policies are as follows:

- A user in a specific group can call any EJB method during business hours
- Only users with the admin role can edit JDBC resources
- Only one specific user can post messages on a JMS queue

And to illustrate one of these examples, we're going to implement a **sign-up user case** for the **Store** application using a protected JMS queue in the next section.

Here is a comprehensive list of the main resources that can be secured in WebLogic:

- **Administrative resources** – Secures actions such as checking server logs, unlocking users, and uploading deployment files
- **Application resources** – Secures any valid Java EE module such as web applications and EJB modules
- **EJB resources** – Secures any specific bean or business method

- **Java Database Connectivity (JDBC) resources** – A set of administrative actions that can manage a JDBC pool

- **Java Messaging Service (JMS) Resources** – Actions such as send or receive a message

- **Java Naming and Directory Interface (JNDI) Resources** – Protect actions such as lookups or modifications on the JNDI tree

- **JMX Resources** – Useful to secure JMX connections from clients that need to monitor or manage WebLogic

- **Server Resources** – Secure actions that change server status

- **URL Resources** – The traditional URL pattern protection specified in deployment descriptors

- **Web Service Resources** – Protects web services and its operations from web service clients

The security policies can be created using the WebLogic console, usually by clicking on the **Security** tab of the specified resource. As an alternative, these policies can be created through WLST scripts or even using **eXtensible Access Control Markup Language (XACML)** documents. For more details on these advanced features, check the WebLogic documentation.

Signing up a user and OpenLDAP

The following diagram illustrates the overall security solution we're going to set up and use in this chapter:

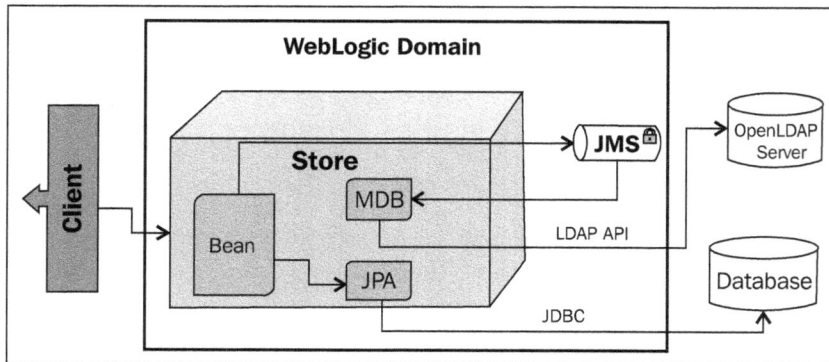

Now let's walk through the actions involved.

1. A visitor clicks on the **Sign-up** button and submits the form to create a new user.

2. A JavaBean will interact with the JPA object and create the entry on the database.

3. Concurrently, this JavaBean publishes a message on the JMS queue, possibly a protected WebLogic resource.

4. Later, a **Message Driven Bean** (**MDB**) listening on the queue reads the message and submits the user information to the LDAP server, completing the user-provisioning process.

Due to the protected resource feature of the WebLogic server, this JMS queue can't be used by other systems, unless of course they match the security policy that will be created to protect the JMS queue.

Now that the solution is clear, let's do the implementation starting with the database step.

Creating a user on the database

We are going to implement a sign-up process so new users can register themselves on the system.

1. Add a **Sign-up** button to the login form we've just created in the previous section of this chapter. Right after the **Login** button in login.xhtml, add the following:

```
<p:commandButton id="signupBtn"
                 value="Not a user? Sign-up"
                 onclick="signupDlg.show()"
                 immediate="true" />
```

2. Then, after the `</center>` tag, create a PrimeFaces `dialog` box. This dialog will be displayed when a user clicks on the **Sign-up** button. Copy and paste the following code:

```
<p:dialog id="dialog" header="User Sign-up" widgetVar="signupDlg">
    <h:form>
        <h:panelGrid columns="2" cellpadding="5">
            <h:outputLabel for="name" value="Name" />
                <p:inputText id="name" required="true" value="#{login.
customer.name}"
                    label="name" />
```

```
<h:outputLabel for="email" value="E-mail" />
<p:inputText id="email" required="true"
            value="#{loginBean.customer.email}"
            label="email" />

<h:outputLabel for="password"
                value="Password:" />
<h:inputSecret id="password" required="true"
            value="#{loginBean.customer.password}"
            label="password" />

<f:facet name="footer">
    <p:commandButton id="signup" value="Sign-up"
        oncomplete="handleSignup(xhr, status, args)"
        actionListener="#{loginBean.signup}" />
</f:facet>
</h:panelGrid>
</h:form>
</p:dialog>
```

3. As you might have noticed, we're using some JavaScript calls in order to show or hide the dialog. In order to do that, copy and paste the following code right after the `</p:dialog>` tag:

```
<script type="text/javascript">
    function handleSignup(xhr, status, args) {
        if (args.validationFailed) {
            jQuery('#dialog').effect("shake", {
                times : 2
                }, 100);
        } else {
            signupDlg.hide();
            jQuery('#signupBtn').fadeOut();
        }
    }
</script>
```

4. We need a service bean that will interact with the JPA and perform transaction handling. Create a new class named `CustomerBean` under the package `com.packt.store.customer` and extend our `AbstractRepository` class in order to have standard **CRUD** operations.

```
@Stateless
public class CustomerBean extends AbstractRepository<Customer> {

    @PersistenceContext(unitName = "StoreBO")
```

```
private EntityManager em;

@Override
protected EntityManager getEntityManager() {
      // TODO Auto-generated method stub
      return em;
}
      }
```

5. Open the `LoginBean.java` class and let's inject the EJB created earlier as a new class attribute.

```
@EJB
CustomerBean customerBean;
```

6. Before creating the `signup()` method, we need to hash the password we're going to store on the database and on the LDAP server later. So let's create a `generatePassword()` method that will do just that using `SHA-1`, a common hashing algorithm.

```
private String generatePassword(String text) {
  MessageDigest md;
  try {
    md = MessageDigest.getInstance("SHA-1");
    byte[] hash = new byte[40];
    md.update(text.getBytes("iso-8859-1"), 0,
                        text.length());
    hash = md.digest();
    return "{SHA}" + DatatypeConverter.printBase64Binary(hash));
  } catch (NoSuchAlgorithmException e) {
    e.printStackTrace();
  } catch (UnsupportedEncodingException e) {
    e.printStackTrace();
  }

  return text;
}
```

The `javax.xml.bind.DatatypeConverter` class is part of the JDK since Version 1.6.

7. Still at `LoginBean`, create a `signup()` method. Here we're going to save the new user to the database using the data received from the sign-up form.

```
public void signup() {
  try {
    customer
    .setPassword(
      generatePassword(
        customer.getPassword()));

    customerBean
    .create(getCustomer());

    addSuccessMessage("Thanks! Your user should be ready in a few
seconds. Try to log in using the form below.");
  } catch (Exception ex) {
    ex.printStackTrace();
    addErrorMessage("An unknown error occurred and your user was
not created.");
  }
}
```

> We're not doing any specific validations on the data received at this step because it was done through the Bean Validations framework at the entity level.

8. Save all files and deploy.

9. Access the URL `http://localhost:7001/store/login.jsf`. Your **Login** form should look similar to the following screenshot. When you click on the **Sign-up** button, a dialog will be displayed and you can type your e-mail and password to create a new user on the system.

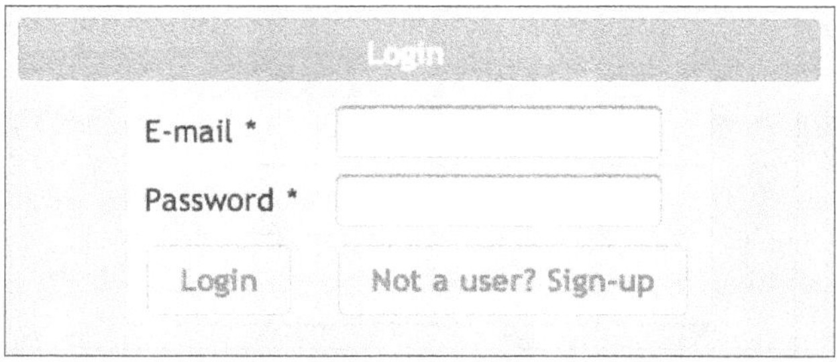

The system is inserting a new entry in the `customer` table of the `store_db` schema of MySQL. But there are still some flaws in this implementation that we're going to fix in the next sections. For example, this new entry in the `customer` table is not even being considered for authentication since we're using only the **OpenLDAP** authentication provider and the information is only at the database for now. Let's complete the solution by publishing the message to the JMS queue and getting the data into the LDAP server asynchronously.

Publishing a customer to a JMS queue

In this section, we are going to publish a JMS message with a `Customer` object that will be used to create a new customer on the system.

1. Create a JMS queue using the WebLogic console or WLST. This was already explained in *Chapter 7, Remote Access with JMS*. Name it `UserQueue` and use `jms.userQueue` as the JNDI name.

2. Open the class `LoginBean` and add two Java EE resources as class properties; we're going to inject a JMS queue and a connection factory through the CDI mechanism.

   ```
   @Resource(mappedName = "jms.userQueue")
   private Queue queue;

   @Resource(mappedName = "weblogic.jms.XAConnectionFactory")
   private ConnectionFactory connectionFactory;
   ```

3. Still at `LoginBean`, create a new method called `publish()` as shown in the following code snippet:

   ```
   public void publish(Customer entity) throws JMSException {
     Connection con = null;
     Session session = null;
     MessageProducer sender = null;

     try {
       con = connectionFactory.createConnection();
       session = con.createSession(true,
                      Session.AUTO_ACKNOWLEDGE);
       sender = session.createProducer(queue);
       Message message =
                  session.createObjectMessage(entity);
   ```

```
                sender.send(message);
                        session.commit();

        } catch (JMSException e) {
            // do something with exception
            e.printStackTrace();
            throw e;
        } finally {
            // Doesn't support try-with-resources yet...
            try { sender.close(); } catch (Exception e) { }
            try { session.close(); } catch (Exception e) { }
            try { con.close(); } catch (Exception e) { }
        }
    }
}
```

At this point, the method is ready to publish the `ObjectMessage` message containing a `Customer` object to the JMS queue. But we still need to protect the queue so that unauthorized users are unable to publish messages to it. This is a common requirement in enterprise environments where multiple applications share the same instance of the application server but have security concerns.

Security policies for the JMS queue

WebLogic provides **security policies** that are very useful for such situations, allowing a fine control of specific functions on a resource. For example, we're going to create a policy that allows only users from **admin** group to publish a message on a JMS queue.

1. Open the WebLogic administration console, expand **Services**, then **Messaging**, and click on **JMS Modules**.
2. Click on the **JMSModule-Tickets** module and select **jms.userQueue**.
3. In **Settings** for **jms.userQueue page**, click on the **Security** tab and then **Policies**.
4. Here you can compose conditions and the method you want to protect. The methods available are according to the resource. In this case, a JMS queue has three methods: **browse**, **send**, and **receive**.

Settings for jms.userQueue

Configuration **Security** Monitoring Subdeployment Notes

Roles **Policies**

Save

Use this page to manage the security policy of your Uniform Distributed Queue resource.

Providers

These are the authorization providers an administrator can select from.

Authorization Providers: XACMLAuthorizer ↕

Methods

This is the list of available methods for this Uniform Distributed Queue resource.

Methods: ALL ↕

Policy Conditions

These conditions determine the access control to your Uniform Distributed Queue resource.

Add Conditions Combine Uncombine Move Up Move Down Remove Negate

No Policy Specified

5. For this example, select the method **send** on the **Methods** combobox. It's important to select the method before adding the conditions, since you can have different conditions for each method.

6. Click on **Add Conditions** and select the predicate **Group**. Click on **Next**.

7. Type admin as group name, click on **Add**, and then **Finish**.

8. At this point, you should be redirected to the settings page for the queue and can double-check the changes. If everything looks good, click on **Save**. The following screenshot shows what the policy should look like:

Methods

This is the list of available methods for this Uniform Distributed Queue resource.

Methods: send ↕

Policy Conditions

These conditions determine the access control to your Uniform Distributed Queue resource.

Add Conditions Combine Uncombine Move Up Move Down Remove Negate

Group : admin

Add Conditions Combine Uncombine Move Up Move Down Remove Negate

Save

Overridden Policy

Group : everyone

Updating the login bean

Now update the `LoginBean` class to use our new method and publish the customer to the JMS queue. First, let's check if the security policy we've created really works.

1. Open the `LoginBean` file, comment the call to the `create()` method of `CustomerService`, and add a call to the `publish()` method we've created.

```
public void signup() {
    //service.create(getCustomer());

    publish(getCustomer());
    addSuccessMessage("Thanks! Your user should be ready in a few
seconds. Try to login in the form below.");
```

2. Save all files and deploy the application.

3. Open `http://localhost:7001/store/login.jsf` and click on **Not a User? Sign-up**, fill the form, and click on **Sign-up** to submit.

4. Now take a look at the server logs from Eclipse or at the domain's log directory. Click on the **Console** tab if you're using Eclipse. You should see the following messages, confirming that the **send** action is **denied** to anonymous users:

```
...
Caused by: weblogic.jms.common.JMSSecurityException: Access
denied to resource: type=<jms>, application=myModule,
destinationType=queue, resource=jms/userQueue, action=send
```

```
   at weblogic.jms.dispatcher.Request.handleThrowable(Request.
java:87)
   at weblogic.jms.dispatcher.Request.getResult(Request.java:52)
   at weblogic.jms.frontend.FEProducer.
sendRetryDestination(FEProducer.java:1072)
   at weblogic.jms.frontend.FEProducer.send(FEProducer.java:1426)
   at weblogic.jms.frontend.FEProducer.invoke(FEProducer.java:1487)
   at weblogic.messaging.dispatcher.Request.wrappedFiniteStateMachi
ne(Request.java:961)
   ...
```

5. So let's configure the necessary resources to authenticate using the application administration user before publishing the message. Start by creating two new entries in the web.xml descriptor with the administrator user that is already in the preloaded users of our OpenLDAP configuration.

```xml
<env-entry>
   <env-entry-name>signupUser</env-entry-name>
    <env-entry-type>java.lang.String</env-entry-type>
    <env-entry-value>superuser@example.com</env-entry-
     value>
 </env-entry>

 <env-entry>
    <env-entry-name>signupPassword</env-entry-name>
    <env-entry-type>java.lang.String</env-entry-type>
    <env-entry-value>welcome1</env-entry-value>
 </env-entry>
```

6. Now add these resources to the LoginBean class attributes.

```java
@Resource(lookup = "signupUser")
private String signupUser;

@Resource(lookup = "signupPassword")
private String signupPassword;
```

7. Then add the authentication needed to publish the message. Replace the signup() method body with the following code:

```java
public void signup() {
  try {
    getCustomer()
       .setPassword(
           generatePassword(getCustomer().getPassword()));
    request.login(signupUser, signupPassword);

    publish(getCustomer());
```

```
        customerBean.create(getCustomer());
        addSuccessMessage("Thanks! Your user should be ready in a few
seconds. Try to log in using the form below.");
    } catch (Exception ex) {
        ex.printStackTrace();
        addErrorMessage("An unknown error occurred and your user was
not created.");
    } finally {
      try {
        request.logout();
      } catch (ServletException e) {
        e.printStackTrace();
      }
    }
  }
}
```

> **A very important note**
> Do not use hardcoded passwords in the production code.

8. Access the **Login** page and the **Sign-Up** form again. Try to create a new user, but this time no errors should occur since superuser@example.com is a valid user that is a member of the admin group, which complies with the security policy.

9. To complete the test, check the messages on jms.userQueue from the **Monitoring** tab, according to the instructions in the *Queuing messages* section in *Chapter 7, Remote Access with JMS*.

> Note that it's not possible to check the content of the message since it's an ObjectMessage message, not a text message. In order words, there is a serialized Customer object in the message and the WebLogic console can't read this object from the **Monitoring** tab. Still, you can see the message size and count to confirm that there is a valid message in there.

From the JMS queue to the LDAP server

Even though the first part of the sign-up process is done, we need to consume the message from the JMS queue and send it to the LDAP server. The consumption part is pretty straightforward, as already presented in the *Consuming messages with an MDB* section in *Chapter 7, Remote Access with JMS*.

Creating the LDAP client

To build the LDAP client, we're going to rely on a few APIs provided by the JDK used to access **Java Naming and Directory Interface (JNDI)** objects, since both models define the same mechanisms of having hierarchical namespaces and objects trees, which can also hold attributes and other related information.

> For more details about this API, check *JNDI as an LDAP API* in the *Web resources* section of this chapter.

Let's create the LDAP client using the JNDI APIs that will be used from the MDB we will create in the next section.

1. Create a new class named `LDAPClient`.

    ```
    @Named
    public class LDAPClient {
    ```

2. Create some properties in the class that we're going to need in order to connect to the LDAP server. This is the same information you have already used to set up the authentication provider in the WebLogic server.

    ```
    final static String ldapServerName = "localhost";
    final static String rootdn =
                        "cn=Manager,dc=example,dc=com";
    // This is not recommended for production code
    final static String rootpass = "welcome1";
    final static String rootContext =
                        "ou=people,dc=example,dc=com";

    // create getters/setters for this property
    private DirContext ldapCtx;
    ```

    > Note that the values of `ldapServerName` and `rootpass` could be externalized into the `web.xml` file just like we already did in many other areas of the application. This is just an example.

3. Create a method named `connect()` that consumes the properties we've defined.

    ```
    public DirContext connect() throws NamingException {
        Properties env = new Properties();

        env.put(Context.INITIAL_CONTEXT_FACTORY,
                    "com.sun.jndi.ldap.LdapCtxFactory");
    ```

```
    // Consider SSL
    env.put(Context.PROVIDER_URL, "ldap://" +
            ldapServerName + "/" + rootContext);
    env.put(Context.SECURITY_AUTHENTICATION, "simple");
    env.put(Context.SECURITY_PRINCIPAL, rootdn);
    env.put(Context.SECURITY_CREDENTIALS, rootpass);

    setLdapCtx(new InitialDirContext(env));
    return getLdapCtx();
}
```

4. Now let's add more two methods: `createUser()` and `prepareUserObject()`. These will create the object that will be sent to the LDAP server, extracting data from the `customer` entity.

```
public void createUser(Customer customer) throws NamingException {

  Attributes attrs = prepareUserObject(customer);
  try {
    getLdapCtx().bind("cn=" + customer.getEmail(), null, attrs);
    log.info("User created in LDAP server");
  } catch (NameAlreadyBoundException nae) {
    log.severe("User already exists on LDAP server.");
    throw nae;
  } catch (NamingException ex) {
    log.severe("Unknown error occurred with LDAP communication");
    throw ex;
  }
}

private Attributes prepareUserObject(Customer customer) {
  Attributes attrs = new BasicAttributes(true);
  Attribute basicObjectClass = new BasicAttribute("objectclass");

  basicObjectClass.add("inetOrgPerson");
  basicObjectClass.add("organizationalPerson");
  basicObjectClass.add("person");
  basicObjectClass.add("top");

  attrs.put(basicObjectClass);
  attrs.put("sn", customer.getEmail());
  attrs.put("userPassword", customer.getPassword());

  return attrs;
}
```

This creates the LDAP client and exposes it to be injected on any other class through CDI, since it's using the @Named annotation. Also note that the createUser() method already connects to LDAP and creates the user.

Creating the MDB

The final part is to create a message bean (MDB) that will consume the message from the queue jms.userQueue and, through the LDAP client, send the customer to the LDAP server.

1. Create a new **Message Driven Bean (MDB)** named UserConsumer in the com.packt.store.security package with the following properties:

   ```
   ...
   @MessageDriven(name = "UserConsumer",
     activationConfig = {
     @ActivationConfigProperty(
         propertyName = "destinationType",
         propertyValue = "javax.jms.Queue")},
         mappedName = "jms.userQueue")
   public class UserConsumer implements MessageListener {
     Logger log = Logger
                 .getLogger(UserConsumer
                             .class.getCanonicalName());
     ...
   ```

2. Inject the LDAPClient and MessageDrivenContext classes as follows:

   ```
   @Inject
   private LDAPClient client;

   @Resource
   private MessageDrivenContext mdc;
   ```

3. In the onMessage() method, we will use the LDAP client class to redirect the user to the LDAP server:

   ```
   public void onMessage(Message inMessage) {
     ObjectMessage msg = null;

     try {
         if (inMessage instanceof ObjectMessage) {
             msg = (ObjectMessage) inMessage;
             Customer customer = (Customer) msg.getObject();
               client.createUser(customer);
         } else {
             log.severe("Message of wrong type: "
                 + inMessage.getClass().getName());
   ```

```
        }
    } catch (JMSException je) {
        mdc.setRollbackOnly();
        je.printStackTrace();
    } catch (NamingException e) {
        mdc.setRollbackOnly();
        e.printStackTrace();
    }
}
```

4. Save all files and deploy the application.

The usage of MessageDrivenContext is important to avoid message loss. Through this context class, we can call setRollbackOnly() and return the message to the queue and retry in case of errors. Through the WebLogic console, you can set a number of rules such as number of retries, delays, and even an **error destination** queue that the container will use to send messages that exceed the number of retries. All these settings are under the **Delivery Failure** tab of the queue.

Settings for UserQueue

| **Configuration** | Monitoring | Control | Security | Subdeployment | Notes |

| General | Thresholds and Quotas | Overrides | Logging | **Delivery Failure** |

Save

Use this page to define message delivery failure parameters, like specifying redelivery limits, sele for undeliverable or expired messages.

Redelivery Delay Override: 100

Redelivery Limit: 3

Expiration Policy: Discard ⬍

Expiration Logging Format:

Error Destination: None ⬍

Save

Testing LDAP user provisioning

Now, to test the whole solution, perform the sign-up process again to submit a new message to the queue, but this time it will also be consumed and published to the LDAP server. So, right after the success message, you can try to log in to the application with you brand new user.

Remember that you are actually performing authentication against the LDAP server and have the same information duplicated into the database. This can lead to complex maintenance, but at the same time, you now also have a way to set up authentication on the database if needed or in a failure scenario, where your LDAP server might be down and you set up the database as a second option to authenticate using what you've learned so far in this chapter.

Completing the application

The application has a login form as part of the `top.xhtml` file in the `templates` folder, under `WEB-INF`. So use all you have learned in this chapter in order to make that form functional. It's just a matter of wiring up the components with the classes, as we have done in `login.xhtml`.

Web resources

The following is a list of resources:

- JNDI as an LDAP API
    - http://docs.oracle.com/javase/tutorial/jndi/ldap/jndi.html
- WebLogic security realms
    - http://docs.oracle.com/middleware/1212/wls/SCOVR/realm_chap.htm
- The Java Authentication and Authorization Service (JAAS) reference guide
    - http://docs.oracle.com/javase/7/docs/technotes/guides/security/jaas/JAASRefGuide.html
- Java EE 6 Tutorial – security mechanisms
    - http://docs.oracle.com/javaee/6/tutorial/doc/bnbwy.html
- LDAP v3 models
    - http://docs.oracle.com/javase/jndi/tutorial/ldap/models/v3.html

- Security fundamentals
  - ○ `http://docs.oracle.com/middleware/1212/wls/SCOVR/concepts.htm`
- Understanding WebLogic resources security
  - ○ `http://docs.oracle.com/middleware/1212/wls/ROLES/understdg.htm`
- SHA-1
  - ○ `http://en.wikipedia.org/wiki/SHA-1`
- Authentication
  - ○ `http://en.wikipedia.org/wiki/Authentication`

Summary

In this chapter you've learned some of the basics of the Java security model with step-by-step instructions on how to configure it on the WebLogic server. We have also created an authentication mechanism on the example application, including a sign-up process for user self-registration. There were examples of how to protect Java EE resources and the configuration of an LDAP client.

This chapter presented a solution for user provisioning in multiple stores leveraging Java EE 6 native APIs and WebLogic services that can help protect and manage security in many ways. It illustrates the usage of the WebLogic security framework and how to protect Java EE applications and resources.

In the next chapter we're going to explore web technologies such as Servlets, Java Server, Faces, and Web Sockets.

9
Servlets, Composite Components, and WebSockets

Our applications are fully operational by now, using several WebLogic Server features that enable us to expose and consume web services and JMS queues, secure access to these components, read and write business entities from and to a database, and so on.

In this chapter, we're going to check out some features of the presentation layer:

- A very interesting JavaServer Faces resource that helps us improve development speed and composite components and provides a way to create and use reusable pieces of code by applying templates
- Deprecated and new features of Servlet 3.0, such as asynchronous request processing and dynamic component creation
- How to open a direct communication channel between server and browser with **WebSockets**, a new feature introduced by Version 12.1.2

Overview of JavaServer Faces

The main presentation layer technology of Java EE 6 is JSF Version 2.0, which brings a couple of interesting enhancements to the previous version (Version 1.2), such as:

- Composite components that give us the flexibility to combine existing UI tags with new ones
- Native Ajax support

JSF 2.0 has been around for quite some time now, so its features have matured before getting packaged into WebLogic Server 12c, giving us a solid and reliable implementation.

WebLogic Server has native support for JSF Version 2.1 and JSTL 1.2, and these libraries are enabled by default when a server is started; it is available from the classpath. Although the framework is enabled by default, we added it as a **shared library** to our environment in *Chapter 2, Setting Up the Environment*, mostly to show how it is done. Also, this approach avoids having to deal with server configuration when you need to update the library, so use it whenever possible.

> The JavaServer Faces implementation that is shipped with Oracle WebLogic Server 12c is the **Oracle Mojarra JavaServer Faces 2.0**, which is the reference implementation of this technology.

There's also a shared library for JSF 1.2, in case you're porting an application that needs an older version. You just need to deploy this package that can be found inside `/wlserver/common/deployable-libraries` of your WebLogic Server installation.

Using composite components

With this JavaServer Faces feature, we can create (compose) new reusable components, which are pretty much like small templates, by aggregating other existing JSF components, such as the ones available in PrimeFaces that gives us a flexible and quick way to group these in a common reusable unit that can even be shared as a component library between projects for speeding up development. Basically, this is all done through the **Facelets** framework, so any XHTML page can be converted into a composite component having input data, validators, converters, or even listeners.

A composite component is declared by using a few extra markup tags. Here's an example of a simple one:

```
<!DOCTYPE html PUBLIC "-//W3C//DTD XHTML 1.0 Transitional//EN"
"http://www.w3.org/TR/xhtml1/DTD/xhtml1-transitional.dtd">
<html xmlns="http://www.w3.org/1999/xhtml"
      xmlns:h="http://java.sun.com/jsf/html"
      xmlns:composite="http://java.sun.com/jsf/composite">
<head />

<body>
  <composite:interface>
      <composite:attribute name="label" required="true"/>
```

```
        <composite:attribute name="value" required="false"/>
    </composite:interface>

    <composite:implementation>
        <span>
        <h:outputText value="#{cc.attrs.label}" style="font-weight:bold"
/>:  <h:inputText value="#{cc.attrs.value}" style="width: 300px;"
/>
        </span>
    </composite:implementation>
</body>
</html>
```

The preceding declaration creates a component that expects two parameters, `label` and `value`, and the output is a `span` tag with an input field preceded by its label. We just need to declare the attributes expected by the component and their names in the `interface` tag and the necessary code in the `implementation` tag.

The name you give the file, which must have the `.xhtml` suffix, will be used as the tag name; `field` is going to be the name of the sample composite. Also, you have to save it inside a specific folder named `components` that is inside the `resources` folder of your project:

This way, it will be recognized automatically by both Eclipse (at development time) and WebLogic Server (at runtime).

> You can create subfolders inside the `components` folder; the entire directory tree is checked in order to discover the composite tags.

To use the new tag, we have to add a namespace declaration on our JSF page that reflects the folder structure created inside the `component` folder. For your example, the namespace would be `http://java.sun.com/jsf/composite/components` as the tag is at the base folder. Here's the complete declaration using the `index.xhtml` file of the **Store** project as its basis:

```
<html lang="en" xmlns="http://www.w3.org/1999/xhtml"
  xmlns:f="http://java.sun.com/jsf/core"
  xmlns:h="http://java.sun.com/jsf/html"
  xmlns:ui="http://java.sun.com/jsf/facelets"
  xmlns:p="http://primefaces.org/ui"
  xmlns:store="http://java.sun.com/jsf/composite/components">
```

You can use any prefix you want to reference your folder, so we will use `store` — the name of the project — as the alias.

With this declaration in place, go ahead and use the tag in your page. Here's what it would look like:

```
<store:field label="Some field" value="initial value"/>
```

After declaring the namespace in the page, OEPE recognizes it as a component folder and enables code completion for tag names declared in it. Unfortunately, there's no autocomplete for the tags' attributes yet.

That's it; just publish the project and open the page to check the result. This is a pretty easy feature to use, giving developers a very quick and easy way to create complex user interface components.

In another practical example, we have created a `<store:login/>` component that's capable of rendering the login form on the `login.xhtml` page and on the `top.xhtml` page. So, in cases where the same components and logic are used in different places, you have an opportunity to leverage the composite components. This example is part of the code bundle of this chapter.

> There are other features associated with composites, such as listeners, actions, and validators that you can explore — take a look at `http://javaserverfaces.java.net/nonav/docs/2.0/pdldocs/facelets/composite/tld-summary.html` to learn more about them.

Learning a few Servlet tricks

The Java Servlet API has been around for quite some time now — more than 10 years — and is the base for technologies such as JavaServer Pages, the one we just discussed. WebLogic Server 12c comes with Java Servlet 3.0, defined by JSR 315, which brings some new features, such as:

- Annotations support, which helps in easing the task of configuring components
- Dynamic component registration
- Asynchronous request processing

Deprecated features

Up to Version 11*g*, WebLogic Server provides proprietary annotations to ease the development of servlets — instead of declaring them in the web.xml configuration file, you could use the @WLServlet, @WLFilter, and @WLInitParam decorations to set the attributes of servlets and filters. These annotations are deprecated in Version 12c as we can now use the standard ones defined by Servlet 3.0 specifications: @WebServlet, @WebFilter, and @InitParam, respectively.

> If you're migrating @WLServlet to @WebServlet decorations, remember that the runAs attribute of the former is now implemented through a specific annotation, javax.security.RunAs. All other attributes have direct correspondence.

The weblogic.servlet.http.AbstractAsyncServlet class that enables us to write asynchronous servlets is also deprecated and you're supposed to use the asyncSupported attribute of @WebServlet, which defines a servlet, or the corresponding entry at the web.xml deployment descriptor async-supported (which is part of the servlet tag).

Identifying the default name of a servlet

As happens with most annotations, there's always the possibility of overriding the parameters via the deployment descriptor, specifically the web.xml file, when dealing with a web application. This is also true for the @WebServlet decoration, but there's a detail about it that can pass unnoticed and give us a headache down the road.

What happens is that the `name` parameter of the annotation `@WebServlet` is optional. You can declare your servlet as shown in the following code (without a name entry):

```
package com.packt.servlets;

import javax.servlet.annotation.WebInitParam;
import javax.servlet.annotation.WebServlet;

@WebServlet(
   urlPatterns = { "/StoreFront" },
   initParams = { @WebInitParam(name = "maxValue", value = "1000") }
public StoreFront {

   ...

}
```

The container will fill the `name` attribute for you and this is done by using the fully qualified class name. So, the sample servlet above will be named `com.packt.servlets.StoreFront` by WebLogic Server.

As we usually name the servlet with just the class name, `StoreFront`, when we create the deployment descriptors entry to map the servlet, most likely we will do something similar to this:

```
<servlet>
   <servlet-name>StoreFront</servlet-name>
   <servlet-class>com.packt.servlets.StoreFront</servlet-class>
   <init-param>
      <param-name>autoApproveThreshold</param-name>
      <param-value>3000</param-value>
   </init-param>
</servlet>
```

If this is the case, we will end up with two servlets available—`StoreFront` and `com.packt.servlets.StoreFront`—each with its own set of initial parameters. This can lead to unpredictable behavior.

> As a best practice, always declare a name attribute when adding decorations such as `@WebServlet` or `@WebService`, as each one uses a different algorithm to decide how to name a component.

Asynchronous request processing

As said earlier, there's a new Servlet 3.0 feature that enables us to asynchronously process a request. The following diagram shows a basic scheme of how it works:

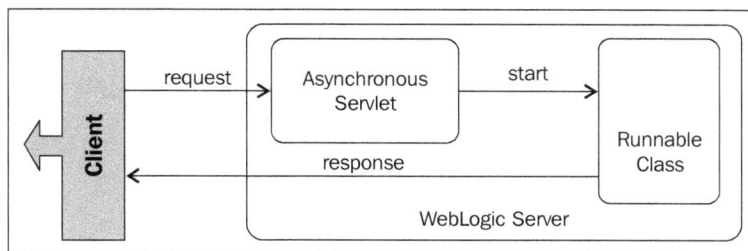

The client makes a request to the asynchronous servlet and it doesn't know a thing about the servlet's characteristic—from its point of view, it's just a regular synchronous request/response invocation. When the servlet receives the request, it must create an **asynchronous context**, which is the component that deals with the associated structure, and inform the context about which piece of software will be responsible for actually processing the request. This component does its work and produces the response that the client is waiting for.

The servlet acts as a dispatcher, setting up the necessary environment and forwarding the request to the actual processor. Here's a very simple implementation of such a servlet:

```
@WebServlet(name = "AsyncServlet",
            urlPatterns = { "/async" },
            asyncSupported = true)

public class AsyncServlet extends HttpServlet {
  @Override
  protected void service(HttpServletRequest req,
                         HttpServletResponse resp)
      throws ServletException, IOException
      {
    AsyncContext ctx = req.startAsync();
    ctx.start(new SomeBasicTask(ctx));
  }
}
```

Notice that the WebServlet annotation has an asyncSupported attribute set to true to tell the container about our intention—if we don't do so, at runtime, an IllegalStateException exception is thrown.

In the `service` method, we acquired the asynchronous context via the `startAsync` request method and then passed a `Runnable` instance to the `start` method, passing the context as a constructor parameter. Here's the general structure of this executor class:

```java
public class SomeBasicTask implements Runnable {
  private AsyncContext ctx;

  public SomeTask(AsyncContext ctx) {
    this.ctx = ctx;
  }

  @Override
  public void run() {
    // Do some long running work

    // Set up the result
    ctx.getResponse().setContentType("text/html");

    try {
      ctx.getResponse().getWriter().write("done");
    } catch (IOException ioe) { }

    // Wrap up processing
    ctx.complete();
  }
}
```

As you may have noticed, the result output is generated here, accessing the response object via the asynchronous context. You could put something into the response buffer from the servlet; but if the goal is to release its thread as soon as possible, this doesn't make sense, so try to keep the output generation in the executor class.

The single most relevant line in this class is the `ctx.complete()` call. This method tells the container that the processing is done and it can release the connection to the client. If you don't do so, the connection will be kept open indefinitely, which brings us two problems:

- The client will wait for a signal that tells that the execution will require more time for completion, basically until a timeout, bringing sluggishness into your application.

- The TCP socket will be kept open at WebLogic Server. Eventually, they will be *recycled*, but this is not an optimal scenario.

> Make sure that your execution flow always sends a call to `asyncContext.complete()` to avoid server contention and client locks.

We can also attach a listener to the asynchronous context we're dealing with and get notifications about the context's state. The list of events published by the context that can be captured by a `javax.servlet.AsyncListener` instance are as follows:

- `onStartAsync`: This event is raised when the container starts the asynchronous context.

- `onTimeout`: When the configured timeout value is reached, this event is raised. From this event you can release the client's connection or notify it about the current status of the execution.

- `onError`: When the thread throws an exception, the listener is notified through this event.

- `onComplete`: This event is raised when the execution is completed without any errors.

This listener is especially useful when we configure the context's timeout to avoid keeping the client locked for more than the usual time the request takes to get processed. When this is the case, the `onTimeout` method is called, and we can inform the client about it.

Here's the servlet updated to set a timeout limit and to deal with the corresponding event:

```
public class AsyncServlet extends HttpServlet
                          implements javax.servlet.AsyncListener {
  @Override
  protected void service(HttpServletRequest req,
                         HttpServletResponse resp)
    throws ServletException, IOException
  {
    AsyncContext ctx = req.startAsync();
    ctx.setTimeout(2000);
    ctx.addListener(this);
    ctx.start(new SomeBasicTask(ctx));
  }
  @Override
  public void onTimeout(AsyncEvent ae) throws IOException {
    // Format some response …
```

```
    // … and release the client's connection
    ae.getAsyncContext().complete();
}

// Other listener methods suppressed
}
```

> Notice that even when we send a response to the client and complete the context, the spawned thread will continue to run until its processing is complete.

A point worth mentioning is that WebLogic Server's default timeout value is 120 seconds, which is a rather large time to keep a user/client waiting for a response. This value can be overridden individually by the `setTimeout` method of `AsyncContext` or at the application level at the `weblogic.xml` deployment descriptor:

```
<wls:async-descriptor>
    <wls:timeout-secs>5</wls:timeout-secs>
</wls:async-descriptor>
```

Another parameter we can configure via `weblogic.xml` is the interval at which the asynchronous mechanism will check if a timeout situation has been reached for every context created. The element that defines this value is named `timeout-check-interval-secs`.

> The default check interval value is 30 seconds, so if you set up timeouts shorter than this, chances are the engine will not generate the `onTimeout` events.

If you set up a 10-seconds timeout and leave the default check interval, your code may end up waiting for about 30 seconds to get the `onTimeout` event or be completed before that. Here's a graphical representation of this scenario:

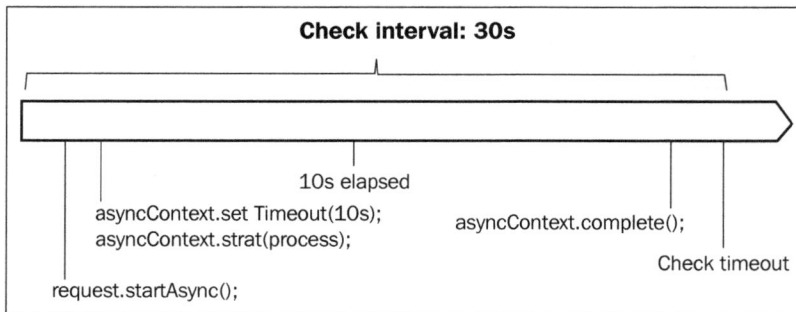

> Keep in mind that the timeout is attached to the start of the asynchronous context, not its `start()` or `dispatch()` methods. You can have an async context with no associated operation that will receive a timeout event in the same way.

If you need to control the timeout of short processes, consider adjusting the timeout check interval value to a smaller value at `weblogic.xml`:

```
<wls:async-descriptor>
    <wls:timeout-secs>5</wls:timeout-secs>
    <wls:timeout-check-interval-secs>1</wls:timeout-check-interval-
secs>
</wls:async-descriptor>
```

Creating dynamic components

Another nice new feature of Java EE 6, or more specifically Servlet 3.0, is the possibility to dynamically create and bind **servlets**, **filters**, and **listeners**. This is a somewhat advanced procedure, but it is good to know about as it can be very handy if you ever need to create a more flexible structure to load your servlets. Let's say you need to create a structure that reads servlet binding information from a data source; when a mapping has to be changed, you don't have to change the deployed application—by just restarting the deployment, the new mapping will be processed and available.

Here's a sample servlet created at the **Store** project, referencing the project's entity manager and a singleton bean of the same project to test context injection:

```
public class DynamicServlet extends HttpServlet {
  @Inject
  ControlGeneratorBean cgb;

  @PersistenceContext(unitName = "StoreBO")
  EntityManager em;

  @Override
  protected void service(HttpServletRequest req,
                         HttpServletResponse resp)
    throws ServletException, IOException {

    List<Movie> movies = em.createNamedQuery(Movie.findAll).
                                getResultList();

    for (Movie movie : movies) {
```

```
       System.out.println(movie.getName());
   }

   System.out.println("Next control # is " +
                             cgb.getNextId(2, 0, 0));
   }
}
```

Notice that the servlet doesn't have the `WebServlet` annotation; this is because if you declare it with the same name as the dynamic procedure, the annotation engine will process the class upon deployment and the dynamic registration will not be considered.

We can't register a servlet from another servlet because, at this point, the servlet context—the engine that instantiates and controls this kind of component—is already closed to changes. So, we do it using a **servlet context listener** that has its `contextInitialized` method called when the application is deployed, as shown in the following code:

```
@WebListener
public class DynamicSetupListener implements ServletContextListener {
@Override
public void contextInitialized(ServletContextEvent event) {
   ServletRegistration.Dynamic servlet =
event.getServletContext().addServlet("DynamicServlet",
       "com.packt.store.DynamicServlet");

   servlet.addMapping("/dynamic");
}
}
```

As the listener is decorated with `@WebListener`, we don't need to change any deployment descriptors; the package is scanned upon deployment and the listener is found and processed accordingly.

After publishing the project, go to the appropriate address—for the sample code, this would be `http://localhost:7001/store/dynamic`—and the list of movies will be printed at the console window.

> Even though the official documentation states that no dependency injection is done for dynamic components, the tests done using the preceding sample code showed that the annotations are processed. The statement can be found in the *Limitations* section on the *WebLogic Annotation for Web Components* page at `http://docs.oracle.com/middleware/1212/wls/WBAPP/annotateservlet.htm`.

Using WebSockets

The WebSocket protocol, defined by IETF's RFC 6455, is a TCP-based protocol that enables two-way communication between a web page running on a browser and a server; even though it uses a single socket connection, both ends of the channel can send and receive information simultaneously, thanks to the full-duplex nature of the protocol. This connection is controlled by your application's code, unlike the HTTP protocol, where the browser itself manages the connections. This control is possible by the use of W3C's WebSocket API, which declares an interface to use the protocol.

With this feature we can directly communicate with a server in real time, bringing a whole new level of possibilities and sophistication to what can be accomplished on web applications.

> To check which browser version has WebSocket support, access `http://caniuse.com/websockets` and look for the **Current** line on the table.

Let's see how to implement and test a really simple WebSocket that receives a message from a client and echoes it back.

Creating the server component

There are two ways to create a WebSocket: you can either extend the `WebSocketReader` class or implement the `WebSocketListener` interface. Either one will get you to the same point, but as `WebSocketReader` already implements this interface, you just have to override what you will actually use instead of implementing all 13 methods of the interface. So, extending `WebSocketReader` should be the preferred way to go.

Here's the complete code of a class that extends `WebSocketReader`; we just need to override the `onMessage` method to echo the received message back to the client:

```
@WebSocket(pathPatterns = {"/wsock"},
           timeout = 30,
           maxConnections = 1000,
           maxMessageSize = 4096)
public class WebSocketListener extends WebSocketAdapter {
  @Override
  public void onMessage(WebSocketConnection connection,
                        String payload) {
      try {
         connection.send(payload);
      } catch (IllegalStateException e) {
```

```
        } catch (IOException e) {
          try {
              connection.close(ClosingMessage.SC_GOING_AWAY);
          } catch (IOException ioe) { }
        }
    }
}
```

A few pointers about this code:

- The WebSocket annotation declares the basic functionality of the WebSocket:
  - The `pathPatterns` attribute declares the relative URL that will be mapped by the component and accepts several entries

  > You can set the path as a wildcard, in which case anything that matches the prefix you gave will be directed to that WebSocket, or you can create a *terminal* path that must match exactly, as we did here.

  - The `timeout` indicates for how many seconds the server should hold an idle connection before closing and releasing it

- You can limit the size of the messages received by the component by setting the `maxMessageSize` attribute. The value is expressed in bytes and only applies to incoming messages from the client; this is useful to keep the consumption of server resources in check, as the server automatically closes the offending connection when a message larger than the maximum value is received.

  > When defining the value for this parameter, remember that the WebSocket protocol has a 6-byte header when messages are sent from client to server; this can be neglected if your maximum size is set to 4 KB, but if really short messages are expected, the header's size must be taken into account.

- If an error occurs when trying to send a message to the client, the connection is closed passing `ClosingMessage.SC_GOING_AWAY` that indicates to the client that the server is deliberately closing the connection. There are other informative values defined by this interface that can be used by the client to take specific actions when being disconnected from the server.

Testing the component

To test the component we just created, we're going to use a web page that is already available that connects to a server and sends messages to it:

1. Open the URL `http://www.websocket.org/echo.html` in your browser.

2. The **Echo Test** page will be loaded and displayed. After a few seconds, a green box should be rendered just after the **Try it out** phrase, stating that your browser supports WebSocket:

Echo Test

The first section of this page will let you do an HTML5 WebSocket test against the echo server. The second section walks you through creating a WebSocket application yourself.

You can also inspect WebSocket messages using your browser.

Try it out

✓ This browser supports WebSocket.

3. Enter your WebSocket's implementation address, `ws://localhost:7001/store/wsock`, in **Location** and click on **Connect**.

4. A connection is opened and the text **CONNECTED** should be rendered inside the **Log** box.

> If you implemented a WebSocket using the `WebSocketListener` interface, make sure that your `accept` method is returning `true`.

5. You can now start sending information to the server by entering it in the **Message** field and clicking on the **Send** button.

6. As the server is echoing the message received, this is what you should see in the **Log** field:

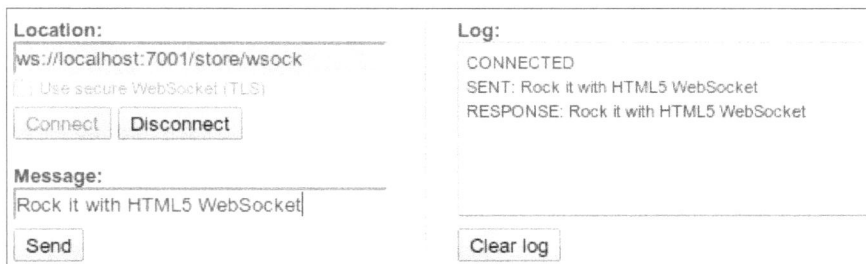

Location:
ws://localhost:7001/store/wsock
☐ Use secure WebSocket (TLS)
Connect | Disconnect

Message:
Rock it with HTML5 WebSocket

Send

Log:
CONNECTED
SENT: Rock it with HTML5 WebSocket
RESPONSE: Rock it with HTML5 WebSocket

Clear log

7. If you stop sending messages for 30 seconds, a timeout event will occur, the server will close the connection, and the browser will be notified; just wait and a **DISCONNECTED** message will be printed inside the **Log** box.

Using an encrypted connection

The WebSocket specification creates two new schemes to address a resource: ws: and wss:. We used the first one in the previous section where an unsecured connection was opened; the second one uses an encrypted channel to send and receive messages.

To use the secured connection, you must first enable HTTPS in WebLogic. Open the server's **Configuration** screen, find the **SSL Listen Port Enabled** field under the subtab **General**, enable it, change the **SSL Listen Port** to 7002, and save the configuration:

You don't need to restart the server. Just go back to the browser, adjust the port number at the **Location** field, check the box **Use secure WebSocket (TLS)**, click on **Connect**, and start sending messages to the server:

If you want to see what a JavaScript client code would look like, just scroll down on the page and check the full code of the test page in the **Creating your own test** section.

It's really easy to use WebSockets and this opens up lots of possibilities when creating **Rich Internet Applications** (**RIA**). But, keep in mind that you have a limited number of connections available at any given time, so if the projected usage of your application is high, you have to carefully design how it will use this feature.

Web resources

The following are a few web resources that you can refer to:

- Asynchronous context in Servlets
    - http://docs.oracle.com/javaee/6/api/javax/servlet/AsyncContext.html

- The `weblogic.xml` deployment descriptor elements
    - http://docs.oracle.com/middleware/1212/wls/WBAPP/weblogic_xml.htm

- JavaServer Faces technology
    - http://www.oracle.com/technetwork/java/javaee/javaserverfaces-139869.html

- Application events and event listener classes in Servlets
    - http://docs.oracle.com/middleware/1212/wls/WBAPP/app_events.htm

- Using WebSockets
    - http://docs.oracle.com/middleware/1212/wls/WLPRG/websockets_sse.htm

- The WebSocket protocol
    - http://tools.ietf.org/html/rfc6455

Summary

In this chapter, we checked out some of the resources provided by the presentation layer of WebLogic Server, exploring how to create composite components that can be reused by the application, how to dynamically instantiate servlets, some details about the way the servlet engine works, how to process requests asynchronously, and how to create and test a WebSocket component.

In the next chapter, we will see how to configure an application so it can scale up and support heavy loads. Some of the features we will explore are:

- Configuration of a WebLogic cluster to scale up applications
- Creating a singleton service
- Session Replication with Oracle Coherence (Coherence*Web)
- Using Oracle Coherence along with JPA to speed up access to entities

10
Scaling Up the Application

Most applications must eventually deal with increased workload; some will scale up by adding more memory or CPU to a server and others will scale out by adding more nodes and servers to handle the application load. Here, we're going to cover some of the basic principles to scale your application running on WebLogic Server and understand how to leverage services offered by the container among other tools and products of the WebLogic Suite, such as Coherence.

Scalability is the main theme of this chapter, but inherent in that is high availability; this is a technique to ensure that your application will keep running with an acceptable response time, even when multiple aspects may try to compromise its scalability; for instance, having a huge number of users accessing your application at a given time or simply when one of your servers fail and you need to redirect all requests to the only working node.

To start, we are going to check out the tools and services WebLogic provides to help you manage more than one server and the kinds of changes that can be applied to an application to scale it up.

Introducing the Node Manager

One of the first changes we need to do in order to scale an application is to make the environment where it runs more flexible to accommodate the necessary changes, which usually involves creating WebLogic components such as clusters, servers, and machines. In order to interact with multiple (remote) machines, it's recommended that you set up the WebLogic Node Manager process. The Node Manager is a small Java process that runs standalone and can perform basic operations on WebLogic Server instances like `start`, `stop`, and `restart`.

Until Version 12.1.1, you could have only one Node Manager running on a specific machine and all requests to start or stop Managed Server applications from different domains were sent to it. The concept is really nice, having just one component running to deal with all resources available on that machine. But things would usually get tangled and this topology proved hard to maintain; for instance, different domains are managed by different groups, each having their own patching and downtime schedule.

So, starting with Version 12.1.2, Node Managers are attached to a domain. The most notable effect of this change is that now the script to start the Node Manager is located inside the domain `$DOMAIN_HOME/bin/startNodeManager.sh` on our environment.

As the Node Manager is now part of the domain, all we have to do to enable it is fire up its start script using the following steps:

1. Open a command shell and go to the folder `$DOMAIN_HOME/bin`.
2. Run the `startNodeManager.sh` script (or `startNodeManager.cmd` in Windows) and it's done.

The script will output several items of configuration information and the most relevant is the last one, stating that our domain is mapped by it:

```
Domain name mappings:

tickets -> /opt/packt/domains/tickets
```

Defining machines

Machines represent physical computers or servers that can have multiple WebLogic instances. On every machine you want to use the Node Manager facilities, you need to start a Node Manager instance.

Machines are also important to define replication groups for HTTP sessions when using cluster and backup instances for JMS servers, singleton services, and other critical WebLogic services.

Here's a representation of a cluster that spans over two machines:

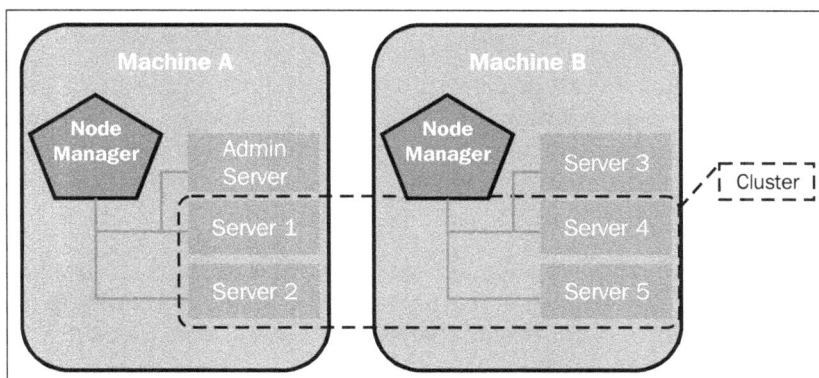

For the examples we're going to run in this book, only one physical machine is enough. In fact, it can be your own computer or laptop since the Node Manager process ensures negligible memory and CPU consumption and with 8 GB of RAM, you can easily run at least two WebLogic Managed Servers simultaneously. Let's set up our machine:

1. Open the WebLogic console at `http://localhost:7001/console`.

2. In the left menu, expand the **Environment** section and then click on **Machines**.

3. Click on the **New** button and fill the information using these values:
    ◦ **Name:** `localMachine`
    ◦ **Machine OS:** `Unix` (choose according to your Operating System)

4. Click on **Next** and on the **Node Manager properties** screen, enter these properties:
    ◦ **Type:** `Plain`
    ◦ **Listen Address:** `localhost`
    ◦ **Listen Port:** `5556`

5. Click on **Finish**.

Using Cluster and Managed Servers

For those who don't have English as their mother language, it can be surprising to discover that the word 'cluster' is actually a noun and a verb; it means a group of similar objects growing closely together (noun) and, also, congregating or being part of a group (verb). Of course, nowadays, the term is popular as computer clusters have become widespread.

Based on that, WebLogic Server cluster or clusters basically means that a group of servers will work together, running at the same time, toward some predefined architectural goals. Clusters can be created to cater to different needs of users, such as scalability, reliability, performance, load balancing, failover, and management. Note that WebLogic clusters can be defined by multiple machines and servers (Managed Servers) but they may also be seen as one single WebLogic Server for applications and clients.

Clustering is a key concept in application scalability and needs to be used in order to scale out (horizontally) by adding more machines to a system or scale up (vertically) by adding more servers or resources to the system. Today, with cloud computing, preparing your application to be scalable in both ways is mandatory and can be a successful factor in determining the number of users or requests your application can handle.

Thanks to the Java EE application server model, clustering is native to most of the Java EE and WebLogic components, for example:

- Servlets (JSF and JSP pages)
- Enterprise JavaBeans (Stateless and Stateful beans)
- **Java Message Service (JMS)** objects (queues, connection factories)
- **Java Management Extensions (JMX)** and **Remote Method Invocation (RMI)** objects
- **Java Database Connectivity (JDBC)** data sources and connections

Application developers must be aware that clustering will modify the behavior of the application at runtime and should design the application taking this into consideration. For example, accessing a file when you have only one server and one machine is something easy and simple to do with a Java EE application, but doing this on a clustered environment in a consistent manner may incur different techniques considering that you may need to access the same file or different files from different physical machines.

Also, it's a common mistake to think that by simply clustering an application, you may end up with higher performance. There are cases when applications can run slower on clustered environments due to the heavy exchange of data between nodes; this is an indication that a session is being used without proper considerations such as the size of the objects in the session, and its replication is causing a performance bottleneck.

Clustering an environment or an application requires a detailed analysis of multiple technologies, such as network topologies, sizing, security, application architecture, and so on. Take these into consideration for any real or production system. In this book, we're creating a development environment according to the demo application's needs, for example.

Creating a static cluster

Now, assuming that the machine and Node Manager configurations are in place, follow these steps to create the cluster:

1. Access the WebLogic console at `http://localhost:7001/console`.

2. In the left menu, expand the **Environment** section and then click on **Clusters**.

3. In the `Clusters` table, click on **New**, and then select **Cluster** from the pop-up menu.

4. On the **Create a New Cluster** screen, enter `ticketsCluster` in the **Name** field and leave all other values unchanged.

5. Click on **OK** to create the cluster.

6. Click the cluster name and navigate to the **Servers** tab.

7. Under the **Servers** tab click on the **Add** button.

8. In the **Add a Server to Cluster** window, click on **Create a new server and add it to this cluster** and then click on **Next**.

9. Enter the following values and then click on **Finish**:

   ○ **Server name**: ticketMS_A

   ○ **Server Listen Address**: localhost

   ○ **Server Listen Port**: 8001

10. Click on server name under the **Servers** tab and set the **Machine** drop-down to **localMachine**; notice that the **Cluster** drop-down is already set to **ticketsCluster**. Click on **Save** to conclude this step.

Settings for ticketMS_A							
Configuration	Protocols	Logging	Debug	Monitoring	Control	Deployments	Services

General	Cluster	Services	Keystores	SSL	Federation Services	Deployment	Migration

Save

Use this page to configure general features of this server such as default network communications.

View JNDI Tree

Name:	ticketMS_A
Template:	(No value specified) Change
Machine:	localMachine ▼
Cluster:	ticketsCluster ▼

11. Using the breadcrumbs at the top of WebLogic console, get back to the **Servers** tab and repeat the process from steps 6 through 8 using the following values:

    ○ **Server name**: ticketMS_B

    ○ **Server Listen Address**: localhost

    ○ **Server Listen Port**: 9001

After the last step, you should have the configuration shown in the following screenshot:

Servers (Filtered - More Columns Exist)

	Name ⌄	Type	Machine	Listen Port
☐	ticketMS_A	Configured	localMachine	8001
☐	ticketMS_B	Configured	localMachine	9001

Add   Remove   Showing 1 to 2 of 2   Previous | Next

Add   Remove   Showing 1 to 2 of 2   Previous | Next

This concludes the cluster configuration. Now, let's start the servers.

> Make sure you have the Node Manager up and running. Without Node Manager, none of the following commands will work.

1. On the **Cluster Settings** page, click on the **Control** tab.

2. In the **Managed Server Instances in this Cluster (Filtered - More Columns Exist)** table, select both the servers and notice that buttons will become available. Click on **Start**.

3. The **State** column of the table will change from **SHUTDOWN** to **STARTING**. Wait a few seconds and refresh the page; the state should now be **RUNNING**.

4. Under the **Domain Structure** menu on the left, expand **Environment** and click on **Servers**. You should see all two servers with the state **RUNNING**.

Managed Server Instances in this Cluster (Filtered - More Columns Exist)

Start   Resume   Suspend ⌄   Shutdown ⌄   Showing 1 to 2 of 2   Previous | Next

	Server ⌄	Machine	Listen Port	State	Status of Last Action
☐	ticketMS_A	localMachine	8001	RUNNING	None
☐	ticketMS_B	localMachine	9001	RUNNING	None

Start   Resume   Suspend ⌄   Shutdown ⌄

Congratulations, you have successfully set up and started a WebLogic cluster. To accomplish the steps performed here, WebLogic's administration instance sends instructions to the Node Manager asking it to start the Managed Server instances and, among other details, to exchange some metadata stating that they belong to a specific cluster, `ticketsCluster`.

Creating a dynamic cluster

Another way to accomplish the same outcome as in the previous section is by creating a dynamic cluster and two dynamic servers. This is a concept introduced in Version 12.1.2 of the product and is closely aligned to the **Cloud Application Foundation (CAF)** initiative. In a nutshell, it gives us a more flexible and quick way to create a WebLogic cluster by just defining the number of servers available. The servers can follow a server template and all other settings, such as listen addresses, ports, and machines are associated properly. This cluster can then shrink or increase the number of servers by just adjusting the maximum number of servers.

To illustrate how this works, let's see how to create and configure the components necessary to set up a dynamic cluster.

> The steps described here are not necessary to configure the remaining components of this chapter; they're just to show how easy it is to create a dynamic cluster and servers.
>
> Of course, if you didn't create the cluster and Managed Servers as outlined in the previous section, you can use the following sequence that is way simpler — just remember to adjust the port values accordingly.

1. At the administration console's home page, click on **Configure a Dynamic Cluster**, located in the **Helpful Tools** list.

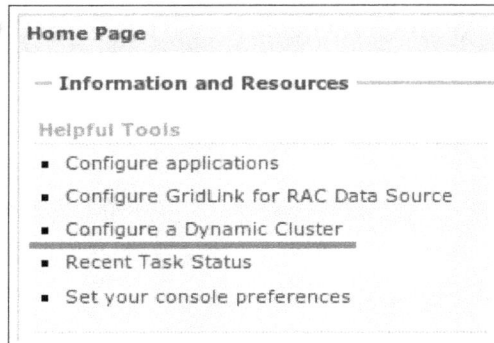

    Home Page

    — **Information and Resources**

    Helpful Tools
    - Configure applications
    - Configure GridLink for RAC Data Source
    - Configure a Dynamic Cluster
    - Recent Task Status
    - Set your console preferences

2. In the **Clusters** table, click on **New**, and then select **Dynamic Cluster** from the pop-up menu.

3. Enter ticketsCluster in the **Name** field and then click on **Next**.

4. The parameters in this page are specific to this kind of cluster; you must enter the number of Managed Servers you want available and the name prefix you want to use. Set the number to 2, enter `tickets-` as the prefix, and then click on **Next**.

5. Now we must tell WebLogic which machines will be part of this dynamic cluster; as we just have one machine available, leave the first option selected and then click on **Next**.

6. We're now asked to inform the initial list of port numbers that must be used by the dynamic servers of this cluster; again, leave the default values and then click on **Next**.

7. A summary screen is shown, with all the information we entered as shown in the following screenshot:

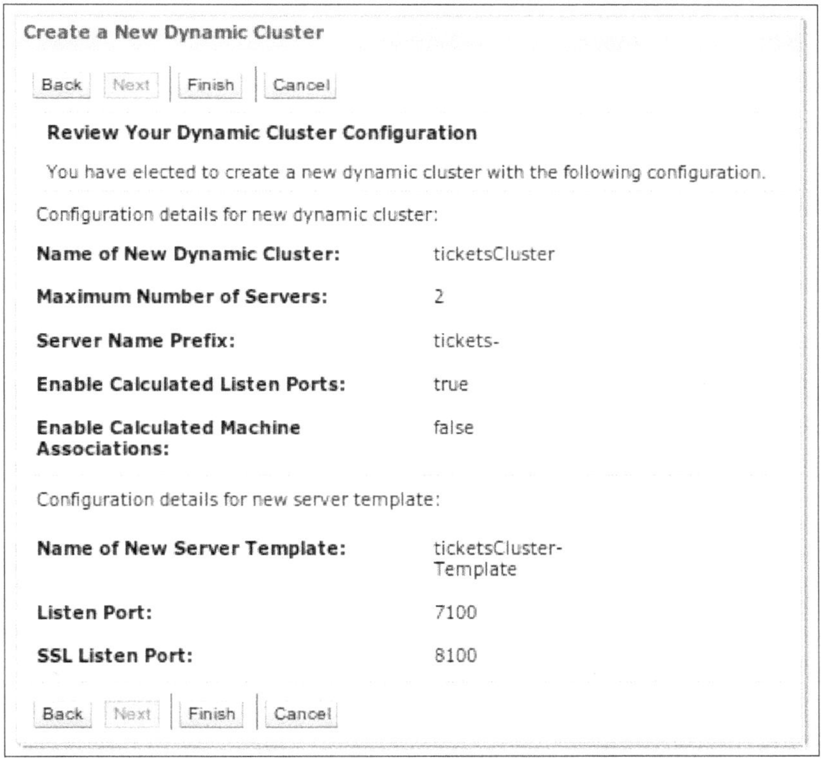

8. Click on **Finish** to create the dynamic cluster.

We covered three concepts associated with this feature by completing the dynamic cluster creation wizard:

- **Server templates**: They hold the common information necessary to configure a dynamic server and are attached to only one dynamic cluster definition.

- **Dynamic servers**: These are Managed Servers created based on a server template and participating on a dynamic cluster. Some of its states aren't directly accessible to the administrator; for instance, we cannot create or delete a dynamic server by selecting it from the **Servers** table and clicking on **Delete** as we would with a regular server.

- **Dynamic cluster**: Putting it simply, a dynamic cluster is one that aggregates dynamic servers based on the same server template. So, it has the features of a regular cluster and also a little more information about how to configure and distribute dynamic servers over the machines bound to it.

Here are a few comments related to these concepts and the dynamic cluster wizard we just executed:

- WebLogic dynamic servers aren't started and stopped automatically by the server itself—the elasticity of the solution goes as far as helping us to create and remove nodes easily, but someone must decide how many instances must be started or stopped to cope with request peaks.

- When the cluster is created, the instances aren't started right away, so you could have entered 100 in the **Number of Dynamic Servers** field; they will be created, but nothing else will be done, so you can go back later and change this value to a more realistic one.

- The instances are distributed among the machines you selected previously, automatically, at the end of the cluster creation process and every time you change the number of dynamic servers of the cluster. If you need to create or retire a machine, go to the **Cluster Configuration** tab, then click on the subtab **Servers**, and change the **Machine Name Match Expression** field accordingly.

- We created both dynamic servers and a server template at the end of the dynamic cluster wizard. You can create templates by accessing the **Server Templates** entry under **Cluster** from the **Domain Structure** tree and, after that, create a dynamic cluster and instruct the wizard to use an existing template.

- Finally, if you want to shrink or expand the cluster by removing or adding dynamic servers, you must change the values in the **Number of Dynamic Servers** field at the cluster's **Servers** configuration page.

Here's the list of servers, showing static and dynamic ones together:

Servers (Filtered - More Columns Exist)

New   Clone   Delete   Showing 1 to 6 of 6 Previous | Next

Name	Type	Cluster	Machine	State	Health	Listen Port
AdminServer(admin)	Configured			RUNNING	✓ OK	7001
loadBalancer	Configured		localMachine	SHUTDOWN		8888
ticketMS_A	Configured	ticketsCluster	localMachine	SHUTDOWN		8001
ticketMS_B	Configured	ticketsCluster	localMachine	SHUTDOWN		9001
tickets-1	Dynamic	DynamicCluster	localMachine	SHUTDOWN		7101
tickets-2	Dynamic	DynamicCluster	localMachine	SHUTDOWN		7102

If you start one of the dynamic servers and click on its name after it starts running, you will see that there are only two tabs available, **Monitoring** and **Control**, both closely related to the current state of the server; neither of them has configuration parameters, only informational values.

All configuration parameters that we can tweak on a standard server are attached to the server template used to create the dynamic cluster; the server doesn't have any proprietary values (other than name, port number, and such, which are controlled by the cluster, not the server itself). So, if you want to change anything, such as logging, debugging, protocols, keystores, and so on, you are supposed to do that on the server template. And this is great because all dynamic servers will be using the same values, making administration a breeze.

Configuring a software load balancer

Although WebLogic Server is an application server used mostly for dynamic content and Java EE applications, it is also a fully-featured web server that's capable of serving static files as HTML and images. A WebLogic instance can even be used as a load balancer to distribute requests between clustered servers and do the necessary failover routing when a server becomes unavailable. In order to leverage such built-in functionalities, you must set up `weblogic.servlet.proxy.HttpClusterServlet` to act as your default web application for the domain. Here are the steps:

1. Create a new dynamic web application in Eclipse named `HttpClusterServlet`.
2. Open or create a `web.xml` deployment descriptor under the `WEB-INF` folder.

3. Copy and paste the following content inside `web.xml`:

```
...
<servlet>
  <servlet-name>HttpClusterServlet</servlet-name>
  <servlet-class>
    weblogic.servlet.proxy.HttpClusterServlet
  </servlet-class>
  <init-param>
    <param-name>WebLogicCluster</param-name>
    <param-value>localhost:8001|localhost:9001</param-
  value>
  </init-param>
  <init-param>
    <param-name>verbose</param-name>
    <param-value>true</param-value>
  </init-param>
  <init-param>
    <param-name>DebugConfigInfo</param-name>
    <param-value>ON</param-value>
  </init-param>
</servlet>
<servlet-mapping>
  <servlet-name>HttpClusterServlet</servlet-name>
  <url-pattern>/</url-pattern>
</servlet-mapping>
<servlet-mapping>
  <servlet-name>HttpClusterServlet</servlet-name>
  <url-pattern>*.jsf</url-pattern>
</servlet-mapping>
<servlet-mapping>
  <servlet-name>HttpClusterServlet</servlet-name>
  <url-pattern>*.html</url-pattern>
</servlet-mapping>
```

4. Now, edit `weblogic.xml` under `WEB-INF` and change the `context-root` value to `/`:

```
<?xml version="1.0" encoding="UTF-8"?>
<wls:weblogic-web-app... >
  <wls:weblogic-version>12.1.2</wls:weblogic-version>
  <wls:context-root>/</wls:context-root>
</wls:weblogic-web-app>
```

5. Save both files.

6. Export the application as a war file named `HttpClusterServlet.war`.

Let's focus on explaining the set of parameters required by the `HttpClusterServlet` that we added in step 3 previously:

- `WebLogicCluster`: It is the most important parameter because it's where the servers that will be part of the cluster are defined. For example, `localhost:8001|localhost:9001`.

- `DebugConfigInfo`: If it's set to `ON` you will be able to query information about the cluster by adding a special URL parameter, `?__WebLogicBridgeConfig`. The use of this parameter is discouraged for production systems.

- `servlet-mapping`: Notice that we're explicitly mapping the servlet to match specific URL patterns. Only requests made with these extensions will be load balanced through `HttpClusterServlet`.

Creating a new Managed Server for load balancing

In this section, we propose the creation of a new Managed Server that will be responsible exclusively for load balancing and will host the `HttpServerCluster` application. Also note that this server will not be part of the cluster and doesn't need to have the same memory sizing as other managed nodes since it will not handle application objects and it only hosts one servlet.

Here's a diagram of the proposed topology:

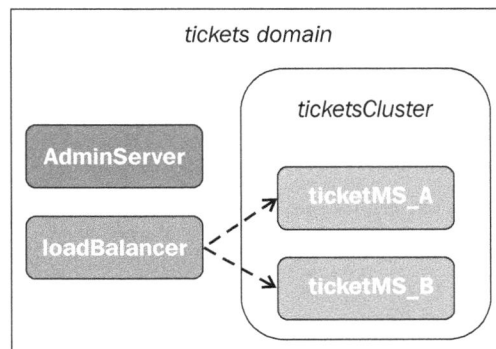

To create this new WebLogic Server instance, follow these steps:

1. Open the WebLogic console at `http://localhost:7001`.

2. Under the domain structure (left menu) expand **Environment** and click on **Servers**.

3. Click on **New** and then enter the following values:

   ° **Server Name**: loadBalancer

   ° **Server Listen Port**: 8888

4. Make sure the server is marked as a standalone server and then click on **Finish**.

5. Back on the **Servers** table, check the **loadBalancer** checkbox under the **Servers** heading.

6. Set the **Machine** drop-down to **localMachine**.

7. Save the changes and start the server using the button under the **Control** tab.

> The preceding steps are optional, so if you don't have available memory to start another server, you can use the AdminServer as a load-balancer server by deploying the HttpServletCluster application on it. Just remember to use the AdminServer port in the steps of the following sections.

Enabling the load balancer

Next, you must enable the **WebLogic Plug-In Enabled** property under the **Advanced** tab in the cluster configuration section; this action will allow WebLogic to use its own proprietary header to balance requests received through a WebLogic Proxy Plug-In.

> If you're going to configure an external load balancer – Apache HTTP Server, Oracle HTTP Server, and Oracle Traffic Director among others – remember that you must enable the WebLogic Plug-in just like we did here.

Now deploy the `HttpServletCluster.war` application and use the **loadBalancer** server as target. To check that the configuration is right, access the URL `http://localhost:8888/?__WebLogicBridgeConfig` and check that an output like the one shown in the following screenshot is generated:

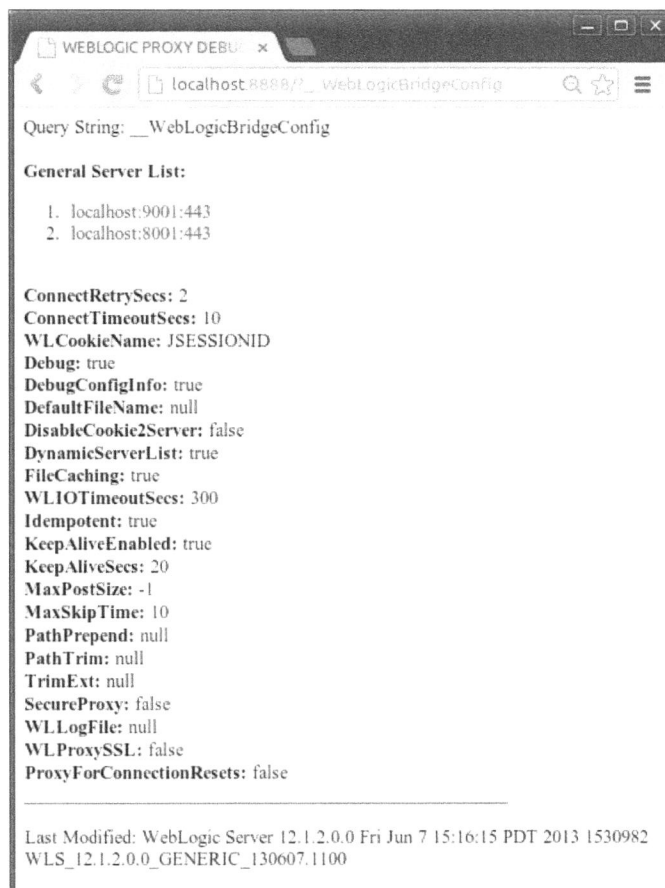

In the next section, we're going to update the application in order to enable the necessary settings for deployment on the cluster.

Retargeting applications and resources

Although we have the cluster and servers up and running, our applications and resources are still deployed only on the Admin server and that's not acceptable anymore. In WebLogic, these resources can be targeted to a specific server, a whole cluster, or even part of the cluster.

Here's what the configuration should look like:

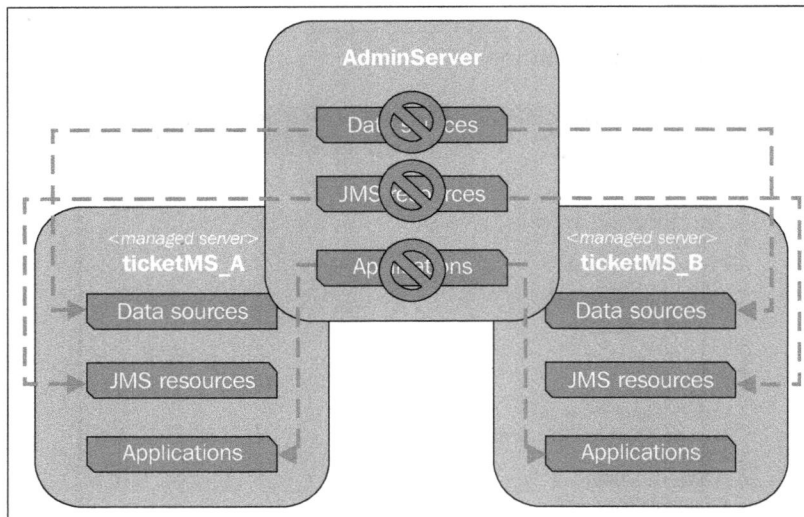

There are a couple of options to achieve these changes and we're going to explore some of the available ones.

Updating web.xml of clustered web applications

One of the key features of Java EE web applications running on a cluster is HTTP Session replication. This functionality can be briefly described as the mechanism of sharing applications' state (HTTP session) between multiple servers and machines, having the application server responsible for decisions regarding where (in which server) the HTTP session will be stored; this usually means defining two servers that will be responsible for a session—the primary one, which will get the incoming requests of that specific session, and a backup server, which will receive the requests in case of the primary server failing.

In order to enable HTTP session replication, WebLogic does not follow the Java EE deployment descriptor web.xml. It instead uses its own runtime deployment descriptor, weblogic.xml, to enable HTTP session replication. Let's enable the standard mechanism of session replication on our web applications, performing the following steps:

1. On Eclipse, in the **Store** web project, open the weblogic.xml file under WEB-INF folder.

2. Go to the **Design** tab of weblogic.xml.

3. Expand the **Session** section on the left and then click on **Persistent Store**.

4. From **Store type** select **Replicated if clustered**.

5. On the left, click on **Session Disposal** and change the **Session Timeout** value according to your specific needs. We are going to set it to 300 seconds.

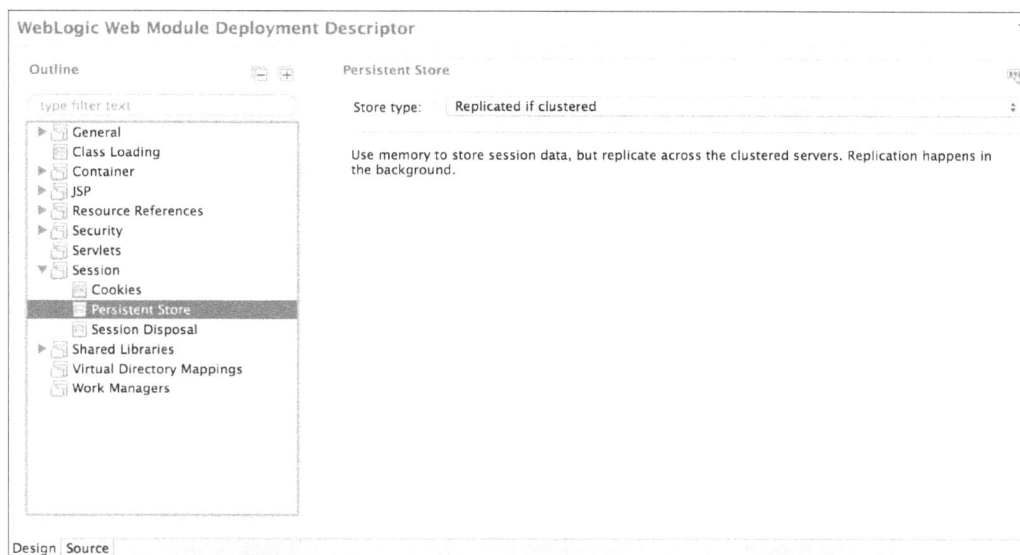

6. Save the file and check the **Source** tab. The steps performed here will add the following lines to the weblogic.xml content:

```
<wls:session-descriptor>
  <wls:timeout-secs>300</wls:timeout-secs>
  <wls:persistent-store-type>
    replicated_if_clustered
  </wls:persistent-store-type>
</wls:session-descriptor>
```

7. Repeat the complete process for the **Theater** web application.

Also, edit web.xml and add a context-param tag in order to enable the JSF application state to be stored on the client. This will prevent some issues with Ajax processing and will decrease the server memory usage with a slight increase in the network bandwidth usage. Add the following parameter:

```
<context-param>
  <param-name>javax.faces.STATE_SAVING_METHOD</param-name>
  <param-value>client</param-value>
</context-param>
```

Do not attempt to deploy the application now since we still have to update the target of other resources such as JDBC data sources and JMS queues, which will be performed in the next sections.

> As stated in the documentation, WebLogic Server does not use the `<distributable>` element of `web.xml`.

> Note that WebLogic has five different session persistence mechanisms: Memory (non-replicated), File system, JDBC-based, Cookie-based, and In-memory (across a cluster). For clustered environments, In-memory and JDBC-based persistence are the best options since they offer effective replication mechanisms.

Retargeting auxiliary components

Let's retarget the data sources to the cluster so that we can later do this with the applications that use them:

1. Access the WebLogic console at `http://localhost:7001/console`.
2. On the left menu, expand **Services** and then click on **Data Sources**.
3. Select **Store DS** and then click on the **Targets** tab.
4. Un-check the **AdminServer** checkbox and then check **ticketsCluster**.
5. Click on **Save**.

Repeat the process for the other data source, **Theater One DS**.

After this procedure, WebLogic Server will destroy the data source created on **AdminServer** and create a new connection pool and JDBC data source on each Managed Server of **ticketsCluster**.

Data Sources (Filtered - More Columns Exist)

New ∨   Delete   Showing 1 to 2 of 2 Previous | Next

	Name ⌃	Type	JNDI Name	Targets
☐	Store DS	Generic	jdbc/tickets/store	ticketsCluster
☐	Theater One DS	Generic	jdbc/tickets/theater	ticketsCluster

New ∨   Delete   Showing 1 to 2 of 2 Previous | Next

> Repeat the process in this section with the JMS resources that are part of the application: JMS Servers, sub-deployments, queues, and connection factories should all be retargeted to the cluster.

Now, let's adjust the shared libraries and optional packages. In order to do so, follow these steps:

1. In Eclipse, under the **Servers** tab, right-click on the server and click on **Add and Remove**.

2. Click on **Remove All** and then click on **Finish**. This will remove the **Theater** and **Store** applications from the Admin server, which is required since they reference the shared libraries **storeBO** and **theaterBO**.

3. Open the WebLogic console and, on the left menu, click on **Deployments**.

4. In the `Deployments` table, click on **storeBO** and then click on the tab **Targets**.

5. You should see a list of servers and clusters available on the domain. Uncheck **AdminServer** and check **ticketsCluster**.

Servers
☐ AdminServer

Clusters
☑ ticketsCluster
⦿ All servers in the cluster
◯ Part of the cluster
☐ ticketMS_A
☐ ticketMS_B

6. Click on **Save**.

Now, go back to the deployments page and repeat steps 4 through 6 for components **TheaterBO** and **primefaces**.

> It's very important to change the target of all deployable resources on the application server. If you get any errors during this process, try to first un-deploy both applications, **Store** and **Theater**, and then retarget all resources.

In this section, we've performed the steps to change the target for all shared libraries we created. Now, we just need to adjust the targeting of the web applications.

Making the application cluster friendly

Until now, the application has been deployed only to a single server, although some features such as HTTPSession were used, the session was not being distributed to different servers. Since the session serialization process is triggered only during the distribution, a common mistake is when a developer leaves non-serializable items on a session-scoped bean, where the application will behave fine without distributed sessions, but issues will arise when the application is used on a clustered environment with distributed sessions.

Other situations related to concurrency can also appear, such as how to serialize database access or distributed transactions. In order to prevent some of these issues, some measures are necessary to be taken while using this application and most of them are pretty easy to apply. For example:

1. Open `SearchManager.java` and remove the `EntityManager` injection. By default, `EntityManager` is not serializable and at this point we actually don't need it here since we already have dedicated beans, such as `TheaterManager` and `MovieManager` that are request-scoped and can be safely injected here.

   ```
   . . .
   // at SearchManager.java
   @Inject
   private TheaterManager theaterManager;
   @Inject
   private MovieManager movieManager;

   . . .
   ```

2. Edit the `search.xhtml` page in order to use `TheaterManager` and `MovieManager` in the box components.

3. Make sure every attribute used in a session-scoped bean is serializable. For example, `TheaterClient` needs to implement the `Serializable` interface and use the `@Dependent` scope to make sure that every instance of this bean is bound to the lifecycle of the parent object.

4. And the last step is to replace all host entries in the `web.xml` file for `theaterServiceEndpoint` and `reservationServiceEndpoint` with `localhost:8888`, which is our software load-balancer address.

> As a general rule, if you are planning to have your application use distributed sessions, consider revisiting the basics about Java Serialization and understand the concepts and requirements related.

Changing deployment target from Eclipse

To retarget the applications, we could perform the same procedure used to adjust the shared libraries, but, for didactic reasons, we're going to illustrate how to change a deployment target from Eclipse in the following steps:

1. Under the **Servers** tab, right-click on the **tickets** server and then click on **Properties**.

2. In the **Properties** window, expand the **WebLogic** entry and then expand **Publishing**.

3. Under **Publishing**, select **Advanced**. You should see the **ticketsCluster** and **loadBalancer** entries on the left side and **AdminServer** on the right.

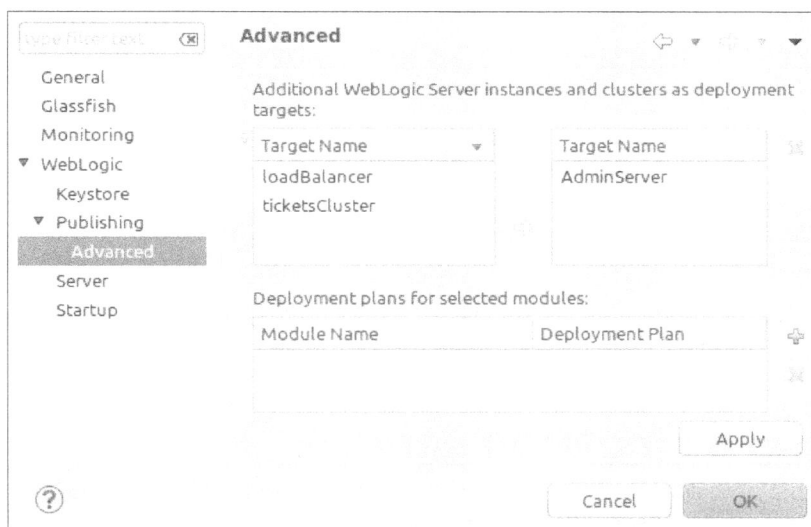

4. Select **AdminServer** (on the right) and click on the red **X** icon.

5. Select **ticketsCluster** (on the left) and click on the yellow arrow.

6. Click on **Ok** to close the window and save the changes.

7. Right-click on the server again and click on **Add and Remove...**.

8. Select the **Store** and **Theater** applications and click on **Add**. Then click on **Finish**.

9. Wait a few seconds and both applications will be available on both Managed Servers. In order to test them, access the following URLs:

   ° `http://localhost:8001/store/`

   ° `http://localhost:9001/store/`

Finally, to test the load balancer, open the URL `http://localhost:8888/` `store/`, which will distribute the requests to the Managed Servers present at its configuration.

Using a singleton service

Java EE provides singletons through the use of the `@Singleton` annotation. In practice, this annotation will guarantee that your class will be loaded only once per JVM or per application server instance. Although this is a powerful feature, if your business scenario can't cope with this behavior (duplicate component instances, one per JVM), you need another approach; the singleton service offered by WebLogic can offer an elegant solution for such cases. This feature guarantees that a given singleton class will have only one instance across a cluster, automatically managing failover and migration to another server instance in case of failure.

In the singleton `ReservationCodeBean` class there is a functionality that generates control numbers used to identify the reservations. The actual implementation is perfectly fine for a single server application, but running this application on multiple servers will end up creating several instances of `ReservationCodeBean`, one per JVM and each with its own counter variable, which may generate duplicate control numbers.

This functionality will be moved to a WebLogic singleton service, which will make it a cluster-wide singleton providing the necessary business function in a safe manner.

Creating a singleton service

To enable this new service, we're going to create a simple JAR file to hold it and then set it up as a domain library. Follow these steps:

1. On Eclipse, create a new Java project named `TokenService`.

2. Since this service will be remotely called through an RMI call, it's necessary to implement the `java.rmi.Remote` interface. Create a new Java Interface named `ITokenService` under the `com.packt.store.services` package using the following content:

```
public interface ITokenService extends Remote {
  public static final String JNDI_ENTRY = "TokenService";
  public String generate() throws RemoteException;
}
```

3. It's also required to implement the `weblogic.cluster.singleton.SingletonService` interface so WebLogic can manage the class. Create a new Java class named `TokenService` under the same package, with the following content:

```
public class TokenService implements ITokenService,
  SingletonService {

  // ideally would be moved to an external source, like a
  DB
  private int counter = 0;

  private Logger logger = Logger.getLogger(
  TokenService.class.getCanonicalName());
  private SimpleDateFormat now = new
  SimpleDateFormat("yyyyMMdd-hhmmss");

  @Override
  public String generate() {
    return String.format("%1$s-%2$06d", now.format(new
  Date()), ++counter);
  }

  @Override
  public void activate() {
    logger.fine("Attempting to bind TokenService...");

    Context jndiCtx = null;
    try {
      jndiCtx = new InitialContext();
      jndiCtx.rebind(JNDI_ENTRY, this);

      logger.info("TokenService activated on this server.");
    } catch (NamingException e) {
      logger.severe("Error during TokenService activation: " +
  e.getMessage());
    } finally {
      if (jndiCtx != null)
        try {
          jndiCtx.close();
        } catch (NamingException e) {
          e.printStackTrace();
        }
    }
  }
```

```
@Override
public void deactivate() {
  logger.fine("Attempting to unbind TokenService...");

  Context jndiCtx = null;
  try {
    jndiCtx = new InitialContext();
    jndiCtx.unbind(JNDI_ENTRY);

    logger.fine("TokenService was deactivated on this server.");
  } catch (NamingException e) {
    e.printStackTrace();
  } finally {
    if (jndiCtx != null)
      try {
        jndiCtx.close();
      } catch (NamingException e) {
        e.printStackTrace();
      }
  }
}
```

> Besides the activate() and deactivate() methods, the content of the generate() method was extracted from ReservationCodeBean.

4. Some of the required classes are missing on the classpath. To fix it, add weblogic.jar into the build path of the application. The file can be found under $MW_HOME/wlserver/server/lib.

5. Export this Java project as a JAR file using Eclipse. This project doesn't have any special requirements like a MANIFEST file does, for example. Save the JAR file as TokenService.jar.

6. The file must be available to the WebLogic classpath, so copy TokenService.jar into the tickets domain /lib folder.

> If you are running the solution using different physical machines, the JAR file must be physically copied to all of them.

7. Restart all running WebLogic servers so they can load the singleton class into the server classloader.

8. Open the WebLogic console at `http://localhost:7001/console`.

9. Under domain structure (left menu) expand **Environment** and then click on **Clusters**.

10. Click on **ticketsCluster**, browse to the **Migration** tab, and change the **Migration Basis** field to `Consensus`.

When running services or applications on a cluster, WebLogic tries to balance instances of these subsystems into all server instances of such a cluster. There are some other services that must run pinned to a single instance and, depending on the runtime situation, they migrate these services to a different server. But, there must be a way to store and keep the information about who owns that particular component; to avoid a **Single Point Of Failure (SPOF)**, WebLogic offers two options for leasing these services: Database leasing and Consensus leasing. Database leasing would require a **High Availability (HA)** database, such as Oracle RAC, but for our examples we're going to use Consensus, which is basically a less sophisticated mechanism that relies on Node Manager information about the health of our servers.

11. Still on the **ticketsCluster** page, click on the **Singleton Services** tab.

12. Click on the **New** button and use the following values:
    ° **Singleton Service Name**: `TokenService`
    ° **Class Name**: `com.packt.store.services.TokenService`

13. Click on **Next** and, in the next screen, select which server will be the preferred or primary server for this service. Every time the environment is restarted, the service will bind to this selected server. Select **ticketMS_A**, as shown in the following screenshot:

Singleton Service Properties

Singleton Services must be associated with a preferred server.

What server would you like to initially associate this Singleton Service with?

User Preferred Server: ticketMS_A ⬍

Back | Next | Finish | Cancel

14. Click on **Finish**. You should have the following singleton service settings:

Settings for ticketsCluster											
Configuration	Monitoring	Control	Deployments	Services	Notes						
General	Messaging	Servers	Replication	Migration	**Singleton Services**	Scheduling	Overload	Health Monitoring	HTTP		

This page lists the singleton services that are configured to migrate automatically within this cluster. You can use this page to add or remove singleton services from a cluster.

▷ **Customize this table**

Singleton Services (Filtered - More Columns Exist)

New	Delete				Showing 1 to 1 of 1 Previous	Next

	Name ⌄	Class Name	Preferred Server	Candidate Servers
☐	TokenService	com.packt.store.services.TokenService	ticketMS_A	ticketMS_A, ticketMS_B

New	Delete				Showing 1 to 1 of 1 Previous	Next

At this point, you can check the `ticketMS_A` log file and you should see the activation log message indicating that the configuration was successful and that the service is currently running on this server. In order to test the failover capabilities, kill or shutdown the `ticketMS_A` Managed Server and monitor the `ticketMS_B` log.

```
Jun 10, 2013 1:56:32 PM com.packt.store.services.TokenService activate
INFO: ReservationService activated on this server.
```

Adjusting the service client

Now, we need to modify the `ReservationCodeBean` class to consume the singleton service. This is a very straightforward process:

1. Open Eclipse, right-click on the project the **Store**, and select **Properties** from the context menu.

2. Click on **Java Build Path** on the left of the window and then click on the **Libraries** tab on the right side of the window.

3. Click on **Add External JARs...** and look for the `TokenService.jar` file.

4. Click on **OK** to confirm and close the **Properties** window.

5. Open the `ReservationCodeBean` class and create an attribute as follows:
   ```
   ITokenService tokenService;
   ```

6. Still in the class, add the following method:

```
private String getControlNumber() throws Exception {
  if (tokenService == null) {
    try {
      Context ctx = new InitialContext();
      tokenService = (ITokenService)
ctx.lookup(TokenService.JNDI_ENTRY);
    } catch (NamingException ex) {
      ex.printStackTrace();
      throw new Exception("Control number was not
generated!");
    }
  }

  return tokenService.generate();
}
```

7. Now, in the `generate()` method, replace the code at the control variable with a call to `getControlNumber()`:

```
String control = this.getControlNumber();
```

8. Save and close the file.

9. Publish the **Store** web application.

At this point, the **Store** web application, deployed on multiple nodes, will consume the singleton service `TokenService` that is primarily hosted on `ticketMS_A` Managed Server. If `ticketMS_A` goes offline due to a failure or simply during a normal shutdown process, the service will be migrated to `ticketMS_B` automatically and any new request to the bean will be able to find it, even if the bean is on a different server now.

Using Oracle Coherence

Oracle Coherence is a distributed data grid solution, keeping data available in memory, and using sophisticated distribution algorithms and protocols to synchronize and transfer information between its nodes. This model gives us amazing access times by having data readily available and improved reliability by distributing the data between several instances and machines, adding redundancy to avoid loss of information.

The most recent version of WebLogic, 12.1.2, comes with the newest Coherence version, also numbered 12.1.2, and tighter integration between the two products; Coherence is now enabled by default at the server's classpath, working as a regular subsystem like JMS, for instance.

> If you are familiar with previous versions of WebLogic Server using Coherence, the concept of a Coherence Server has been dropped, and now what we have is a regular WebLogic Managed Server with Coherence enabled in it. This makes management simpler, normalizing the server concept.

Also, we are able to create and configure Coherence clusters from the administration console (and related technologies such as JMX and WLST). Finally, there's a new deployment package, **Grid ARchive (GAR)**, that encapsulates Coherence configuration files, for instance, cache declarations and operational parameters, into a consistent unit, making administrative tasks more streamlined.

> For more details on this, check out the documentation at `http://docs.oracle.com/middleware/1212/wls/WLCOH/create-application.htm`.

Replicating sessions with Coherence*Web

As you may recall, we configured the web applications to use in-memory HTTP Session replication when configuring a WebLogic cluster. Another alternative for session replication on WebLogic is to use Coherence*Web. This module enables WebLogic session data to be distributed (replicated) among multiple machines, which is basically the same functionality provided by the in-memory session replication feature, but using Coherence as the engine. This allows different applications and even servers to access session data, and, as we can configure standalone Coherence servers to be part of a cluster (each running on their own JVM instance), the application server heap space isn't cluttered with session data.

> Coherence*Web can be used with several other application servers, such as Oracle Glassfish and Apache Tomcat among others. For a complete list of benefits and the possibilities of Coherence*Web, check out the product's documentation at `http://docs.oracle.com/middleware/1212/coherence/COHCW/start.htm`.

We are going to configure an in-process topology for Coherence*Web, meaning that Coherence is going to share the JVM of a WebLogic server, running as its subsystem.

> Up to Version 12.1.1, this integration wasn't available out of the box. It was possible to set it up, but the process involved copying libraries around. Now, `coherence.jar` and `coherence-web.jar` (the files that enable Coherence*Web) are loaded by default at server startup, making the configuration process easier.

To use this feature, we need to enable a Coherence cluster, configure a WebLogic instance to be Coherence's data repository, and, finally, we must adjust the web application that will use this mechanism.

Creating a Coherence cluster

To show how to use Coherence*Web, we're going to use the default cluster configuration provided by Coherence.

> Using the default configuration is a great way to get up and running quickly, but keep in mind that for real-world systems this is not an option; aspects like environment isolation and network latency must be addressed by specific configurations. You can find more information about the parameters available by checking the official documentation at `http://docs.oracle.com/cd/E24290_01/coh.371/e22837/cluster_setup.htm`.

These are the steps to add a Coherence cluster to the domain:

1. At the administration console, expand the **Environment** section at the **Domain Structure** box and then click on **Coherence Clusters**.

2. On the **Summary** screen, click on **New**.

3. Enter `sessionDataCluster` in the **Name** field and then click on **Next**.

4. We don't need to change the way Coherence instances communicate, so just click on **Next** here.

5. Add both the **loadBalancer** server (or **AdminServer** if you didn't create the dedicated instance) and WebLogic's **ticketsCluster** cluster to it by selecting the appropriate entries.

6. Click on **Finish** and it's done.

> Another way to create a basic Coherence cluster is by selecting the entry WebLogic Coherence Cluster Extension when creating or updating a domain using the Configuration Wizard (`config.sh` or `config.cmd`). You just have to add the servers to the cluster afterwards.

Enabling Coherence*Web storage

Another change introduced by Version 12.1.2 is that every WebLogic Server is now potentially also a Coherence node; as the libraries are enabled at the server's classpath, all we have to do to start using Coherence is to add a server to a Coherence cluster.

The most important configuration associated with this step is deciding if that specific server will hold data in it or if it will act as a client in relation to data; in other words, we have to decide if the instance will have local storage enabled. Also, there's a specific Coherence*Web parameter that indicates if the node will act as a storage tier for this feature.

When a server is added to a Coherence cluster, local storage is enabled by default and Coherence*Web storage isn't. To edit Coherence-related parameters of a specific server, the following steps must be followed:

1. In the administration console, select the desired server from the **Servers** list.

2. In the **Configuration** tab, click on the last inner tab **Coherence**.

3. As we want to store all data into the node **loadBalancer**, we must configure it to allow Coherence*Web by enabling the parameter **Coherence Web Local Storage Enabled**.

4. If the servers are already running, restart them.

Adjusting the application to use the cache

Now that we already have a server configured to store session data, we need to modify the application deployment descriptors and change the actual HTTP session state replication mechanism to use Coherence*Web:

1. Start Eclipse and open the file `weblogic.xml` under `/WebContent/WEB-INF` in the project **Store**.

2. Change the value of the entry `persistent-store-type` to `coherence-web` to instruct WebLogic to use Coherence*Web and add a new tag, `coherence-cluster-ref`, to reference the cluster we created in the previous section.

```
<wls:session-descriptor>
  <wls:persistent-store-type>
    coherence-web
  </wls:persistent-store-type>
</wls:session-descriptor>

<wls:coherence-cluster-ref>
  <wls:coherence-cluster-name>
    sessionDataCluster
  </wls:coherence-cluster-name>
</wls:coherence-cluster-ref>
```

3. Save the file.

4. Make sure that the server configured as Coherence*Web storage is running; at least one node of the Coherence cluster we specified at the deployment descriptor must be up when deploying an application that uses it or else the deployment procedure will fail.

5. Deploy the project to the cluster.

In order to test that your sessions are now stored on an external cache server, put some information on the session, shutdown one or both Managed Servers, and start them again. Since the data persists outside these servers, the cache kept the data, even though the application went down.

> Due to the resource limitations of a normal developer workstation or laptop (physical memory, basically), the example used only one node to hold session data. On a production system, or when the memory or number of servers aren't constraints, you can follow the same procedures to scale the cache to use multiple nodes, giving it better performance and increased reliability. As Coherence's is naturally a distributed data grid, having more nodes will contribute to the overall experience.

Caching JPA objects with TopLink Grid

TopLink Grid is a feature that enables Java Persistence API (JPA) to use Coherence to cache object instances, bringing performance gains to an application.

As you may remember, TopLink is WebLogic's JPA implementation, so enabling this cache function basically involves deciding which kind of caching is a best fit for the business scenario and configuring it.

There are a few different strategies that can be used when attaching Coherence to the JPA layer. Here's a quick description of each one:

- **Grid Cache**: This is the simplest way to integrate JPA and Coherence, where the latter acts as an L2 cache; data is read from the database and stored at the cache and subsequent queries can use data from there, speeding up response times.

- **Grid Read**: On this topology, Coherence is promoted to a more central role, being the source of data when JPA runs a query. The cache is loaded with object instances read from the database and the idea is that they should remain there longer, eventually serving all queries using only in-memory data. When an instance is updated, JPA does it first at the database, and then automatically updates Coherence.

> The main difference between Grid Cache and Grid Read is that the former assumes that data can't be preloaded to Coherence, building the cache on the fly, and the latter relies on having the data in-memory, possibly using a mechanism to populate the cache.

- **Grid Entity**: This is an evolution of the Grid Read topology, where all queries and updates are made directly to Coherence. Insertions and updates are sent to Coherence, and this layer propagates them to the database, ideally using its write-behind capability to get even better response times.

> If you want to read details about each topology, check out the following document: http://docs.oracle.com/middleware/1212/coherence/COHIG/tlg_integrate.htm.

The following figure shows how such a configuration would work; Coherence would be at the front of the database, intercepting and serving requests from or to it.

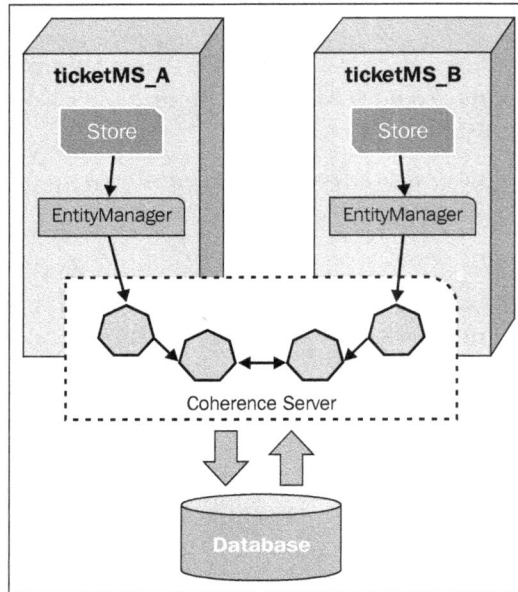

Since this is considered an advanced feature of a more complex WebLogic topology, the configuration of such features is out of the scope of this book, but at the following URL you can find documentation and step-by-step instructions on how to enable it: `http://docs.oracle.com/cd/E24290_01/coh.371/e23131/toc.htm`.

This integration between JPA and Coherence is a powerful feature when scaling up your application, but keep in mind that a new set of considerations must be taken, such as how many Coherence instances must be set up, how to distribute the load over them, for how long a specific object must be kept in the cache, how to invalidate it, and so on.

Web resources

The following are a few web resources that you can refer to:

- TopLink Grid home page
    - `http://www.oracle.com/technetwork/middleware/ias/tl-grid-097210.html`

- TopLink Grid documentation
  - ° `http://www.oracle.com/technetwork/middleware/toplink/documentation/index.html`

- Accessing data caches from applications
  - ° `http://docs.oracle.com/middleware/1212/wls/COHWL/coh_wls.htm`

- Active Cache—Coherence integration with CDI
  - ° `http://docs.oracle.com/middleware/1212/coherence/COHTU/activecache.htm`

- Singleton design pattern
  - ° `http://en.wikipedia.org/wiki/Singleton_pattern`

- Service migration
  - ° `http://docs.oracle.com/middleware/1212/wls/CLUST/service_migration.htm`

- WebLogic clusters & Multi-tier architectures
  - ° `http://docs.oracle.com/middleware/1212/wls/CLUST/setup.htm`

- Java EE XML schemas for DDs
  - ° `http://www.oracle.com/webfolder/technetwork/jsc/xml/ns/javaee/index.html`

Summary

In this chapter, you've learned how to create a cluster with two Managed Servers, the procedure to migrate a Java EE Singleton to a Singleton Service, how to use WebLogic Server as a load balancer through the `HttpClusterServlet` component, how to set up and use Coherence*Web to scale out HTTP Sessions, and how to integrate your JPA entities with TopLink Grid. By doing all this, we were able to scale up a web application by leveraging several WebLogic services and functionalities. This content is very important for production systems and applications that want to provide high availability and high performance.

In the next chapter, we're going to see features of WebLogic that speed up the development process, how to monitor server resources by using a **Representational State Transfer (REST)** API and how to troubleshoot classpath problems using the **Classloader Analysis Tool (CAT)**.

11
Some WebLogic Internals

Now that we have seen how to scale and optimize our application, let's take a look at some features of WebLogic Server that help the developer in his/her job of creating, delivering, and testing applications. More specifically, we're going to check:

- The different kinds of packaging, and how to benefit from them at development time
- How to optimize redeployment by enabling the FastSwap feature
- How to package modules (a JDBC data source, for instance) into an application
- How to troubleshoot classloader problems using WebLogic's **Classloader Analysis Tool (CAT)**
- How to monitor WebLogic resources using WebLogic's RESTful management service

Understanding deployment structures

There are different ways to package and deploy an application, and each one has a specific set of benefits and challenges. When using Eclipse to publish projects, as we have been doing here, the archived file model is the only format that can't be used by the IDE — we can choose either from the exploded archive directory or the split development directory (also known as a virtual application).

Let's check each available option and when they can be used.

Packaging as an archived file

This is the most common way of packaging one or more projects—just create a JAR, WAR, or EAR file with all application resources and compiled code inside, and deploy it to the server. From Eclipse, we can create a deployment unit by using the **Export...** context menu of a project.

Using an exploded archive directory

This option is pretty close to the archived file one—the structure is basically the same, but instead of using a single packaged file, we use a folder with the same contents. The benefit of using it is that we have direct access to the files, and some of them can be changed directly without the packaging procedure. Static files such as images and web pages (the Store project's .xhtml files, for instance) can be changed without the need to redeploy the application; just save the file, and it's already available.

The downside of this approach while developing the application is that the IDE must duplicate all files and folder structures to make them available to WebLogic, and this step can take some time, depending on the size of the projects involved.

> We can use this structure even when deploying to a production environment, as it's a WebLogic Server feature. If the application requires constant changes to static files, this is the best way to go, as there's no downtime associated to a deploy procedure.

When you look up your application at WebLogic's administration console, there's no noticeable difference between this approach and an archived file—you need to check the **Path** field in the **Overview** tab of a specific deployment in order to know which one is being used. It would look something like the following screenshot:

Settings for Store							
Overview	Deployment Plan	Configuration	Security	Targets	Control	Testing	Monitoring

Save

Use this page to view the installed configuration of a Web Application.

Name:	Store
Context Root:	/store
Path:	/ opt/ packt/ workspace/ . metadata/ . plugins/ org. eclipse. core. resources/ . projects/ Store/ beadep/ tickets/ Store
Deployment Plan:	(no plan specified)

[💡 An archived file deploy would list `/opt/packt/deploy/Store.war` as **Path**.]

Using a virtual application

The last option, also called split development directory, uses the same concept of the previous one, exploded archive directory, but doesn't have the copy operation overhead — the deployment creates a direct reference to the current development directories instead of creating a stage area. Direct updates to static files are also immediately available to the server.

This configuration is applied to a server, so it changes the way in which all **Oracle Enterprise Pack for Eclipse (OEPE)** projects are targeted to that specific server; these projects will be bundled as a single enterprise application (EAR) when deployed to WebLogic, hence the name *virtual application*. This rule applies to Java EE projects that aren't explicitly bound to EAR projects — in this case, the EARs are created and deployed as usual. The following screenshot shows how both projects, **store** and **theater**, are presented as a single deployment on WebLogic's administration console while using this strategy:

Deployments

| Install | Update | Delete | | Start ∨ | Stop ∨ | | Showing 1 to 4 of 4 | Previous | Next |

	Name △	State	Health	Type	Deployment Order
☐	📦 primefaces(3.4,3.4.1)	Active		Library	100
☐	📦 storeBO(1.0,1.0.0)	Active		Library	100
☐	📦 theaterBO(1.0,1.0.0)	Active		Library	100
☐	⊟ 📦 _auto_generated_ear_	Active	✅ OK	Enterprise Application	100
	⊟ Modules				
	🗔 store			Web Application	
	🗔 theater			Web Application	
	⊟ EJBs				
	⬡ ExhibitionBean			EJB	
	⊟ Web Services				
	None to display				

| Install | Update | Delete | | Start ∨ | Stop ∨ | | Showing 1 to 4 of 4 | Previous | Next |

Configuring the deployment model

By default, OEPE uses the virtual application model. If you want to change it to use exploded archives, the following steps can be performed:

1. Right-click on the server name in the **Servers** view and select the last entry, **Properties**.

2. The configuration screen will show up. Expand the **WebLogic** entry on the left-hand side, and then click on **Publishing**.

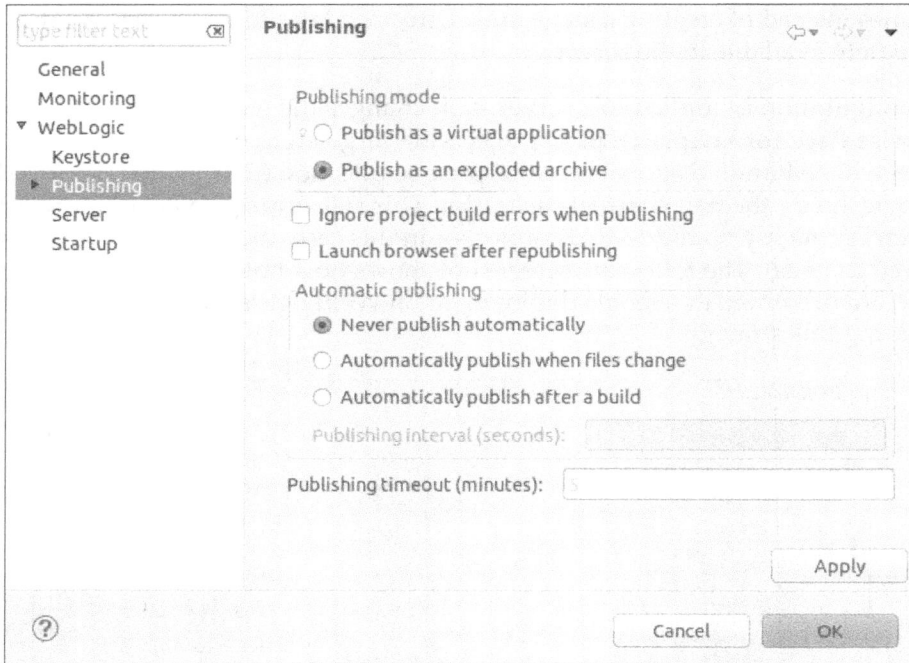

3. Select the appropriate option under the **Publishing mode** group on the top of the **Publishing** screen, and click on **OK** to close the window and redeploy the projects using the selected approach.

> We are changing the server configuration, so this behavior is applied to all projects attached to that server. This can be obvious, but it can also be overlooked and forgotten, hence the reminder.

Using FastSwap to reduce deployment time

To speed up the deployment process, we can enable the FastSwap feature, instructing the container to update bytecode without dropping the existing instances of the affected classes or reloading the classloader. This means that a class binary can be loaded into the container's memory without dropping the class' instances that are already in use—it's like updating a static file using the exploded directory archive (explained in the previous section) and making it immediately available to the container, but we're actually replacing binaries.

> Remember that this doesn't mean you don't have to publish a project after changing the source code—FastSwap only makes the deployment process quicker, but you still have to command Eclipse to execute the deployment procedure (if automatic publishing is disabled, obviously).

Not every change made to a class is a candidate to use the FastSwap feature, though. Here are a few requirements and constraints we need to observe to use this feature:

- The application must be deployed as an exploded archive—this is configured when you map the server in OEPE, as we just saw in the previous section
- Classes inside packaged files aren't eligible to use it
- Changing enums isn't supported

> The complete list of supported changes and limitations can be found here: `http://docs.oracle.com/cd/E24329_01/web.1211/e24443/deployunits.htm#i1054385`

To show how to enable FastSwap, let's do it for the project **theater**:

1. Open the `weblogic.xml` file located in the folder `/WebContent/WEB-INF`.
2. In the **Outline** tree, click on **General**, and then click on **FastSwap**.

3. Check the **Enable class redefinition** checkbox as shown in the following screenshot:

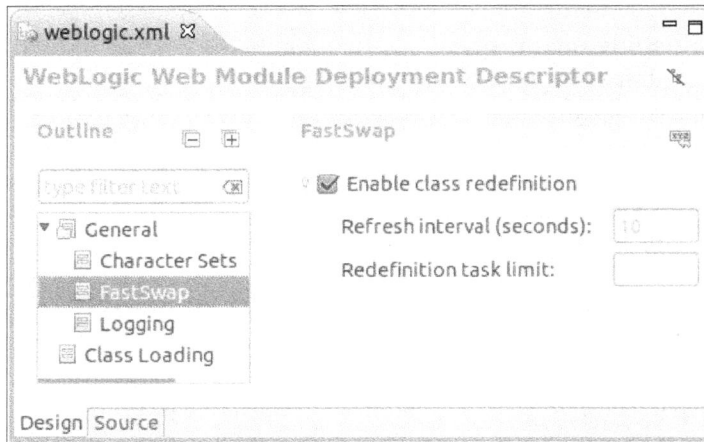

4. Save the file.

The other parameters available on the **FastSwap** configuration screen are:

- **Refresh interval (seconds)**: This value sets the interval at which FastSwap's engine will check for changes in the application classes, and fire up redefinition tasks, if needed. This parameter is only applied when using automatic publishing and an exploded archive deployment. The default value is **10** seconds.

- **Redefinition task limit**: This sets the maximum number of redefinition tasks (the act of changing the bytecode) that can be monitored by JMX interfaces. Only the most recent tasks are kept available—when this limit is reached and a new redefinition task is created, the oldest task being monitored is discarded.

The configuration we just changed will create the fast-swap tag in the project's weblogic.xml file as follows:

```
<wls:weblogic-web-app>
  <wls:weblogic-version>12.1.1</wls:weblogic-version>
  <wls:context-root>store</wls:context-root>
    . . .
  <wls:fast-swap>
    <wls:enabled>true</wls:enabled>
  </wls:fast-swap>
</wls:weblogic-web-app>
```

While publishing a module, you should see messages similar to the ones shown in the following screenshot in Eclipse's Error Log window, stating that the FastSwap feature is active:

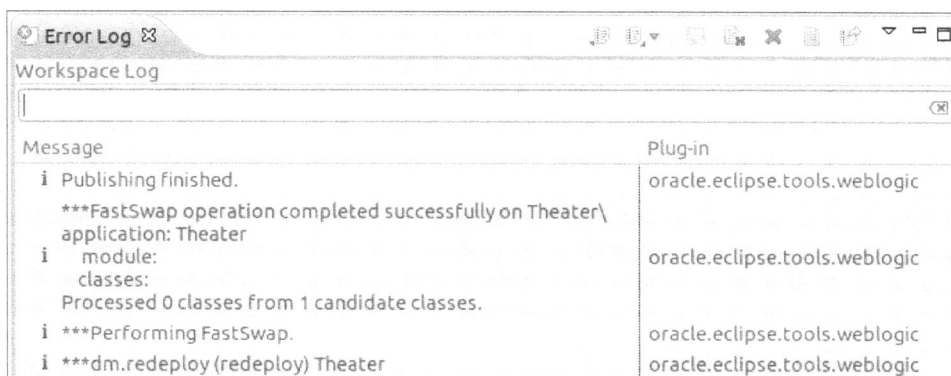

If you make a change to a class that is not supported by FastSwap, an error message is shown, and the regular deployment procedure is executed.

> There is an issue with FastSwap and **Contexts and Dependency Injection** (CDI) that renders some projects unable to use the FastSwap feature—if a project contains classes annotated with `ApplicationScoped` or `SessionScoped`, for instance, the deployment procedure may raise an error and abort. At the time of writing, there was no definition about this issue being a problem or a design decision (bug # 13572166 at Oracle Support).

Packaging modules into an application

First, let's define what a module is on the context at hand; apart from the usual Java EE modules deployed in WebLogic Server—our applications and shared libraries, for instance—there are modules that group server resources such as JDBC and JMS components.

When we create a data source using WebLogic's administration console, we're actually creating a module inside the domain's configuration folder. This structure is read at the server's startup procedure to configure it properly.

> You can check the folder `/opt/packt/domains/tickets/config/jdbc` to see the JDBC modules, Ticket and Theater, defined in our server.

There are two kinds of such modules, classified according to the way they are defined: globally-scoped (also called system modules) and application-scoped. The first is the most commonly found and used module—resources are created using WebLogic's administration console or **WebLogic Scripting Tool (WLST)** scripts, and are available to any application deployed and targeted to the same servers of the module. The other module, application-scoped modules, refers to modules that are declared as part of a Java EE application. As you are packing everything together, there's no need to instruct WebLogic administrators or operators to create the resources before deploying the application.

While looking up these application-scoped resources using WebLogic's administration console, you will not find them at the usual places—as they are part of a deployment, you will find them listed inside the deployment that defines it. The following screenshot shows the structure of an enterprise application that packages a data source and a web module:

Deployments

| Install | Update | Delete | Start ⌄ | Stop ⌄ | Showing 1 to 4 of 4 | Previous | Next |

	Name ⌃	State	Health	Type	Deployment Order
☐	⊟ ▣ TestDataSourceEAR	Active	✅ OK	Enterprise Application	100
	⊟ Modules				
	☐ Test-DS			JDBC Configuration	
	▣ Test			Web Application	
	⊟ EJBs				

> When you click on the resource name, the configuration pages specific to its category, in our example, data source, are shown. From this point on, there's no difference between a global- or application-scoped resource, meaning that you have all configuration options available to both scopes.

Creating an application-scoped module

To create this kind of module, the easiest way is to define everything you need using WebLogic's administration console, and then copy the generated XML files to your application, which must be an Enterprise Application (EAR). You can create a new folder inside it, and keep all module declarations inside it.

Remember that the system modules' declarations are created into specific folders using /opt/packt/domains/tickets/config/ as the root. Basically, you will work with the jms and jdbc subfolders.

Then, you just need to add a reference to the module from within the weblogic-application.xml descriptor file, shown as follows:

```
<wls:module>
   <wls:name>StoreDS</wls:name>
   <wls:type>JDBC</wls:type>
   <wls:path>jdbc/StoreDS-jdbc.xml</wls:path>
</wls:module>
```

The previous sample shows that a folder jdbc has been created in the project's root, and the module descriptor StoreDS-jdbc.xml can be found there.

The -jdbc suffix at the end of the filename is a requirement. If you forget to add it, the deployment procedure will fail with the message "Data source descriptor filename [name] does not have the required suffix "-jdbc.xml"".

Restricting access to an application-scoped resource

Even though we declare modules inside an application, it doesn't mean that the resources cannot be accessed by other applications. For JDBC data sources, for instance, the visibility depends on a parameter, scope, as shown in the following code snippet, which is taken from the configuration file and changed to reflect it:

```
<jdbc-data-source-params>
   <jndi-name>Ticket_DS</jndi-name>
   <scope>Application</scope>
</jdbc-data-source-params>
```

The default value for the scope parameter is Global, meaning that all applications running on the same server as the application declaring the resource have access to it.

You can use this setting to restrict external access to the resource, but there are a few collaterals that can make even the application defining the resource unable to use it.

- If you reference the app-scoped data source from a `persistence.xml` file, the JNDI name resolution will fail, so it cannot be used when declaring JPA persistence units

- References (either by lookup or the `@Resource` injection) will only work when used inside enterprise beans, and the relationship between classes and resources must be explicitly declared using the `ejb-jar.xml` and `weblogic-ejb-jar.xml` deployment descriptors

So, if you are considering this option to make access to a resource more secure (as there's no possibility of access from other applications) by setting the scope of the application, you may want to check the security features provided by WebLogic, leaving the scope with its default value.

> For more details on how to secure access to a resource, check *Chapter 8, Adding Security*.

Declaring data sources using annotations

The limitation involving web projects can be tackled with another feature, if all you need is to declare a data source; the annotations `DataSourceDefinition` and `DataSourceDefinitions` allow us to create a data source without resorting to the application-scoped module feature.

Here's how a web service declaring a data source pointing to our store database would look like:

```
import javax.annotation.Resource;
import javax.annotation.sql.DataSourceDefinition;

@DataSourceDefinition(
  name = "java:module/env/jdbc/tickets",
  className = "com.mysql.jdbc.Driver",
  portNumber = 3306,
  serverName = "localhost",
  databaseName = "store_db",
  user = "store_user",
  password = "store",
  properties={"create=false", "weblogic.TestTableName=SQL SELECT
  1"})
```

```
@WebServlet(value="/hello")
public class SomeServlet extends HttpServlet {
  private static final long serialVersionUID = 1L;

  @Resource(lookup = "java:module/env/jdbc/tickets")
  DataSource ds;

  public void service(ServletRequest req, ServletResponse res)
  throws IOException, ServletException {
    Connection con;

    try {
      con = ds.getConnection();
      ...
      con.close();
    } catch (SQLException e) {
    e.printStackTrace();
    }
  }
}
```

Notice that we used the prefix module to declare the JNDI name. There are a few different prefixes we can use, each defining a different level of visibility for the resource.

Prefix	Meaning
java:comp	The resource is available only to the component that declares it.
java:module	The component can be accessed by other components in the same module, a web project, for instance.
java:app	All modules inside an application, an EAR for instance, can access the component.
java:global	Any application running on the same server(s) can reference and use the component.
	This is the same visibility you have if you declare the resource using the administration console, but with the downside of not having the corresponding management and monitoring pages available.

As usual, you can declare the same object using deployment descriptors. As the previous sample is from a web project, this block could be added to the `web.xml` descriptor file:

```
<data-source>
  <name>java:module/env/jdbc/tickets</name>
  <class-name>com.mysql.jdbc.Driver</class-name>
  <server-name>localhost</server-name>
  <port-number>3306</port-number>
  <database-name>store_db</database-name>
  <user>store_user</user>
  <password>store</password>
  <property>
    <name>create</name>
    <value>false</value>
  </property>
  <property>
    <name>weblogic.TestTableName</name>
    <value>SQL SELECT 1</value>
  </property>
</data-source>
```

This feature cannot be used in pure named beans—only enterprise beans, servlets, and web services support it.

Using the Classloader Analysis Tool (CAT)

One feature of WebLogic Server that helps developers to pinpoint class conflicts and other classloader issues is the **Classloader Analysis Tool (CAT)**. Here's the description of what it does, taken from its main page:

> *CAT is a small web application that is designed to help application developers understand, analyze, and resolve classloading issues in their applications.*

It does so by showing all applications and modules on the server where you're running CAT, and from there, you can drill down and check which classes were loaded by each classloader, searching for potential conflicts.

Starting CAT

In order to use CAT, there are a few points that must be observed:

- Your server must be running in the development mode. By default, CAT is not enabled on production servers

- You cannot run CAT on servers running over IBM SDK for Java, as some functions depend on implementation provided by HotSpot

- A console credential is required to access it, so if you're not able to access the administration console, you will not be able to access CAT either

If all the previously mentioned requirements apply, just open a browser and direct it to `http://localhost:7001/wls-cat` to load the application. The package is deployed on demand, so wait for a few seconds for this process, and a credential pop up will be displayed, asking for the username and password, and the main page will be loaded.

Another way to start it is by going to the **Testing** tab of any deployed application and clicking on the **Classloader Analysis Tool** link:

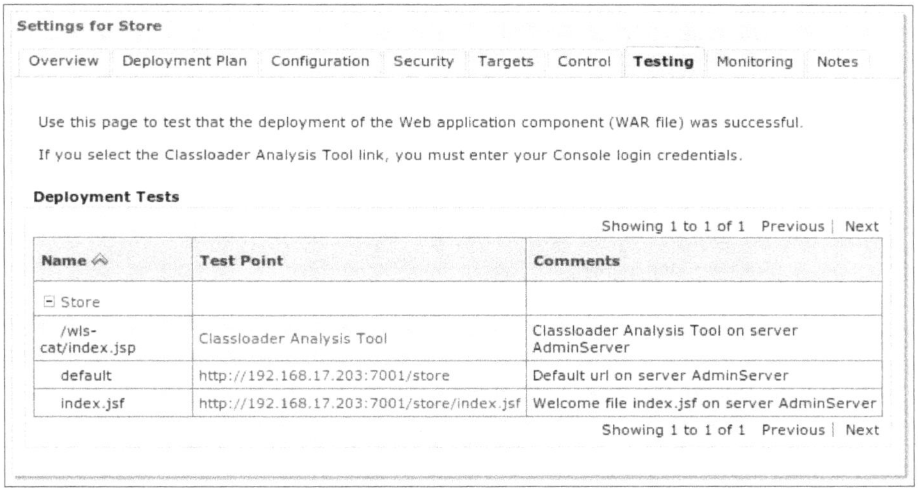

In the top-left corner, you can see a list of the modules and applications enabled on the server where CAT is running, something like the following screenshot:

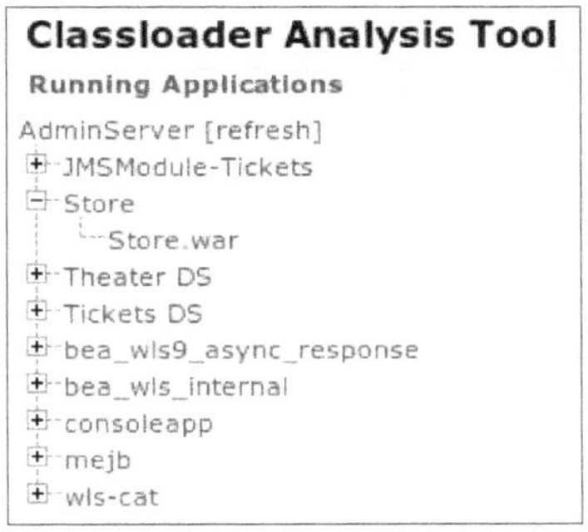

From this tree, you can check the classloaders of each application. Clicking on **Store. war** under **Store** and then clicking on **Classloader Tree** on the blue ribbon will show us details of all classloaders attached to this specific module:

```
Classloader Tree for Application: Store Module: Store.war

  View: basic | detailed
  Actions: Summary | Analyze Conflicts | Classloader Tree | Generate Report

─ Information ──────────────────────────────────────────────────────
Application Info
  • Application: Store.war
  • Version: <Not Set>
  • Module: Store.war
  • Annotation: Store@Store.war

─ System Classloaders ─────────────────────────────────────────────
      Type: sun.misc.Launcher$ExtClassLoader
      HashCode: 29244674

      Type: sun.misc.Launcher$AppClassLoader
      HashCode: 2523263

      Type: java.net.URLClassLoader
      HashCode: 24917264

      Type: weblogic.utils.classloaders.GenericClassLoader
      HashCode: 5027114

─ Application Classloaders ────────────────────────────────────────
      Type: weblogic.utils.classloaders.FilteringClassLoader
      HashCode: 20730504
      Filter: []

      Type: weblogic.utils.classloaders.GenericClassLoader
      HashCode: 18475494

      Type: weblogic.utils.classloaders.ChangeAwareClassLoader
      HashCode: 264825
```

> System classloaders are named after those that involve JVM and WebLogic Server core classloaders. Application classloaders are related to Java EE applications and libraries deployed to WebLogic.

The previous screenshot shows basic information of each classloader. If you click on the **detailed** link on the top blue ribbon, the same list will be presented, along with all libraries loaded by each one. It is great to do a visual check of which libraries are being loaded, but the volume of output can be overwhelming, making it difficult to sort out all the information, so another feature can be used to check for conflicts, as explained in the next section.

Finding potential conflicts

An easier way to look for conflicts is to use CAT's Analyze Conflicts function. To do so, you just need to click on the module name you want to analyze, then on the **Analyze Conflicts** link on the blue ribbon. And it's done!

To show how it works, we left the file StoreBO.jar in the domain's lib folder (we added it in *Chapter 7, Remote Access with JMS*, to be able to see what's inside a JMS message), and we also have a shared library exposing the same classes, and this shared library is explicitly referenced by the Store's web application. When we ask WebLogic to check for possible conflicts, the output generated would look like the following screenshot:

```
Conflict Report for Application: Store Module: Store.war

   View: basic | detailed
   Actions: Summary | Analyze Conflicts | Classloader Tree | Generate Report

─── Report

Conflicts Summary

There are potential conflicts detected and they do not seem to have been resolved. Please
review the potential solutions below.

 • 4 classes are in conflict
 • Those classes are found in the following main packages:
     •    com.packt.domain.*

Suggested Solution

<prefer-application-packages>
    <package-name>com.packt.domain.*</package-name>
</prefer-application-packages>

─── Conflicts

Resource: <select below>

Below is a list of classes that are marked as potential conflicts. By clicking
on a class, further information about this class will be shown in this space.
This information includes the alternative locations this class may be found
and which classloader actually will load this class.

Classes:

 • com.packt.domain.store.Customer
 • com.packt.domain.store.Movie
 • com.packt.domain.store.Theater
 • com.packt.domain.store.Ticket
```

A list with all classes from the library is presented. To check on which files carry a specific class, just click on the class' name to show its details:

```
— Conflicts

Resource: com.packt.domain.store.Customer

Checksum: b198aba5db0a3eb182e8f00d49bde1d6
Load Location: jar:file:/opt/packt/domains/tickets/lib/StoreBO.jar!/com/packt/domain/store/Customer.class
Classloader Type: java.net.URLClassLoader
Classloader Hash Code: 15212479
Classloader Search Order: 12959502 ->15212479
Alternative Locations:

   • /opt/packt/domains/tickets/servers/AdminServer/upload/StoreBO.jar!/com/packt/domain/store/Customer.class


Source:

public class com.packt.domain.store.Customer implements java.io.Serializable {
    public void com.packt.domain.store.Customer();
    public int getId();
    public void setId(int);
    public String getEmail();
    public void setEmail(String);
    public String getPassword();
    public void setPassword(String);
    public java.util.List getTickets();
    public void setTickets(java.util.List);
}
```

Just by looking at the paths of the libraries, we can tell that the first reference comes from the domain lib (/opt/packt/domains/ticket/lib/...), and the other is a standalone deployment (.../AdminServer/upload/StoreBO.jar...). As the classes are being loaded from the domain library, any changes to the shared library (the one we are supposed to use) aren't going to be reflected, and errors may arise — for instance, if there's a new version of a class with a couple more methods that the application can't find, MethodNotFoundException errors are likely to happen.

CAT is a very handy feature, even more so when you don't have full control of the server, and several projects and applications are running and applying changes to it simultaneously.

Using RESTful management services

Starting with WebLogic Server 12c, there is a feature that enables us to monitor several aspects of a running domain, including its clusters, server instances, applications, and data sources, without resorting to the administration console or management scripts.

> For a full list of resources that can be monitored through RESTful management services, check the documentation at http://docs.oracle.com/cd/E24329_01/web.1211/e26722/toc.htm.

WebLogic Server provides an address that can be queried to get information about specific components. The general format of this URL is `http(s)://[host]:[port]/management/tenant-monitoring/[path]` where:

- If the server is configured to enforce SSL communication, you must use `https` to access the service

- The `host` and `port` values must point to the host and port where the administration server is running

- The `path` parameter will tell WebLogic which kind of resource you want to monitor, and also name a specific resource, such as `servers/AdminServer` or only `servers` to list all servers available

Enabling the management service

To enable the service, open the administration console and perform the following steps:

1. Go to the navigation tree—the **Domain Structure** box—and then click on the domain name, **tickets**.

2. Click on the **Configuration** tab, and then click on **General**.

3. Scroll down to show the **Advanced** link, and then click on it.

4. Scroll down to the end of the page and locate the **Enable RESTful Management Services** entry.

5. Click on its checkbox, and then click on **Save**.

6. The page will be reloaded, and a message stating that the server must be restarted will be presented.

> **Messages**
>
> ✅ All changes have been activated. However 1 items must be restarted for the changes to take effect.
>
> ✅ Settings updated successfully.

7. Click on the **Control** tab on the same page, click on the checkbox right next to the **AdminServer** entry, and then click on **Shutdown** and **Force Shutdown Now** from the pop-up menu, or just go to Eclipse's **Server** view and command a restart from there.

With the server running again, we can proceed and test the management services.

Monitoring resources

When you first access the URL, the server asks for a user credential. This user must belong to either the **Administrators** or the **Monitors** group to get proper access. Type `http://localhost:7001/management/tenant-monitoring/servers` in a new browser window and enter the appropriate credentials. A page with the following content will be presented:

```
• body
    ◦ items
            1.      ▪ name AdminServer
                    ▪ state RUNNING
                    ▪ health HEALTH_OK
• messages
```

This command lists all servers of the domain. If you want to see details about a specific server, just add a slash at the end of the URL and type the name of the instance you want to check— for example, `http://localhost:7001/management/tenant-monitoring/servers/AdminServer`. The resulting page will show the basic information already presented—name, state, and health, along with several other entries.

```
• body
    ◦ item
        ▪ name AdminServer
        ▪ state RUNNING
        ▪ health HEALTH_OK
        ▪ clusterName null
        ▪ currentMachine
        ▪ weblogicVersion WebLogic Server 12.1.2.0.0 Fri Jun 7 15:16:15 PDT 2013 1530982
          WLS_12.1.2.0.0_GENERIC_130607.1100
        ▪ openSocketsCurrentCount 6
        ▪ heapSizeCurrent 291504128
        ▪ heapFreeCurrent 95166664
        ▪ heapSizeMax 477233152
        ▪ javaVersion 1.7.0_21
        ▪ oSName Linux
        ▪ oSVersion 3.8.0-27-generic
• messages
```

As you may have noticed, there are two ways of querying the management service— by a collection and by a specific item. The collection view is a condensed one, showing all available objects of that specific kind, for instance, servers.

When querying for a specific item, remember that the resource name appended to the end of the URL is case-sensitive.

Here's a list of all currently available resources — collections and items that can be monitored:

- `/servers`
- `/server/[server name]`
- `/clusters`
- `/cluster[cluster name]`
- `/applications`
- `/application/[application name]`
- `/datasources`
- `/datasource/[data source name]`

Each resource query returns a specific set of information. For instance, a query to a named data source returns this set of live data, among others:

- `activeConnectionsCurrentCount`
- `currCapacity`
- `numAvailable`
- `numUnavailable`
- `prepStmtCacheAccessCount`
- `prepStmtCacheCurrentSize`
- `prepStmtCacheHitCount`
- `prepStmtCacheMissCount`
- `waitingForConnectionCurrentCountx`
- `connectionsTotalCount`

Check the official documentation at `http://docs.oracle.com/middleware/1212/wls/RESTS/index.html` to get a complete list of item attributes and their meaning.

If you want to show the same level of information for a specific entry when listing the collections, just add a parameter, `format=full`, to the query `http://localhost:7001/management/tenant-monitoring/servers?format=full`.

Hopefully, in the future, the development team will add more resources to this list, JMS being the most missed of them.

Formatting the response

As this feature is enabled by Jersey, the JAX-RS reference implementation, the output can be generated as plain HTML—the format we used here is JSON or XML. To receive the response as JSON or XML, you must set the `Accept` header to `application/json` or `application/xml` respectively.

You can't change this flag using the standard features of a browser, so if you don't use a plugin like Tamper Data for Firefox or Request Maker for Google Chrome, you may want to know that WebLogic provides a web client that allows us to test these other formats in an easy way. To use it, just point your browser to `http://localhost:7001/management/ajaxtest.html`.

The host and port must point to the administration server of the domain, as we are already using it to access the RESTful management services.

You just need to enter the query's URL, as you did before, and select the appropriate response data type. Here's how the same query would look like using the Ajax client to retrieve a JSON structure:

URL: `http://localhost:7001/management/tenant-monitoring/servers`

Response Data Type: JSON ▾

Go

Result:

```
{
  body: {
    items: [
      {
        name: "AdminServer",
        state: "RUNNING",
        health: "HEALTH_OK"
      }
    ]
  },
  messages: [

  ]
}
```

Keep in mind that this client is provided as is, so there is no support available. It must be used only for testing purposes.

Web resources

The following are a few web resources that you can refer to:

- Packaging applications and modules for deployment & using FastSwap
    - http://docs.oracle.com/middleware/1212/wls/DEPGD/deployunits.htm

- Creating a split development directory environment
    - http://docs.oracle.com/middleware/1212/wls/WLPRG/splitcreate.htm

- Configuring JDBC application modules for deployment
    - http://docs.oracle.com/middleware/1212/wls/JDBCA/packagedjdbc.htm

- Understanding JMS resource configuration
    - http://docs.oracle.com/middleware/1212/wls/JMSAD/overview.htm

- Using DataSource resource definitions
    - http://docs.oracle.com/middleware/1212/wls/JDBCP/ds_annotation.htm

- Annotation type DataSourceDefinition
    - http://docs.oracle.com/javaee/6/api/javax/annotation/sql/DataSourceDefinition.html

- Understanding WebLogic Server application classloading
    - http://docs.oracle.com/middleware/1212/wls/WLPRG/classloading.htm

- Using RESTful management services with Oracle WebLogic Server
    - http://docs.oracle.com/middleware/1212/wls/RESTS/index.html

Summary

In this chapter, we covered a few features brought by WebLogic Server and Java EE 6 that help the development process by cutting deployment time, optimizing class redefinitions without the need to restart the whole application, finding classloader issues, and how to monitor server resources in a simple way.

The purpose of the book is to refresh or introduce Java EE 6 concepts implemented by WebLogic Server 12c, by showing how to apply them in a real-world scenario, presenting product-specific features that would be relevant to make things easier and more productive, both during design and runtime.

So, we covered topics such as persistence configuration and usage, the mechanics of sending and receiving asynchronous messages by using JMS and remote clients, how to create and use events, interceptors, and validations rules, how to secure an application, the main techniques used to scale up your code to process larger quantities of requests, and how to use communication channels such as Web Services, RESTful clients, and WebSockets, among other things.

There is still a plethora of features and details to explore, but you're on the right track to build enterprise-grade applications by using the book's content as a starting point. Happy coding!

Index

J

Thank you for buying
Getting Started with Oracle WebLogic Server 12c: Developer's Guide

About Packt Publishing

Packt, pronounced 'packed', published its first book "Mastering phpMyAdmin for Effective MySQL Management" in April 2004 and subsequently continued to specialize in publishing highly focused books on specific technologies and solutions.

Our books and publications share the experiences of your fellow IT professionals in adapting and customizing today's systems, applications, and frameworks. Our solution based books give you the knowledge and power to customize the software and technologies you're using to get the job done. Packt books are more specific and less general than the IT books you have seen in the past. Our unique business model allows us to bring you more focused information, giving you more of what you need to know, and less of what you don't.

Packt is a modern, yet unique publishing company, which focuses on producing quality, cutting-edge books for communities of developers, administrators, and newbies alike. For more information, please visit our website: www.packtpub.com.

About Packt Enterprise

In 2010, Packt launched two new brands, Packt Enterprise and Packt Open Source, in order to continue its focus on specialization. This book is part of the Packt Enterprise brand, home to books published on enterprise software – software created by major vendors, including (but not limited to) IBM, Microsoft and Oracle, often for use in other corporations. Its titles will offer information relevant to a range of users of this software, including administrators, developers, architects, and end users.

Writing for Packt

We welcome all inquiries from people who are interested in authoring. Book proposals should be sent to author@packtpub.com. If your book idea is still at an early stage and you would like to discuss it first before writing a formal book proposal, contact us; one of our commissioning editors will get in touch with you.

We're not just looking for published authors; if you have strong technical skills but no writing experience, our experienced editors can help you develop a writing career, or simply get some additional reward for your expertise.

Oracle Enterprise Manager 12c Administration Cookbook

ISBN: 978-1-84968-740-9 Paperback: 324 pages

Over 50 practical recipes to install, configure, and monitor your Oracle setup using Oracle Enterprise Manager

1. Recipes for installing, configuring, and getting up and running with Oracle Enterprise Manager

2. Set up automatic discovery, create and clone databases, and perform provisioning

3. Monitor Oracle Fusion Middleware, and remotely use incident and problem management using iPad/iPhone

Oracle Enterprise Manager 12c Administration Cookbook

Over 50 practical recipes to install, configure, and monitor your Oracle setup using Oracle Enterprise Manager

Foreword by Shashank Patwardhan, Head of Application Management Services, Europe, TechMahindra Limited

Dhananjay Papde   Tushar Nath   Vipul Patel   [PACKT] enterprise 🞘

Oracle APEX 4.2 Reporting

ISBN: 978-1-84968-498-9 Paperback: 428 pages

Learn how to build complex reporting solutions using Oracle APEX

1. Provides an introduction to the APEX architecture and is a step-by-step guide to setting up the APEX environment on Weblogic

2. Integrations of the reports with the most popular reporting technologies and generation of exotic and typical reports alike

3. Packed with complex APEX applications to help you learn newer ways of fulfilling reporting requirements in APEX

Oracle APEX 4.2 Reporting

Learn how to build complex reporting solutions using Oracle APEX

Vishal Pathak   [PACKT] enterprise 🞘

Please check **www.PacktPub.com** for information on our titles

OCA Oracle Database 11*g*: Database Administration I: A Real-World Certification Guide

ISBN: 978-1-84968-730-0   Paperback: 582 pages

Learn how to become an Oracle-certified database administrator

1. Prepare for Oracle Database Administration I certification

2. Learn real world skills in database administration

3. Written in an example driven format with step-by-step real world examples

OCA Oracle Database 11g: Database Administration I: A Real-World Certification Guide

Steve Ries

Oracle Data Integrator 11*g* Cookbook

ISBN: 978-1-84968-174-2   Paperback: 352 pages

Over 60 field-tested recipes for successful data integration projects with Oracle Data Integrator

1. Clear, step-by-step recipes to walk you through some of the most advanced features of Oracle Data Integrator

2. Covers everything from administration, to development, to deployment, including advanced coding techniques using the Oracle Data Integrator SDK

3. Numerous code samples, screenshots, diagrams, and best practice recommendations

Oracle Data Integrator 11g Cookbook

Christophe Dupupet   Denis Gray
Peter C. Boyd-Bowman   Julien Testut

Please check **www.PacktPub.com** for information on our titles

www.ingramcontent.com/pod-product-compliance
Lightning Source LLC
Chambersburg PA
CBHW080714220326
41598CB00033B/5412